THE LABYRINTH OF TIME

THE LABYRINTH OF TIME

The illusion of past, present and future

Anthony Peake

ARCTURUS

ARCTURUS

This edition published in 2012 by Arcturus Publishing Limited
26/27 Bickels Yard, 151–153 Bermondsey Street,
London SE1 3HA

ISBN: 978-1-84837-868-1
AD001779EN

Printed in the UK

CONTENTS

PROLOGUE:
THE HYPOTHESIS

Back in March 2000 I had an idea. It was to write a book.

That was it.

I had no idea what I was going to write about. I knew that it would be non-fiction and that it would probably discuss subjects that would be at the further reaches of science and philosophy. I planned to spend a year writing it and my plan was that by March 2001 I would have a book.

Much to my surprise, exactly 12 months later the book was written. In that year I had been involved in the greatest intellectual adventure of my life. I had learned a huge amount about quantum physics, neurology, theology and esoteric philosophy. More importantly, I had somehow pulled all this information together to create a simply amazing hypothesis about the nature of consciousness, how it related to time and how future events could be perceived before they took place. And there was more. This model, which I decided to call 'cheating the ferryman' (now popularly known as CTF), also contained a possible explanation of the greatest mystery of all: what happens to human consciousness at the point of death.

Eleven years later I find myself writing my fifth book. Each of my previous works has expanded upon the initial cheating-the-ferryman hypothesis. This concept is dynamic in that it has grown and adapted. As I have discovered more information with regard to the nature of consciousness and reality, so this information has been added to, like applying new colours to a still-wet canvas. What started as a simple idea, seemingly drip-fed to me as I wrote my first book, has grown into an international movement involving people from virtually every country on the planet. I have my own web-based forum and I appear regularly on television and radio

7

across the world. My books really seem to have changed many lives and they have facilitated an amazing flowering of creativity. There are now novels, rock albums, poems and paintings based on the cheating-the-ferryman concept. There is even a line of men's underwear that has been developed by a young New York-based Canadian.

Although later books have fine-tuned the CTF concept, it is still the first book, *Is There Life After Death? The Extraordinary Science of What Happens When We Die* (now popularly known as ITLAD), that introduced the hypothesis to the world. It was released in 2006 by the organization responsible for this book, Arcturus of London. It was this small, independent publisher, and more specifically its Managing Director, Ian McLellan, and Editorial Director, Tessa Rose, who saw something in the manuscript and decided to take a gamble with a totally unknown, first-time author based in Harrogate, a small town miles away from London. The rest, as they say, is history.

Which brings me to this book. In it I will be discussing the mysteries of time. For example, what exactly is time and how can we really understand its true nature? More importantly, it will review evidence that under certain circumstances human beings seem to be able to *precognize* the content of the future: that is, perceive events that have yet to take place. Within the generally accepted model of Newtonian science this is simply impossible. Time is something that comes into existence as we perceive it. We seem to travel through it and in doing so we turn the potentiality of the future into the actuality of the present moment and the non-existence of the past. This flow is inexorable and its motion can be measured by clocks, the motion of the planets and even, as we shall discover, the micturition (urination) of baboons.

However, if this is the case then how can anybody have advance knowledge of the future when it hasn't happened yet? The past similarly doesn't exist but it has been experienced and as such it remains in memory. Indeed, those memories can be shared with others to prove that past events actually took place; they are, as those who study consciousness term them, 'consensual'. All involved agree that they took place. But the future is different. We can have no agreement about future events because they are yet to happen. We can make a guess as to what may take place but this is all it is, an extrapolation from available data and information. But some people seem to be able to predict with great accuracy what is about to take place in the near, middle and even distant future.

My cheating-the-ferryman hypothesis suggests an answer. Reflecting on the curious subjective phenomenon known as *déjà vu*, it proposes that this strange sensation of familiarity is, in fact, a memory of a past life in which the subject is experiencing an event for (at least) the second time. Research has shown that more than 70 per cent of humanity have experienced this sensation at least once. This suggests that a similar number of individuals are re-living a life already lived (technically known as *déjà vécu*). If this is the case then it is possible that some of us can 'remember' an event that is yet to take place in this world but has already been experienced in another. We predict the future by remembering the past.

How such a scenario can be accommodated is explained in great detail in my previous books. However, in general terms, I suggest that at the moment of death consciousness falls out of time and continues to exist in a timeless place I call the 'Bohmian IMAX' (named after the physicist and independent thinker David Bohm whose work has influenced me greatly). In this permanent 'now' there is more than enough subjective time for a person to experience many hundreds, if not many thousands, of lives. From the letters and emails I have received and the questions I am usually asked during media interviews and after public lectures, it is clear to me that many find this the most difficult of my concepts to understand. I can appreciate this and I accept it is a possible reflection on my own inadequacies as a writer.

This book is my attempt to put that right. Together we will

explore the mysteries of the all-pervading dimension we call 'time'. I will review the philosophy, the physics and the neurology of temporal flow and then I will turn our attention to the subjective experiences of time. I will discuss evidence that under certain circumstances people can *precognize* things yet to happen, visit the past, journey into the future, slow time down and even speed it up. We will visit the furthest reaches of human understanding and discuss how such ideas have stimulated some of the greatest writers, poets and film-makers. In short, by the end of our journey we should know a great deal more about time. Whether we will be any closer to understanding what it is may be open to debate. However, if you enjoy the adventure half as much as I have then we will have at least not wasted too much of that most precious of commodities – time itself.

INTRODUCTION:
TIME – THE GREATEST MYSTERY

Defining the task

What exactly do we mean when we use the word 'time'?

I was astonished to discover that this word is the most-used noun in the English language. It is a small, four-letter word that contains within it so much mystery. Indeed, the very word itself cannot really be defined in any accurate or meaningful way.

As Michel de Montaigne (1533–92) wrote: 'All we are doing is substituting one word for another, often more obscure.' This is why a fellow Frenchman, the scientist and philosopher Blaise Pascal (1623–62), considered it to be a very primitive word.

St Augustine of Hippo (354–430) wrote: 'If I am not asked I know what time is; but if I am asked, I do not.' This echoed the ongoing fascination that the great thinkers of history have shown with regard to this most precious of commodities. The Roman philosopher and emperor Marcus Aurelius (121–180) stated: 'Time is a river made of events.' But if it is a river what are the banks or the riverbed? What makes this river of time flow? A real river flows because it is affected by gravity. Interestingly enough, time is affected by gravity, too. Time on the sun flows differently from time on the earth and, by implication, also does so for short people in relation to tall people. However, we have no evidence of any external motive force that makes time flow. Do we travel through time or does time flow around us? The great French writer Pierre de Ronsard (1524–85) made this point perfectly when he stated: 'Time is passing, time is passing, Madame. Alas time is not. It is we who are passing.' We feel trapped in this temporal flow that carries us ever forwards to our inevitable death.

As the old saying goes, 'time and tide wait for no man' and so it seems. It is relentless. The sand runs through the hourglass, the clock ticks away the minutes. We cannot control it, slow it down or speed it up. It just follows its own course. It is the agent for change. Without time everything would remain the same, in permanent stasis. You would not age but then again you would also find yourself trapped, immobile, like a statue caught in a timeless nothing. We can never escape from its grasp. However, the problem is that we have no real idea as to what time is. For example, it is the only thing that is measured by itself. Think about it, you can have a pound of apples, a gigabit of data, a cast of thousands or a dozen eggs but you can only have a minute of 60 seconds or an hour of 60 minutes. There is no objective measuring tool. A clock does not measure time, it simply moves its hands. You do not 'pour' 60 minutes into the clock and the minute hand then makes one revolution of the clock face. Though the clock may stop, time continues. Indeed, time never slows down or stops, or does it?

The winged chariot

Do you remember your long school summer holiday? Those hot, sunny days seemed to go on for ever. Do you also remember that endless wait for Christmas or for your birthday? An afternoon in junior school was a lifetime. What has happened? Why is it that now the days rush by and merge into months, while the months blur into years. Time really does seem to be running away from you. You know that an hour is an hour and always has been. The clock on the wall confirms this fact. However, your internal time does seem to vary with your circumstances, mood and age. How many times has it happened that the alarm clock goes off, you come out of doze state, flick the 'snooze' button and slip back to sleep. What seems like minutes or even hours later, the alarm goes off again. What happened then? How could a minute of real time dilate into a much longer period?

Here, author Rian Hughes describes a curious case of time reversal while in a sleeping state:

I dug out an old alarm clock – it had always been faultless in the past, but had not been in use for some years – to wake me up for a morning appointment. My dreams, early that morning, concerned boxing. Despite my protestations, I was to go several rounds with an enormous bruiser who looked ready to settle the business without bothering about my puny frame. Forced into the ring, I took a deep breath – then the bell went. I woke up. The bell was the alarm clock – ringing once and once only (a 'ding'), at exactly the right time in my dream (or my dream had led up to the time the clock went off exactly). It had never rung only once before.[1]

What happened to Rian Hughes is not unusual. However, it does not mean that objective, 'clock time' speeded up, dilated (or expanded). What changed was the observer's perception of time passing. And so it is for all of us; those summer holidays lasted exactly as many clock hours as was recorded, it was our 'inner' time that expanded.

It is clear that there are many different times. There is, as we know all too well, 'clock time'. But is this really time? We all carry within us the 'inner time' as experienced by Hughes. I have often experienced that sensation of 'nowness' – an immediate feeling that time is an illusion and that in reality there is no time, just a permanent 'now'. For me, these incidents happen not only if I see something of great beauty, like the sun setting over the sea at Santorini, but also when I receive bad news or when I have an accident. During times of physical pain, time seems to lose all meaning.

Philosophers have long been intrigued by these two forms of time. Since the ancient Greek era, the greatest minds have pondered on time more than on any other subject. As the centuries have passed this has not changed. For philosophers, time is tied up with the nature of being, and, by implication, also with the framework by which everything we perceive happens. Without time and space to contain all physical objects there simply would be nothing. It is to the philosophy of our temporal experiences that I would first like to turn.

CHAPTER 1
THE PHILOSOPHY OF TIME

Lost in space

In order to understand how a philosophy of time developed, we have to appreciate that time is inextricably linked to a far more immediate element of observed reality, the strange something we call 'space'. Space is something that we all exist within. We move through space and we perceive objects located in space. However, we have no real idea what 'space' is. When asked to reflect on the nature of space, most people understand it to be some kind of 'container'. Within this container there exists all material things. Each object fills up the space in which it is located. This is a very different sort of containment from the way a box 'contains' articles. Plato debated this point in one of his dialogues, *Timaeus*, when he described space as the 'receptacle' of material being.

However, this is only a partial model of the true nature of space. Even if the universe had no objects in it space would still exist, we tend to assume, or is space defined by the objects it contains? Described in this way, it becomes clear that space does not consist of ordinary matter. It is too insubstantial to be considered to be 'in the world'.

As we shall see, Aristotle suggested that each object has a 'place' in space. Motion is a change of space in that an object moves from one place to another. In moving from one place to another that object also moves in time. At one moment it is in one place and at the next it is in another. In this way, time and space are linked. All physical objects must exist in space and all must similarly exist in time. However, there are some things that do not exist in space but do exist in time. For example, our thoughts can be described as being in time but as they do not *extend* into space they cannot be described as 'existing in space'.

We naturally believe that time, too, is a form of container – one in which events take place. Without time nothing would happen. Objects would be frozen in one location in space. However, a major difference between space and time is the 'absence-of-objects' model. It is possible to imagine that if there were no objects in space then space itself would not exist. Yet most people, if challenged, would state that even if nothing existed time would still 'flow'.

We tend to think that if something exists now it will cease to exist in that form as time flows forwards. We happily accept that objects that existed in the past no longer exist now, such as the old St Paul's Cathedral or the original Winston Churchill. What has changed these things from existence to non-existence is the temporal flow. Indeed, we can also state with some certainty that there are things that do not yet exist that will come into existence in the future. For example, the moment we depart for next year's summer holiday. However, this event does not exist in the future. It becomes a reality as the future becomes the present. The event itself (the departure) exists for only a brief moment and then disappears into the past where it becomes non-existent once again. This idea that objects or circumstances exist only in the present moment intrigued St Augustine who pointed out that as the present is a vanishingly small moment of time, can it ever be properly said that anything has any existence at all?

Time also seems to be asymmetric. Past and future have very different aspects. The past is fixed whereas the future has no determinate kind of being until it occurs.

For the ancient Greek philosophers, the greatest mystery of all was the coming to be and the passing away of things. By things they meant every object and every event that exists both in the physical world and in the mind of man. One of the earliest recorded philosophers was Anaximander, who lived in the 6th century BCE. Only one sentence of his work survives:

And into that from which things take their rise they pass away
once more, as is meet; for they make reparation and satisfaction
to one another for their injustice according to the ordering of time.[2]

Anaximander considered that things changed from one state to another, for example, from hot to cold or from wet to dry. These changes take place in time. He called this incessant process 'separation'. For him time involves not just a sequence of identical 'now-points' but also a plurality of beings that exist in each moment.

Around a hundred years later, Parmenides of Elea, in southern Italy, took the ideas of Anaximander and reversed them. Parmenides suggested that the seeming multiplicity of things, both in time and in space, is an illusion and that behind them can be discovered a single, eternal reality that he called 'Being'. Parmenides argued that objects in time are undifferentiated in time. There is a smooth continuation of presence and this can only be taken as evidence that the past and future do not exist. Everything exists within an ongoing 'now'. From this he not only concluded that change is an illusion but also that time itself does not exist.

A follower of his, Zeno of Elea, proposed a series of paradoxes to show why such a conclusion can be reasonably inferred from rational observation. These paradoxes still intrigue and fascinate centuries after they were first written down.

Zeno's paradoxes explore the concept that time and space can be infinitely divisible or that space and time are composed of dimensionless elements. He does this by presenting a series of arguments. The first, known as the 'Dichotomy', presents the idea that there is no motion by pointing out the simple truism that in order for any travelling object to complete a journey it must, by logic, have to arrive at the halfway point before reaching the end. To arrive at any point in the journey it must first cover half of the distance to it – and so on. This leads to the paradoxical conclusion that, in order to cover any distance at all, it is necessary to have first covered an infinite number of halfway points that have no first position, and therefore the travelling object can never actually get started.

Zeno's second paradox is officially known as the 'argument of Achilles' although most readers will recognize it as the story of the race between the tortoise and the hare. In modern times it has also been called the 'bisection paradox'. This asserts that in any race the slower runner can never be overtaken by a faster one who is pursuing. In the popular tortoise-and-hare version there is a 100 metre race. As the hare is a much faster runner than the tortoise, it is agreed that the tortoise will be given a 50-metre start. So it is only when the tortoise passes the halfway stage that the hare is allowed to shoot off in pursuit. The hare then runs 50 metres and arrives at the point that the tortoise had reached when the hare first started to race. In the time it has taken the hare to run that 50 metres the tortoise has strolled another metre. In order to catch up with its opponent the hare has to run the additional metre. However, as it takes an amount of time for the hare to cover this additional metre, the tortoise will have already moved nearer the finishing line. In this model the hare can never catch the tortoise. It is continually arriving at a point in space and time that the tortoise has already moved on from.

Zeno's third argument states that an arrow flying through the air is, in fact, stationary. Indeed, of all his paradoxes, this is the one that really highlights the mysteries of time. If we accept that the 'instant' is the indivisible and constituent part of time then during any specific 'instant' the arrow must be at rest.

This is logically profound. If the arrow was moving at that instant then the arrow must be located at one place in space at the start of the instant and in another at the end of the instant. However, to make such a statement shows that the period in question must have temporal duration. As such, that period is divisible and cannot, by definition, be termed an 'instant' within the true meaning of the word. In other words, the passage of an arrow is made up of an infinite number of individual moments in time when it was stationary and so at no point can it be said to have been truly in motion. This is not simple semantics but a statement of fact.

Such was the power of Zeno's 'arrow paradox' that one of the greatest philosophers of all time, Aristotle (384–322 BCE), was to use this as the basis for his own ideas on the subject.

In attempting an answer to the paradox, Aristotle suggests that there are two ways of defining infinity. He presented an infinity of 'divisibility' and an infinity of 'aggregation' (or addition). As he stated it, an infinite addition cannot be contained within infinite limits but a finite distance can be infinitely divided. This can be applied to Zeno's 'arrow paradox' by observing that the distance covered by the arrow therefore may be infinitely divided but the sum of those infinite divisions is not itself infinite.

Aristotle's philosophy of time was presented in his work *Physics*. In this he follows two lines of enquiry. The first asks whether time exists or not. The second enquires about the true nature of time. He argued that time appears to be made up of things that do not exist. These are the past – which no longer exists – and the future – which is yet to come into existence. He furthermore observed that the present instant is not actually part of time but something quite separate. As usual, his argument is extremely elegant. He points out that a part measures a whole and a whole must consist of parts. However, this does not apply when we consider the relationship between now and the whole of time. Time consists of the past and the future but by definition neither of these entities consist of 'nows'.

In a later argument, he also suggests that each 'now' is different from the one that went before and the one that will follow. So when does this 'change' take place? If one 'now' simply ceases to be and another 'now' appears then there is a discontinuity. However, if each 'now' simply transforms into another 'now' then the two different 'nows' would be simultaneous. Of course the 'now' could simply stay the same but if that was the case there would be no change as each 'now' would be identical to the one before. For Aristotle, time was different from the action of motion or change in the same way that space cannot be considered merely to be made up of the objects it contains. He also argued that if something is said to be continuous then the adjacent parts of that 'something' must be, in some way or other, in contact.

Aristotle also took issue with the views of his own teacher, Plato. In his work *Timaeus*, Plato suggested that time had started with the first motion of the heavenly bodies, such as the sun, the stars and the planets. In this way time and change were closely associated. Aristotle considered this relationship to be impossible. In *Physics*, he points out that change happens at different rates: it can speed up or slow down. Time, however, is perceived at the same rate. He adds that change is also confined to one location in space whereas time is universal.

Aristotle falls into the trap of assuming that time never changes its speed because five minutes will always take five minutes to pass. However, the question is, what is it 'passing'? What is the measurement gauge? Furthermore, time is not measured by anything other than itself. As we shall discover later, this temporal measurement problem was to preoccupy 20th-century thinkers.

Aristotle concluded that time perception is mind-dependent. In *Physics*, Chapter 14, he makes this famous statement:

> Whether, if soul (mind) did not exist, time would exist or not, is a question that may fairly be asked; for if there cannot be someone to count there cannot be anything that can be counted.[3]

Here, Aristotle places the perceiver at the centre of time. Without a perceiver there is no time, just as counted objects need a counter. As we shall see, this idealistic viewpoint regarding the true subjective nature of time has been a central consideration even to the present day.

Although it is generally acknowledged that the period immediately following the fall of the Roman Empire was not the greatest time for philosophical and scientific advancement, it did include a handful of influential thinkers who carried forward the ideals of Ancient Greece. One of these was St Augustine. Like his predecessors, it was the nature of time that particularly fascinated him. Indeed, the latter part of his major work, the *Confessions*, contains a treatise on the nature of this most elusive of subjects.

Augustine asked his readers to contemplate the nature of time. He was in agreement with Aristotle that the very existence of time had to be questioned. For him, the concept of duration made no logical sense. He revisited Aristotle's argument that both the past and the future have duration and yet the present moment does not. In other words, time is never present *in extenso*. It consists of a series of instants that do not coexist. For Augustine, the implications of this observation are clear; nothing that exists has 'duration'.

Enduring duration

Let us pause for a moment and consider Augustine's concept of 'duration'. To have this quality, something must exist as a continuum from instant to instant. But each instant, as it appears from the future and disappears into the past, has no duration. It just exists as a point. Duration is one of three distinct concepts that are covered by the noun 'time'. The other two are 'simultaneity' (she was cooking the evening meal at the time the phone rang) and 'succession' (the time will come when I will have finished this book). 'Duration' simply defines time as it is experienced now.

For centuries after Augustine, the philosophy of time became simply an area of greater theological speculation. For example, the medieval scholars were keen to understand whether God existed in time or observed the world from a position outside time. This was of crucial importance as either conclusion had implications for both the nature of God and the concept of free will. If God exists within time then he cannot be omniscient as he has no idea what will happen in the future. In other words, the future has no reality until it comes to pass. As it has no reality even God cannot know what events will take place in the future. However, as God has a plan for the universe he can only plan with absolute surety if he knows the outcome of all events. For example, the Bible states that there will be a final battle between Good and Evil and Good will prevail. There will also be a 'Last Judgement'. How can God plan for these things if he cannot control what is to be? The solution is that God exists in a place outside of time and space. For him the past, present and future are just one permanent 'now'.

In an intriguing attempt to explain the role of God, Thomas Aquinas (1225–74) wrote the following:

> God is before the world by duration. The term 'duration' here means the priority of eternity, not of time. Or you might say that it betokens an imaginary time, not time as really existing, rather as when we speak of nothing being beyond the heavens, the term 'beyond' betokens merely an imaginary place in a picture we can form of other dimensions stretching beyond those of the body of heavens. [4]

God can therefore observe all events from his vantage point and in doing so he knows the outcome of every action. This gives him the omniscience needed if he is to be the true Supreme Being. However, it also means that he knows the actions of each and every human being. He knows, for example, if somebody will commit sin and, in this knowledge, he is aware of who will be condemned to hell fire and who will enter paradise.

It was this last observation that brought about the concept of Predestination, so popular with the Calvinists of post-Reformation Europe. God knows if we are saved or not from the moment of our birth. There is nothing we can do to change this. As such, this predestination will be intimated by success in this life. Of course, this presents huge problems for the concept of free will. If a person is predestined to do evil acts, in what way can his actions be considered to be his choice? Later we will discover that such an idea may be the actual state of affairs with regard to the workings of the human brain.

As well as focusing upon the implications of a God that predetermines the fate of his subjects, the Protestant Reformation and the Catholic response, the Counter-Reformation, created a social environment in which science could flourish. Suddenly, man was again keen to understand the mechanisms of the universe. In this time of deeply held religious beliefs, here was an attempt to understand the mind of God and to thrill at the power of his designs.

One individual who was both a man of science and a man of the new Protestant God was Isaac Newton (1642–1727). He believed that God had created a universe in which science and logic ruled. Newton's laws of motion suggested a universe in which, with sufficient information, the outcomes of all events could be predicted with absolute accuracy. Newton takes space and time to be something more than mere spatial and temporal relations among material objects and events. What, exactly, he was not sure. Indeed, falling back on the prevailing philosophy of the period, he considered time to be the property of God. This 'property' exists everywhere and is the same in all locations. Time is universal and each 'now' is the same 'now' wherever an object is located in space. However, for Newton and those who followed in his footsteps, time is something that has an independent existence. Even if no physical objects existed in the universe, time – and indeed space – would still exist.

Enter the Monads

Another man living around the same time and within a similar tradition to Newton's had come up with a very different model of time and space. Gottfried von Leibniz (1646–1714) was a German philosopher-mathematician for whom the Aristotelian tradition was the correct one. Space and time have no independence in that they both need ordinary material things and material happenings to give them existence. Leibniz asked us to imagine moments of time where nothing happens, or unoccupied regions of space where nothing is located.

Can these be said to have existence? He argued that in such circumstances they do have existence because they have the potentiality to have events or objects within them. This is sufficient to bring them into existence. From this can be concluded that time is simply the family of temporal relations among material events. Without the material events, potential or actual, time itself ceases to have any real independent existence. Indeed, in his 'deep' philosophy, Leibniz argued that space, time and even matter itself are simply constructs of the mind. The universe actually consists of mind-like objects that he called 'Monads'. Each Monad exists in total isolation from every other Monad and each contains a snapshot of time and space. Although each Monad is timeless and spaceless, they do have relationships with each other. These relationships can be termed 'simultaneous', 'before' and 'after'. So one Monad can be before another, or after another, or two Monads can be simultaneous with each other. Time is simply the relationship between individual Monads.

Over time, the disagreements between Leibniz and Newton became very heated and sometimes acrimonious. Both had their followers who reflected as much as anything else the differences between the Prussian/Germanic philosophies and the more materialistic English approach to the nature of external reality. Of course, there was a subtext to these debates that centred round which of the great thinkers, Newton or Leibniz, had discovered the form of mathematics now known as the Calculus. As with many disputes of ownership, these arguments spread out into other areas of philosophy. Leibniz's argument that space and time only existed when related to physical objects or mental constructs become known as 'Relationist' whereas Newton's belief that time and space existed irrespective of material objects was termed 'Absolutist'.

Leibniz's model of reality as a mental construct was to have a huge influence on another great Prussian philosopher, Immanuel Kant (1724–1804), who was born eight years after Leibniz' death. Many years later, in 1770, Kant was to write the following telling statement about his position regarding the nature of space, and by implication, time:

> *Now what are space and time? Are they actual entities* [wirkliche Wesen]*? Are they only determinations or also relations of things, but still such as would belong to them even if they were not intuited? Or are they such that they belong only to the form of intuition, and therefore to the subjective constitution of our mind, without which these predicates could not be ascribed to any things at all?*[5]

In asking if space and time are 'actual entities', Kant is referring directly to the Newtonian, Absolutist, position and his alternative that they are 'determinations' is a reference to Leibnizian Relationism. He answers these questions by agreeing with Leibniz and rejecting Newton. He argues that time and mind have a subtle relationship in that time is a form of conscious experience rather than an objective reality. It is from subjective perceptions that we sense the flow of time. Yet again we see the influence of Aristotle reaching out across the centuries.

Kant was to refine the idealism of Leibniz and give it a conceptual framework. By 'idealism' we mean that the external world is simply an 'idea' that exists within the mind. This is not to say that there is not an external world out there but simply that we can never perceive that world directly. It is presented to us as an internally generated mental construct. Such was the power of his arguments that his writings had a major impact on many generations of German thinkers. Indeed, during the 19th century the movement he spawned, known as 'German Idealism', was to influence a whole generation of poets, philosophers and writers such as Lessing, Herder, Goethe, Schiller, Fichte, Hegel and Schelling. However, it was the German philosopher Arthur Schopenhauer (1788–1860), who was to put his own stamp on the philosophy of time.

Schopenhauer was one of the most intriguing philosophers of the early 19th century. He was born in the Baltic port of Danzig to a family of Dutch origin. He was educated in Germany, France and England. This gave him an excellent grounding in the prevailing philosophies of these three countries and enabled him to develop his own unique understanding of consciousness and its relationship to the external world. In 1818, he published his major work, *Die Welt als Wille und Vorstellung* (*The World as Will and Representation*). In this work, greatly enhanced in a later edition in 1844, Schopenhauer proposed that there are two aspects to the self: the self as an object of perception and the self as a manifestation of will.

Schopenhauer was also greatly influenced by Kant and shared the opinion that the external world is simply an 'idea' – that is, an object in the mind of a perceiving consciousness. To be a subject is to be a perceiver. Central to this was the idea of the personal relativity of time. He wrote:

> *A man of correct insight among those who are deluded and duped resembles one whose watch is right while all the clocks in town give the wrong time. He alone knows the correct time, but what use is it to him? The whole world is guided by the clocks that show the wrong time, even those are so guided who know that his watch alone states the correct time.*

According to the commentator René Trintzius, Schopenhauer's fascination with relativity was stimulated by a curious incident that took place when the philosopher called one of his maids to deal with a spillage he had caused by knocking over his inkwell. When the maid entered she looked totally shocked. Schopenhauer asked her why. She replied that she had dreamed the whole event the night before. The philosopher was intrigued by this and called in the maid's room-mate. The second maid confirmed that they had discussed the dream that morning. For Schopenhauer, this was strong evidence that time itself is a form of illusion created by the mind and that the natural state of time was a form of permanent 'now'.

Presentism and Eternalism

Schopenhauer had been fascinated by the teachings of the ancient Hindu and Buddhist texts that were in circulation from the early 19th century. A German translation of a Persian version of the 50 Upanishads – philosophical commentaries on ancient Indian works called the *Vedas* – had been published by the French scholar Anquetil Duperron in 1804. The German Orientalist Friedrich Majer's *Life and Teachings of the Buddha* had also been published around this time. Both proved to be highly influential on the developing philosophy of Schopenhauer. It is in this way that Vedic and Buddhist philosophy were to find their way into the mind of one of the most original, some would say iconic, thinkers of the 19th century.

In our review of how philosophers have approached the mystery of time throughout the centuries, two themes seem to be central: that time is a form of mental construct and that, in actuality, there is no time but the 'instant'. These two themes can be reduced to one simple statement: all that exists is the instant and that is being perceived by an observer. This position is now known as 'Presentism'. The opposite of this is called 'Eternalism', which proposes that all times are equally real.

It was John McTaggart Ellis McTaggart (1866–1925) who took this viewpoint on the nature of time and created an intriguing philosophy that still arouses debate within certain circles. In a seminal paper published in 1908, this iconoclastic thinker suggested that time was unreal.

McTaggart had been elected to a fellowship at Trinity College Cambridge in 1891 when he was 25. By 1908, this profoundly odd man had become a great influence upon his younger contemporaries such as the philosophers Bertrand Russell (1872–1970) and George Edward Moore (1873–1958). Indeed, it was during one tea-time meeting that took place in Russell's rooms in Cambridge that McTaggart introduced his ideas on time to Moore, then a student of his. One can imagine the scene in 1893, with Moore choking on his crumpets as McTaggart proposed the notion that time was an illusion. Later, Moore was to describe McTaggart's announcement as a 'perfectly monstrous proposition'.

It is important to appreciate that, for McTaggart, everything that exists is real and that nothing can be real without existing. For him, there was no such thing as a non-existent reality. Indeed, for something to exist it must also have a quality besides its own existence. A quality may be a simple one, a compound one or a complex one. By its nature, a simple quality is singular and, as such, indefinable. A compound quality may be defined as an aggregate of other qualities. This compound quality can be called the nature of that thing. To be called 'a substance' a thing must have a number of qualities and must relate in some way to other things. In this model, matter is anything that has size, shape, position, mobility and impenetrability.

This meant that he had great difficulty with the notion of the 'existence' of time. For McTaggart, our thinking about time had become confused. He suggested that we need a radical reworking of what we mean when we use the term 'time'. For example, he wrote:

Positions in time, as time appears to us prima facie, *are distinguished in two ways. Each position is earlier than some, and later than some, of the other positions. And each position is either past, present, or future. The distinctions of the former class are permanent, while those of the latter are not. If M is ever earlier than N, it is always earlier. But an event, which is now present, was future and will be past.*

McTaggart said this suggests two different states of time. He called these the 'A-Series' and the 'B-Series'. This differentiation is of profound significance because it helps us appreciate what St Augustine meant by his famous statement. We all feel we understand what time is until we have to sit down and think about it.

For McTaggart, these two types of time, or more accurately, ways of thinking about time, were of profound significance. The 'A-Series' can be described as containing specific moments that move through time in a sequence. By this he meant that the present must move along with the present moment. We have the concept of 'now' and 'now' moves through time. In the same way, three hours ago moves through time, two weeks from now moves through time, and so on. This concept is very different from specific dates in time, such as 8.45 pm on 12 October 1981. That is a specific point in time that remains in that place. It does not move forwards or backwards within time's flow. This is an example of the 'B-Series'. Lockwood calls this 'clock time'.

McTaggart's present

In her book *Representing Time: An Essay on Temporality and Modality*, the Cambridge professor of linguistics and philosophy Kasia Jaszczolt gives two excellent analogies to facilitate our understanding of these two complex concepts. Professor Jaszczolt compares the 'A-Series' to a ski lift, the type that is in continuous motion. She asks us to imagine each skier latching on to the ski lift as it goes past. Each event in time is like the skier in that only one skier at a time can latch on at any one point. For Professor Jaszczolt, the 'B–Series' is likened to a long washing line, which allows a person to hang different articles of clothing at different positions on the line. Unlike the ski lift, the washing line is static and it is the person who moves up and down.

The first metaphor is probably how most people understand time, or more specifically, its motion. It flows from the future, becomes the present moment, which then fades away into the past. This is 'internal time'. However, the washing line analogy represents 'real time'. If we were to stand at a distance from the washing line we would see it as an object that contains the past, the present and the future in a sequence-free 'now'. This is what McTaggart termed the 'C-Series'. However, McTaggart observed that the 'C-Series' is not actually a form of time because no change is taking place. Indeed, what turns the static 'A-Series' into an in time 'B-Series' is the addition of a conscious agent – an observer – who interprets the series in a before-and-after structure that imposes motion.

From this we can see that 'A-Series' expressions help us to locate events taking place in the B-Series. Within the English language, almost all sentences will contain 'A-Series' expressions. This is because in English, as with most European languages, verbs are used to describe the position of the subject within the 'A-Series'. For example, the phrase 'I am writing this chapter' conveys the present tense, that my 'writing' is taking place now. If I expressed this sentence in the past tense it would be 'I wrote this chapter two weeks ago'. The past tense of the verb 'to write' is used to locate the event in the past. Indeed, it is very difficult to express an event that is located outside of the 'A-Series'.

More importantly for our discussion on the nature of time, McTaggart argued that because relations in the 'B-Series' are permanent they cannot account for change.

As time itself seems to be an agent for change, it is logical to conclude that the 'B-Series' cannot be considered a form of time. However, McTaggart then went further and suggested that even the 'A-Series' must be unreal.

His logic goes as follows:

1. To have a property of being 'the future', 'the present' and 'the past' is impossible. It is only possible for a thing to be in one of these states. One cannot be in the future and the past at the same instant. Nor is it possible to be in the present and the past or the present and the future. Anything in time can only be in one of these states.

2. However, when perceived as being 'in time', every event appears to possess properties of each state.

3. But the two propositions above are contradictory.

The central issue here is one of succession. Any event is initially located in the future as a potential, then manifests in the present and disappears into the past. For McTaggart, this is impossible because it is contradictory. Indeed, this brings us straight back to the two conflicting models touched upon earlier: Presentism and Eternalism.

As we discussed, Presentism suggests that only objects that exist in the present instant can truly exist. According to this viewpoint, if we were to make a list of all things that exist it would include all the things that exist at this instant. This includes you, me, David Beckham and the Grand Canyon. However, and this is important to appreciate, what would not be on the list would be any objects that are non-present. I am using the word 'present' in its literal sense as a word that describes things that are here in this 'present'. So, by definition, a non-present object cannot be placed on the list of things existing now. For example the old St Paul's Cathedral was 'present' until the Great Fire of London of 1666 and then it became a thing of the past; it was non-present. A new St Paul's Cathedral was then built to take its place. The same thing can be stated about John Lennon or Elvis Presley. Photographs and films of these two iconic individuals are 'present' but these are simply images of Presley and Lennon. The same could be said about future things that do not exist at the moment, such as a bound copy of this book in paperback format. Now, what is strange about that statement is that for me, as I type these words on a computer screen, the book does not exist. It is not present. However, for you as the reader in some future time, the book has total reality. It is held in your hands (or, if it is an e-book, it appears on the screen of your e-reader). However, from my temporal point of view, this book does not exist, any more than the old St Paul's, or John Lennon or Elvis Presley exist.

The contrary position to Presentism is Non-Presentism, one version of which is Eternalism. For somebody who holds to this philosophy, the old St Paul's and a paperback version of this book exist in exactly the same way that David Beckham and the Grand Canyon do. It is simply that these things are not currently present. As such, an Eternalist would place all the things that have ever existed and all the things that have the potential to exist on their list of existing things.

Clearly this seems to be a difficult position to hold. However, an Eternalist would argue that we are simply confusing what we mean by 'exist'. They would focus in on the 'ontological' reality of things and point out that we are confusing temporal location with actual location. 'Ontology' is defined as the study of the nature of being, existence and reality. The current discussion is profoundly ontological in that we are analyzing what we mean when we say that something exists. In an ontological sense, John Lennon still exists but is located in another place in time. He is not here at this moment but he was in New York until December 1980. Similarly, old St Paul's Cathedral existed in 1665.

On the other hand, future things do not exist in this way because they never have had existence, simply potentiality. The book you hold in your hand is, for me, only a potentiality (my publisher may decide not to publish it, for example) but for you, in your temporal location, it is a real thing.

Interestingly enough, as we will discover later in this book, a modern particle physicist by the name of John G. Cramer (1934–), a professor of physics at the University of Washington, has suggested a model of quantum physics that uses Eternalism as its central concept.

It is Presentism that is used for an argument against the possibility of time travel. If all that exists is the present instant then only the things that share the present instant can exist. As such, 1981 does not exist any more and therefore can never be visited.

Nietzsche's question

In October 1865, a young student by the name of Friedrich Wilhelm Nietzsche (1844–1900) found himself in a second-hand bookshop in the German city of Leipzig. He had recently arrived in the city from his home in Bonn and he was stocking up with books. Much to his delight, he discovered two volumes of *The World as Will and Representation* by Schopenhauer, who had died just five years previously. The young Nietzsche had long been intrigued by the work of this great thinker. Nietzsche was later to write in one of his autobiographies that after the discovery of Schopenhauer's book he felt like he was 'walking on air'.

At the time, Nietzsche was a first-year student at the University of Leipzig studying classical philology but he was already developing a reputation as an outstanding scholar. His tutor, Friedrich Ritschl, the leading German philologist of the time, had heaped praise upon his young protégé, declaring that he had never had such a talented student. However, Nietzsche was not at all sure that this was the route he wished to take. On 30 August 1865 he wrote in his journal: 'To be guided by men like Ritschl, is to get pulled away on perhaps the very paths most alien to one's own nature.'

Reading Schopenhauer's *The World as Will and Representation* was to bring about Nietzsche's 'conversion'. His letters and diary entries from 1866 onwards show how his world view was radically changing. In a letter to his friend, Hermann Mushacke, on 11 July 1866, he wrote that Schopenhauer had removed the 'blindfold of optimism' from his eyes and that life seemed 'more interesting, albeit uglier'. From then onwards, Nietzsche was to follow a course of logic that would lead him to his most controversial of ideas, that of the 'Eternal Return' (known by some philosophers as the 'Eternal Recurrence').

While it is clear from his later writings that Nietzsche's fascination with the cyclical nature of life was stimulated by his readings of Schopenhauer in the mid 1860s, these ideas had already been playing upon Nietzsche's mind. In 1862 he wrote an essay entitled 'Fate and History'. In this he asks the question:

Does the eternal becoming ever reach an end? . . . Hour by hour, the hand of the clock moves along, only to begin its passage all over again after twelve; a new cosmic era dawns.[6]

However, it was in his discovery of Schopenhauer's writings that he was able to find both support and initial structure. In a later work, *The Birth of Tragedy*, he makes a reference to his idea of an 'eternal life at the core of existence, with the perpetual destruction of phenomena'. This was a reflection of a similar idea proposed by Schopenhauer when the earlier philosopher likened time to an 'endlessly revolving sphere'. This description had profoundly affected Nietzsche, as had Schopenhauer's suggestion that the present moment, the 'now', is a vertically streaming sun of an 'eternal noon'.

By this he meant that the present moment can never be lost because our perception of it, the window to the world, remains consistent. Schopenhauer considered that the present is the tangent that has one point of contact with the circle of time. The circle moves but the point of contact remains stable. As an analogy, this is similar to the way a laser beam reads a CD or DVD. The CD/DVD revolves and the laser remains in one place, reading the data. The laser is equivalent to the present moment, the 'now', or, as Schopenhauer termed it, the 'eternal noon', and the CD/DVD represents the circle of time.

In this way, Schopenhauer divorced conscious awareness from

the circle of time. We are creatures that exist in the physical universe, the phenomenal world in which time and matter exist. But there is also a part of us, the non-physical spirit or *Geist*, that observes from outside of space-time in the same way that a laser beam 'perceives' the digital data encoded on a CD/DVD.

Such was the power of this model that Nietzsche took Schopenhauer's imagery and used it in his masterwork *Also Sprach Zarathustra*. The terms 'great noon' and 'noon and eternity' both appear in this work. However, Nietzsche took this much further in that he attempted to create a scientific model to accommodate the idea that time has to be circular and in doing so involve an Eternal Return.

Interestingly enough, Nietzsche was of the opinion that his model of the Eternal Return was entirely original. Indeed, in his work *Ecce Homo: Wir Man Wird, Was Man Ist* (*Behold the Man: How One Becomes What One Is*) he describes how, on a walk in the woods near Lake Silvaplana in August 1881, the idea forced itself upon him.

His logic was simple. He pointed out that the universe is an enclosed system. There is nothing outside of the universe. As such, it must contain a finite number of particles. From this it is fair to say that at any one moment all particles will be in particular positions in relation to each other. In the next moment one or more of these particles will have moved to another position within this finite space. However, as all this movement is taking place within a finite space then there must also be a finite number of positions that all particles can be in relation to each other. As such, and given enough time, there must be a point where all the particles will again find themselves in the same relational positions. Then, by the laws of causality, each subsequent position must follow the same logical pattern and progress as they did the last time. For example, if two snooker balls impact each other in exactly the same way, and all surrounding conditions are identical, then the outcome of that impact will also be identical. Each snooker ball will move off in the same direction and at the same speed as last time. In turn, each subsequent impact and outcome will also be the same. And so it is that as the outcomes of all the impacts spread out so everything is repeated in exactly the same way and history repeats itself. Nietzsche was writing in a period where Newtonian determinacy was the overriding scientific paradigm. Therefore, what he stated was, for the time, an absolute scientific proof. Indeed, as all objects are made of smaller particles (atoms and molecules) it is therefore reasonable to conclude that this Eternal Return involves everything that has existed, exists or will exist. This model has close similarities with a concept known as 'Poincaré's Recurrence', proposed by the French mathematician and philosopher Jules Henri Poincaré (1854–1912) in 1890.

Nietzsche describes this as follows:

If the world may be thought of as a certain definite quantity of force and as a certain definite number of centres of force ... it follows that, in the great dice game of existence, it must pass through a calculable number of combinations. In infinite time, every possible combination would at some time or another be realized; more: it would have been realized an infinite number of times. And since between every combination and its next recurrence all other possible combinations would have to take place, and each of these combinations conditions the entire sequence of combinations in the same series, a circular movement of absolutely identical series is thus demonstrated: the world as a circular movement that has already repeated itself infinitely often and plays its game ad infinitum. *This conception is not simply a mechanistic conception; for if it were that, it would not condition an infinite recurrence of identical cases, but a final state. Because the world has not reached this, mechanistic theory must be considered an imperfect and merely provisional hypothesis.*[7]

From this, Nietzsche concluded that as we are all part of the physical universe so it will be that each one of us will be reborn and will be reborn again and again to live an identical life to the one before and the one after. His initial feelings on this were of absolute horror. He describes it in this way:

> *What if a demon were to creep after you one night, in your lone-*
> *liest loneliness, and say, 'This life which you live must be lived by*
> *you once again and innumerable times more; and every pain and*
> *joy and thought and sigh must come again to you, all in the same*
> *sequence. The eternal hourglass will again and again be turned*
> *and you with it, dust of the dust!' Would you throw yourself down*
> *and gnash your teeth and curse that demon? Or would you answer,*
> *'Never have I heard anything more divine'?*[8]

It is clear from this passage that Nietzsche was in two minds about this possibility. In one way he regarded it with fear and yet in another he found it to be profoundly liberating. He concluded that the difference between these two conditions can be explained by one factor, memory. The concept of living the same life over and over again is only terrifying for us if we are aware that this is taking place. If we live each life as if it is the first time – and with no memories to tell us otherwise – then it might as well be the first time.

Indeed, Nietzsche allowed himself to divide mankind into two groups: those who could deal with the insight in a positive way and those who could not. For those who embraced the idea, a form of liberation could be found. He suggested that while engaged in any activity we should reflect on this and ask one simple question: 'Is this something I want to be doing countless times?' He added:

> *Let us etch the image of eternity on to our own lives! In this way*
> *humanity is forced to live in the here and now at every moment*

because each moment is, in a very real sense, but one of an infinity of identical moments. To live in the now is to become liberated from time. We must live always in 'The Moment'.

In typical fashion, this is how he describes living in 'The Moment':

'Behold this gateway, dwarf!' I went on: 'It has two aspects. Two paths come together here: no one has ever reached their end. This long lane behind us: it goes on for an eternity. And this long lane ahead of us that is another eternity. They are in opposition to one another, these paths; they abut on one another: and it is here at this gateway that they come together. The name of the gateway is written above it: "Moment".'[9]

And this is why Nietzsche was in two minds about the concept of living one's life over and over again. By living each moment as if it is a moment that you will have to repeat one is forced to ensure that that moment, and every subsequent one, is as perfect as possible. Of course, it will be the case that this is exactly what one did every other time, but the central issue is that we believe we are acting as beings that have free will and as such to ensure the perfection of each moment must still be the aim. For Nietzsche, this is the approach taken by the Übermensch, the Superman who takes control and transcends such nihilism.

Nietzsche's work was of great interest to many similarly motivated intellectuals of the time. One such deep thinker was the Austrian philosopher and social reformer Rudolf Steiner (1861–1925). In his book *Friedrich Nietzsche, Ein Kämpfer Gegen Sein Zeit* (*Friedrich Nietzsche, One Fighter Against His Time*) he describes the power of Nietzsche's writing:

In the words in which he expressed his relationship to Schopenhauer, I would like to describe my relationship to Nietzsche: I belong to those readers of Nietzsche who, after they have read the first page, know with certainty that they will read all pages, and listen to every word he has said. My confidence in him was there immediately... I understood him as if he had written just for me, in order to express all that I would say intelligibly but immediately and foolishly. 'One can speak thus and yet be far from acknowledging oneself as a "believer" in Nietzsche's world conception.'[10]

The fighter for freedom

Steiner encountered the writings of Nietzsche in 1889 and immediately recognized the older man's spiritual pre-eminence as a 'fighter for freedom'. Later he was to meet Nietzsche's sister, Elizabeth Foerster-Nietzsche, and through this association Steiner was able to visit the philosopher in his sick room. This allowed him a fascinating insight into Nietzsche's thought processes long after the philosopher's writing days were over. At this time, Nietzsche was well into the profound mental illness of his last years. This brought about a fascination with his writing that Steiner describes below:

A penetrating conception of Nietzsche's final creative period shone clearly before me as I read his marginal comments on Eugen Dühring's chief philosophical work. Dühring there develops the thought that the cosmos can be conceived at a single moment as a combination of elementary parts. Thus the course of the world-process would be the succession of all such possible combinations. When once these should have been exhausted, the first would have to return, and the whole series repeated.[11]

In other words, if we conceive of the world as simply an agglomeration of a finite number of deterministic atoms, with each state of the entire system being absolutely determined by the relations present in the previous state or the preceding moment, everything is not only predetermined, but bound to repeat eventually, forever, and throughout eternity, again and again in exactly the same way.

If such a thing represents reality, it must have occurred

innumerable times in the past and must occur again innumerable times in the future. We should thus arrive at the conception of the eternal repetition of the same states of the cosmos. The German philosopher Eugen Karl Dühring (1833–1922) had rejected this thought as an impossibility. Nietzsche read this and he received from it an impression that worked further in the depth of his soul and finally took form within him as 'the return of the same', which, together with the idea of the 'superman', dominated his final creative period. Steiner explains:

> I was profoundly moved – indeed, shocked – by the impression I received from thus following Nietzsche in his reading. For I saw what a contrast existed between the character of Nietzsche's mind and that of his contemporary, Dühring, the extreme positivist, who rejects everything that is not the result of a system of reasoning directed with cold and mathematical regularity, considers 'the eternal repetition of the same' as an absurdity, and sets up the idea only to show its impossibility; but Nietzsche must take this up as his own solution of the world-riddle, like an intuition arising from the depths of his own soul.[12]

He continues:

> Nietzsche's ideas of the 'eternal repetition' and the 'superman' remained long in my mind . . . Nietzsche looked upon the evolution of humanity as if everything that occurs at any moment had already occurred innumerable times in the same form and would occur innumerable times in the future. The atomistic structure of the universe makes the character of the present moment seem to be a certain combination of the smallest entities; this must be followed by another, and this in turn by another – until, when all possible combinations have beem formed, the first must again appear. A human life, with all its individual details, has been present innumerable times and will return with all its details innumerable times.[13]

In my opinion there is an ongoing misunderstanding about exactly what Nietzsche meant by the Eternal Return. In 'On the Vision and the Riddle' section of *Thus Spoke Zarathustra*, it is made clear that he is not advocating perfectly repeating cycles but cycles that subtly change with every revolution. As Zarathustra climbs the mountain the dwarf sits on his back, a symbol of how the mind is held down by what Nietzsche termed 'The Spirit of Gravity'. Together they approach the gateway that is called 'Moment' (*Augenblick*, literally 'eye blink') that we encountered in an earlier quotation. On each side of the gateway they see two paths running off into infinity in either direction.

One represents the future and the other the past. Zarathustra asks the dwarf what would happen if a person followed one of the paths for its full length. The dwarf replies that the person would return to the gate from the opposite direction stating that 'time itself is a circle'. This prompts an angry response from Zarathustra who chides him for taking the thought of Eternal Return 'too lightly'. The dwarf vanishes shortly thereafter, presumably vanquished by Zarathustra.

Many years later the mid-20th-century German philosopher Martin Heidegger (1889–1976) argued that a very profound lesson could be drawn from this section of *Zarathustra*. He wrote:

> *So the dwarf has not really grasped the riddle; he has made the solution too easy. Accordingly, the thought of eternal recurrence of the same is not yet thought when one merely imagines 'everything turning in a circle'. . . That is precisely the thought of circling as the dwarf thinks it, the dwarf who, in Zarathustra's words, makes things too easy – inasmuch as he absolutely refuses to think Nietzsche's stupendous thought.*[14]

French philosopher Gilles Deleuze (1925–95) come to a similar conclusion in the 1960s when he observed:

Every time we understand the Eternal Return as the return of a
particular arrangement of things after all the other arrangements
have been realized, every time we interpret the Eternal Return as
the return of the identical or the same, we replace Nietzsche's
thought with childish hypotheses. No one extended the critique of
all forms of identity further than Nietzsche.[15]

Indeed, in a profoundly influential book written in 1972, Professor Joan Stambaugh, a recognized world authority on Buddhist and existentialist philosophy, focuses on Nietzsche's use of the expression *das Gleiche*. She argues that this word does not strictly translate into English as 'the same', suggesting that it sits somewhere between 'the same' and 'similar'. She gives an example of two women wearing hats that resemble each other to such an extent that on first glance the hats would be thought to be the same. However, on careful examination they are seen to be subtly different. In this way the hats would be the 'same' in the usage of the German word *Gleiche*. 'This is more than similarity, but it is not indentical.'[16]

It is evident from Nietzsche's writings that he was of the opinion that his model of the Eternal Return was unique and was solely his discovery. In many respects this is true. Nietzsche described his model of circular time in a specific way, reflecting 19th-century science. However, all Nietzsche was really doing was clothing in modern (for the time) philosophical language a concept that goes back as far as written records are available. The idea that time is cyclical may have been one of the earliest philosophical concepts of mankind. It is to a review of the history of this curiously beguiling concept that we now turn.

CHAPTER 2

THE ETERNAL RETURN

The myth of Sisyphus

There is an old saying that states: 'There is nothing new under the sun'. In many ways this can be seen as a reference to the Eternal Return but it is also a true statement with regard to the concept itself. In Europe it was the ancient Greeks who first recorded a view of the universe based on circularity. Through the ages, one of the most evocative images of this belief, which is seen as encapsulating the tragedy and nihilism of Eternal Return that so fascinated and horrified Nietzsche, is the legend of Sisyphus.

Sisyphus was the son of Aeolus, the ruler of the winds, and husband of Merope, one of the seven daughters of Atlas. As was the will of the gods, Zeus decided it was time for Sisyphus to die and sent Death, in the guise of Thanatos, to kill him. However, Sisyphus took Thanatos by surprise and held him prisoner so that no mortals would ever die again. This enraged Zeus who forced Sisyphus to release Thanatos and allow Death to return to humanity. In revenge, Thanatos decided to make Sisyphus the first victim of his return. However, once again Sisyphus was extremely cunning and hatched a plan to thwart Death once more. He persuaded his wife that should he die she should not allow any funerary honours to go ahead. When Sisyphus died and entered the Underworld he pointed out to the gods that Merope had deliberately withheld the honours due to him and requested that he be allowed to return to earth to punish his wife for her omission. The gods agreed to this and Sisyphus returned from the dead. He was reunited with his wife and lived to a great age. When eventually he died for the second time, the gods of the Underworld were determined that not only should he never escape again but also that he should suffer for tricking them. He was given a task that involved rolling a huge stone up a hill. Just as he was about to reach the top the stone would slip out of his grasp and roll all the way to the bottom again. He was doomed to perform this task for all eternity as a punishment for cheating Death.

This wonderful myth seems to somehow sum up the human condition. Indeed, so evocative was its imagery that the French-Algerian existentialist writer Albert Camus (1913–60) used it as a simile for man's absence of hope in the face of an unintelligible universe. For Camus, there is still hope for man, as there is for Sisyphus. Whatever else, Sisyphus still has his rock, his awareness of his fate, and his futile struggle towards the heights, which is, in Camus' opinion, enough to fill a man's heart and thus make him happy.

The idea that the universe in some way involves cycles that return everything back to the same place can be found in many cultures across the globe. Indeed, this circularity is often used to explain human immortality in that it is believed that when someone dies that person is reborn to re-live that same life. This is a form of reincarnation but into one's own body, rather than transmigration into another person or creature. One of the most intriguing belief systems is that of the N'Kongo people of central Africa. According to anthropologist Wyatt MacGaffrey, these people believe not in circularity but a spiral of birth and rebirth. In this way there is no death and change can still be accommodated, a concept embraced by many Western philosophers.

It has been suggested that the idea of the Eternal Return was imported into ancient Greece by travellers from India, where belief in reincarnation is strong. Many scholars disagree with this position and it is possible that the concept was developed by the Greeks independently. Of course, this idea of 'eternal cycles of time' has its own inner logic. Indeed, there are really only two alternatives when it comes to understanding the ultimate nature of time; either it started at some specific point in the past and will come to an end at some point in the future or it has always existed and always will exist. If we accept the idea that time started at some point then the question has to be asked: what was there before? A similar question can be asked about the end of time. What follows that? Cyclical time over-comes this problem because the distant past is the distant future, or more specifically the distant future becomes the distant past.

The ancient Hindu texts deal with huge time cycles. For example, the *Vishnu Purana*, written about 1,000 BCE, describes a series of cosmic cycles known as *mahyugas*, with each one made up of four *yugas*. Each *mahyuga* lasts 4,320,000 years. One thousand *mahyugas* constitute a *kalpa*, a single day in the life of the ultimate god-figure of Hinduism, Brahma.

Not surprisingly, a similar belief can be found in the Buddhist tradition known as the 'Lesser Vehicle'. Once again this involves truly enormous time scales yet still follows a cyclical pattern. The large cycle is called the *mahakalpa* and goes through a process of evolution and decline. Each cycle has four great periods called *asankhyeya*. There are 'Buddha' cycles and 'Empty' cycles. There have been four Buddha cycles. In each one a different Buddha teacher has been manifest. We will soon be entering a fifth featuring a new Buddha, called the Maitreya.

The Japanese writer Keiji Hishitani considers that these great cycles are a form of Eternal Return (or, as he calls it, 'Eternal Recurrence'). He writes:

> *A recurrent world process, as a cyclical movement, implies infinity to the extent that it lacks beginning or end. But to the extent that it does arrive at an end, in a sense, by going back to the begin-ning, its recurrent character signals a finiteness. It thus possesses, we might say, a finitude of a higher order – what has been called Eternal Recurrence.*[17]

Hishitani suggests that the Buddhist concept is similar to the Eternal Return/Recurrence but with subtle differences. He writes:

> *What I am speaking of here is something other than the endlessly recurring system of identical time, in which the same world process*

returns again and again in Eternal Recurrence. In Eternal Recurrence, a before and an after are imagined in the successive repetitions of the same world-time in that recurrence time is represented purely and simply as a straight line without beginning or end. But in Buddhism time is circular, because all its time systems are simultaneous; and, as a continuum of individual 'nows' wherein the systems are simultaneous, it is rectilinear as well. . . in newness without ceasing, we see two simultaneous faces of time; one of creation, freedom, and infinite possibility, and one of infinite burden, inextricable necessity. Newness is essentially equivocal; thus, so is time.[18]

The *Tao Te Ching* of Lao Tzu

This is a fascinating concept; the idea that all times exist in a permanent 'now'. In other words time itself is an illusion. As we shall see later, this particular philosophy has been updated by the Cambridge mathematician Julian Barbour.

In ancient Chinese philosophy, the Eternal Return was known as 'the Way'. This is the route of everything, the ultimate philosophy. The Chinese word for 'the Way' is *Tao* or *Dao*, and it represents the essentially unknowable nature of the universe. The central philosophy of *Tao* was described in the classic Chinese text known as the *Tao Te Ching*. According to tradition, this was written by the sage Lao Tzu, believed to live in the 6th century BCE. How this concept may be told to people and how people receive it is poetically described in a section of the *Tao Te Ching*:

On hearing the Way, the best of men will earnestly explore its length. The mediocre person learns of it and takes it up and sets it down. But the vulgar people, when they hear the news, will laugh out loud, and if they did not laugh, it would not be the Way.[19]

Further on it states:

> *Touch ultimate emptiness, Hold steady and still. All things work together: I have watched them reverting, and have seen how they flourish and return again, each to his roots. This, I say, is the stillness: A retreat to one's roots; or better yet, return to the will of God, which is, I say, to constancy. The knowledge of constancy I call enlightenment and say that not to know it is blindness that works evil.[20]*

However, with regard to the Western concept of the Eternal Return, we have to acknowledge that the major influence was that of the ancient Greeks. Indeed, some of the greatest thinkers of the classical period spent a good deal of their time wrestling with the import of this subject. For example, Aristotle observed the cyclical nature of the heavens reflected in the natural world here on earth:

> *There is a circle in all other things that have a natural movement and coming into being and passing away. This is because all other things are discriminated by time and end and begin as though conforming to a cycle; for even time itself is thought to be a circle.[21]*

A very influential group of philosophers, collectively known as the Stoics, believed that everything would start again when the planets returned to the positions they occupied at the beginning of time. The universe would then start a new cycle that would follow the exact course of the old cycle. This doctrine was known as *Apokatastasis*.

The pre-Socratic philosopher Empedocles (*c.*490–430 BCE) stated that the universe had started in a state of supreme harmony in which the four elements (earth, air, fire and water) existed in homogeneity. This state was pure 'love'. As the cycle unwinds, the system loses this state of homogeneity and moves to disorder and heterogeneity.

It is clear that such ideas were not forgotten after the fall of the Roman Empire. The 4th-century historian Eusebius (*c.*263–339 CE), Bishop of Caesarea, wrote the following:

Socrates and Plato and each individual man will live again, with the same friends and fellow citizens. They will go through the same experiences and the same activities. Every city and village and field will be restored, just as it was. And this restoration of the universe takes place not once, but over and over again – indeed to all eternity without end. Those of the gods who are not subject to destruction, having observed the course of one period, know from this everything which is going to happen in all subsequent periods. For there will never be any new thing other than that which has been before, but everything is repeated down to the minutest detail.[22]

It is evident that Eusebius was not alone in commenting on the concept of *apokatastasis*. In another tract, Nemesius (*c.*390 CE), Bishop of Emesa, now Homs in Syria, remarked:

Socrates and Plato and each individual man will live again with the same friends and fellow citizens. They will go through the same experiences and the same activities. Each city, village and field will be restored, just as it was. And this restoration of the universe takes place not once, but over and over again – indeed all eternity without end.[23]

It has long been suggested that it was Judaism that placed time in a linear format and that Christianity and Islam followed on from this. This freed humanity from the fear that progress was impossible because all journeys simply lead back to the beginning. However, there is evidence that Judaism too had its own system of cyclical time. There is a very intriguing section in Ecclesiastes 1.1–11 which opens with the line 'vanity of vanities, says the

Preacher. All is vanity'. This suggests that whatever man tries to do he will be defeated by time. This is a specific type of time, one that returns again and again. Later in the section, in verse 9 it states: 'What has been will be, and what has been done is what will be done, and there is nothing new under the sun.' This is followed by another, even more cryptic, statement in verse ten which states: 'Is there a thing of which it is said "see this is new"? It has been already in the ages before us.'

What possible interpretation can be taken from this verse other than that this moment will be experienced again in the future?

However, by the time St Augustine was writing down his own ideas on time it is clear that for him there was no question that whatever time was its basic flow is linear. He made this point strongly when he wrote:

> God forbid that we should believe in this for Christ died once for us for our sins and rising again dies no more.[24]

Ma fin est mon commencement

Yet even the great thinkers of the Church sometimes used the circle as an example of time. Earlier we encountered the great medieval scholar Thomas Aquinas explaining how God can exist beyond time. In his *Summa Contra Gentiles* he makes the following statement when trying to explain how God's eternity is not simply an everlasting existence but a dimension outside of human time:

> *Furthermore, since the being of what is eternal does not pass away, eternity is present in its presentiality to any time or instant of time. We may see an example of sorts in the case of a circle. Although it is indivisible, it does not co-exist simultaneously with any other point as to position, since it is the order of position that produces the continuity of the circumference. On the other hand, the centre of the circle, which is no part of the circumference, is directly opposed to any given determinate point on the*

circumference. Hence, whatever is found in any part of time co-exists with what is eternal as being present to it, although with respect to some other time it be past or future.[25]

Of course, the reason why these early Christian writers were preoccupied by this concept is that it ran contrary to classical Christian teachings and so had to be dismissed as heresy. As we have already seen in the words of St Augustine, a central tenet of Christian belief is that time is linear rather than cyclical. This has to be the case for Christian theology to be correct. For example, crucial to Christian doctrine is the belief that the birth and crucifixion of Christ were unique, one-off events and so will never occur again. The concept of circularity then seemed to disappear from philosophical discourse for centuries until, as we have already seen, young Friedrich Wilhelm Nietzsche walked into that bookshop in October 1865. But that is not strictly true. The idea had remained an intellectually attractive, if somewhat disturbing, alternative explanation for life after death. This is evidenced by a curious motto embroidered on the Chair of State at Holyrood Palace in Edinburgh. This reads: *'Ma Fin est Mon Commencement'* (French for 'my beginning is my end'). This was woven at the request of Mary Queen of Scots. Mary is known to history as being a devout Catholic and yet here we have her suggesting that, contrary to the teachings of the Church, she believed in the Eternal Return.

The same phrase had originally been woven into the 'Cloth of State' that Mary kept with her during her uncomfortable imprisonment in Tutbury Castle in England's East Midlands. Mary found her accommodation cold and damp and regularly complained of the draughty conditions. Scholars have suggested that this phrase reminded Mary of her happy childhood in France. It is reasonable to conclude that during this time she would have heard a piece of music written by Guillaume de Machaut in the mid-14th century. This song cycle, written in the style of a rondeau, uses the phrase *'Ma Fin est Mon Commencement'* over and over again. Machaut's piece consists of three voices. The lyrics are as follows:

> (A) *Ma fin est mon commencement,* (B) *Et mon commencement ma fin,* (a) *est teneüre vraiement,* (A) *Ma, Ma fin est mon commencement.* (a) *Mes tiers chans trois fois seulement,* (b) *Se retrograde et einsi fin.* (A) *Ma fin est mon commencement,* (B) *Et mon commencement ma fin.*

This translates as:

> *My end is my beginning, and my beginning is my end. And this truly holds. My end is my beginning. My third voice just three times reverses itself and thus ends. My end is my beginning and my beginning my end.*

The structure follows a conventional rondeau with certain lines repeating – indicated in the text by the letters **A, a, B, b** and following the pattern **ABaAabAB**. As the song develops we find that the second voice part is the reverse of the first part, and the third part is a palindrome. This is a fascinating example of how the Eternal Return can be conveyed in musical terms.

Machaut's haunting *Ma Fin est Mon Commencement* is a superb example of how the idea that life is a circle of death and rebirth was strongly held in certain sectors of society. Although he was an ordained Catholic priest, it is clear from the lyrics and structure of this piece that Machaut was trying to convey in as many ways as possible that life itself is a circular process. Indeed, this is why he uses the musical form known as a rondeau to really underline the recursiveness.

In doing so he was presenting to his audience a profoundly esoteric and mystic idea. The concept of the Eternal Return was secret but central to the alchemical beliefs of the Dark Ages. One of the key images of alchemy, the 'ouroborus', can be found in many alchemical manuscripts of the period. The word 'ouroborus' is taken from the Greek u ó , which literally translates as 'tail-devourer'. The image usually depicts a serpent eating its own tail. The most famous version of this symbol of recurrence is a drawing found in the early alchemical text *The Chrysopoeia of Cleopatra*. Dating from 2nd-century Alexandria, this image shows the ouroborus enclosing the words *'hen to pan'* ('one is the all'). This profoundly Gnostic statement reflects the belief that all things are linked and that time and consciousness are cyclical in nature. The black and white colouring of the snake depicts the Gnostic belief in the duality of nature.

The link between the ouroborus and Gnosticism was to carry through into the early medieval period when a Gnostic sect known as the Albigensians used the symbol in their printed watermarks. It has been suggested that a link can be made between this group and the symbolism of early decks of Tarot cards which show a similar watermark. The ouroborus symbol also features in the Tarot card the 'ace of cups'. In one version of this card (from the 'Goldschmidt set'), the neck of the cup is encircled by an ouroborus. What is strange about earlier versions of this card is that it is not the cup that is the central theme of the card, but the two fountains that gush from it. This suggests that this card is redolent with Gnostic meaning. We have the Eternal Return symbol of twin fountains ejecting water which then circulates back into the fountain to be ejected again. The choice of depicting a twin fountain also seems to suggest, yet again, the concept of duality.

The Albigensians are also known to history under another name, that of the Cathars. In my first book, *Is There Life After Death? The Extraordinary Science of What Happens When We Die* I suggested that this fascinating group were very aware of both the cyclical nature of life and death and of the concept of human psychological duality. Is it therefore in any way surprising that these latter-day Gnostics wove the symbol of the ouroborus into their writings and philosophy?

Although based in Rheims in northern France, it is reasonable to conclude from his poetry that Machaut was influenced by the troubadour tradition of the Langue d'Oc, a particular style of writing that has long been associated with the Cathar/Albigensian way of life.

The troubadour tradition was to evolve into our modern concept of poetry, using rhyme and rhythm to convey an idea, a feeling or an emotion, and a storytelling tradition that was to become the novel. It therefore comes as no surprise that poets, playwrights and novelists have long been fascinated by the idea of the circularity of life and the way we are doomed to repeat over and over again all the positive and negative elements of our lives.

One of the greatest examples of this is T.S. Eliot's poetic meditation on the nature of time, *Four Quartets*. Each of the four sections of this extended poem focuses on a specific element of our perception of time. For example, in 'East Coker' (the second of the *Four Quartets*), Eliot takes one phrase and weaves it into something enigmatic and beautiful. He opens the first two verses with the same phrase:

In my beginning is my end, in succession
Houses rise and fall, crumble, are extended
Are removed, destroyed, restored, or in their place
Is an open field, or a factory, or a bypass.

And

In my beginning is my end. Now the light falls
Across the open field, leaving the deep lane
Shuttered with branches, dark in the afternoon
Where you lean against a bank while a van passes
And the deep lane insists on the direction.

In 'East Coker', Eliot attempts to convey in poetic format the concept of the Eternal Return, cycles that begin where they finish and finish where they begin. The poem begins with a series of cyclical images. It describes the cycle of the seasons and the circular movement of a country dance. These suggest not a beginning and an end but an endless repetition of the same events, movements and circumstances. The words Eliot chooses are redolent of lazy summer afternoons and the languid flow of time across the English landscape. However, as the poem progresses the feeling becomes more wintry and cold. The first verse ends with this enigmatic section:

> And a time for the wind to break the loosened pane
> And to shake the wainscot where the field-mouse trots
> And to shake the tattered arras woven with a silent motto.

Joyce's fin again awakes

The last line may seem familiar. When read in conjunction with the first line it becomes clear that this poem is referring to Mary Queen of Scots. 'In my beginning is my end' is a subtle reference to the phrase *'Ma Fin est Mon Commencement'* that Mary had woven into her 'Cloth of Estate' (see page 49) and which Eliot calls *'the tattered arras woven with a silent motto'* and which the Queen requested also be embroidered into the Chair of State at Holyrood Palace in Edinburgh. This is the same phrase we discussed earlier in relation to Machaut's rondeau. Such was Eliot's attachment to this concept that on his death in 1965, his ashes were placed in St Michael's Church, in East Coker, a real place set deep in rural Somerset and the village from which Eliot's ancestors set off for America in 1669. In the church can be found a plaque dedicated to the poet. The dedication reads:

> In my beginning is my end. Of your kindness, pray for the
>   soul of Thomas Stearns Eliot, poet.
> In my end is my beginning.

This attaching the end of a life to the beginning is subtly different from the general concept of the Eternal Return, which suggests a return to a starting point after a long period of time. Indeed, the concept of 'Recurrence' as proposed by Nietzsche involves a return after a huge cycle of time. This model is more in keeping with the concept of the ouroborus, the snake eating its tail. Literally MY end is MY beginning. This is a much more personal and immediate interpretation of cycles of existence. It suggests that my death will be my birth and that I am, from my own viewpoint, immortal. This is the cheating-the-ferryman concept I proposed in my first book, *Is There Life After Death? The Extraordinary Science of What Happens When We Die*. Again I claim no originality for this concept. All I have done is tried to present a model by which such a concept can be considered scientifically valid. Indeed, the idea that human life itself is an enclosed circle was first proposed by a 5th-century BCE philosopher called Alcmaeon.

Alcmaeon lived and taught in the southern Italian city of Croton. He was a thinker way ahead of his time. He was fascinated by the workings of the human body and was one of the first to suggest that the brain was the source of consciousness. Later commentators describe how he wrote only one book. Entitled *On the Nature of Man*, this has long been lost to antiquity. The only information we now have regarding his writings is from other ancient Greek scholars such as Aristotle and Theophrastus. It seems that Alcmaeon was particularly interested in the nature of the human soul and what happened to it at death. He noted that the planets and the stars are in continual motion and argued that as the human soul, too, is always in motion it reflects this ongoing movement of the seemingly immortal objects seen in the sky. By motion he meant that the human body was animated by a motive force that gives it vitality and movement. Death seemingly brought an end to this movement but for Alcmaeon this was because, as Aristotle stated in his work *De Anima*, 'Alcmaeon says men die because they cannot attach their beginning to their end'. Alcmaeon declared that each soul was immortal, that its life forms a closed cycle and the same soul undergoes an infinity of reincarnations that are all similar to one another.

Although lost for centuries, this idea of attaching the end to the beginning and in such a way as to ensure seamless continuity suddenly reappeared in the writings of three Irish writers in the mid-20th century, James Joyce (1882–1941), Brian O'Nolan (1911–66) and Samuel Beckett (1906–89).

The opening line of Joyce's masterwork *Finnegan's Wake* is:

riverrun, past Eve and Adam's, from swerve of shore to bend of bay, brings us by a commodius vicus of recirculation back to Howth Castle and Environs.

And the last line is:

A way a lone a last a loved a long the

Now if you look closely you will see something of interest. The first line starts with a lower case letter. This is clearly grammatically incorrect. The last line is incomplete and does not end with a full stop. Likewise this is a grammatical error. Or is it? Change the order of the two lines and run them together. You now get the sentence:

A way a lone a last a loved a long the riverrun, past Eve and Adam's, from swerve of shore to bend of bay, brings us by a commodius vicus of recirculation back to Howth Castle and Environs.

Clearly this is deliberate. Joyce is trying to show that life itself is circular and its real nature is an Eternal Return. Indeed, he cleverly makes puns and clever wordplay to reinforce this idea in such a way that it can only really be picked up by those willing to work their way through the puzzle. For example, it is known that Joyce was heavily influenced by Giambattista Vico (1668–1744), an Italian philosopher who proposed a theory of cyclical history in his major work, *New Science*. That this is the case is evidenced by

Joyce's use of the words *'commodius vicus of recirculation'* in the opening line. Vicus is the Italian form of the Latin 'Vico'. The use of the word 'recirculation' is, for Joyce, fairly straightforward.

The peculiar narrative style that Joyce uses is full of puns and wordplay that employs language, in fact many languages, to convey meaning on many different levels. For example, here is one of the many references to the Eternal Return that can be found in the dense weave of semantic cleverness in which Joyce presents his philosophy:

Life, it is true, will be a blank without you because avicuum's not there at all, to no-more cares from nomad knows, ere Molochy wars bring the devil era, a slip of the time between a date and a ghostmark, rived by darby's chilldays embers, spatched fun Juhn that dandyforth, from the night we are and feel and fade with to the yesterselves we tread to turnupon.

Here Joyce likens life to a letter that is blank, a vacuum (avicuum) between a date and a ghostmark, between the writing and delivery (birth and death, 'ghostmark'). 'Avicuum' is also another reference to Giambattista Vico and his philosophy of Eternal Return. We then have the wonderful description of endless rebirth in the line *'. . .from the night we are and feel and fade with to the yesterselves we tread to turnupon'.*

But for me the cleverest pun of all with regard to Joyce's fascination with the Eternal Return is that the book ends (*fin*) only to begin once more (again). And what do you get if you place the words 'fin' and 'again' together? The word 'finagain', a clear homonym of the title of the book, *Finnegan's Wake*.

Tim Finnegan is a hard-drinking hod carrier who falls from a ladder and breaks his skull. At the wake held after his funeral the mourners get carried away with drinking and, in the course of their rowdy behaviour, whiskey is spilt on to the head of the corpse. As it does so it brings Finnegan back to life and he joins in the drunken revelry. In yet another clever circular reference, we have whiskey being both the cause of Finnegan's demise and also his resurrection. But Joyce does not stop there. The English word whiskey is derived from the Irish phrase '*uisce beatha*', which means 'water of life'. So here we have a baptismal rebirth brought about by the splashing of the alcoholic waters on Finnegan's head. Indeed, even the word 'wake' has a double meaning that reflects the concept of rebirth. A wake is something that takes place after a funeral but is also the verb that describes coming out of a sleep state. In this way, Joyce placed many, many levels of meaning into his carefully chosen book title.

One of Joyce's great admirers was an iconoclastic writer known to posterity as 'Flann O'Brien', the nom de plume of the Northern Irish writer Brian O'Nolan (1911–66). O'Nolan's writing is full of bizarre humour, literary references and characters taken from other works. In many ways his writing style has elements of the South American genre known as 'magical realism' in that the stories meld the fantastic with the mundane and suggest that in some way the stories themselves are narratives written about real events. For example, in his novel *The Dalkey Archive*, O'Nolan/O'Brien includes a character called 'James Joyce', who seems to have forgotten that he had written a novel called *Finnegan's Wake*.

O'Nolan wrote his most intriguing novel, *The Third Policeman*, between 1939 and 1940. However, it remained unpublished until his death in 1966.

This tale of murder and weird science features a narrator and his associate, Divney, who kill somebody called Mathers and steal his cashbox. Divney hides the cashbox and refuses to tell the narrator of its location. In his search, the narrator finds himself walking towards a police barracks and feels oddly disturbed by its appearance:

It looked as if it were painted like an advertisement on a board on the roadside and indeed very poorly painted. It looked completely false and unconvincing.

This feeling of recognition disturbs him, a sensation that continues when he encounters the two policemen who live in the barracks, Sergeant Pluck and Policeman MacCruiskeen. The narrator enters the barracks and is greeted by Sergeant Pluck who asks: 'Is it about a bicycle?'

The narrator has long been an amateur scholar of a famed intellectual called de Selby (who also appears in O'Nolan's novel *The Dalkey Archive*). It seems that this eccentric theoretician philosopher is yet another absent character whose odd theories on the nature of reality are used to explain the bizarre world that exists within O'Nolan fiction. Inside the confines of the police barracks, the narrator discovers many odd and irrational concepts, many of which he refers back to the theories of de Selby. For example, underneath the barracks is a vast underground chamber that the policemen call 'Eternity' where time seems to stand still. After a series of curious events, including a meeting with the mysterious third policeman, Fox, the narrator finds himself walking down a road towards the police barracks once again. As, before, he finds himself oddly disturbed by its appearance (and the previous lines are repeated):

It looked as if it were painted like an advertisement on a board on the roadside and indeed very poorly painted. It looked completely false and unconvincing.

In a device similar to one used by Joyce in *Finnegan's Wake*, we have a complete circularity of events. Joined by Divney, the narrator again enters the barracks and is greeted by Sergeant Pluck asking the same question: 'Is it about a bicycle?'

In a letter dated 14 February 1940, O'Nolan sought to explain the strange plot:

When you get to the end of this book you realize that my hero or main character (he's a heel and a killer) has been dead throughout the book and that all the queer ghastly things which have been

*happening to him are happening in a sort of hell which he earned
for the killing... It is made clear that this sort of thing goes on
for ever... When you are writing about the world of the dead –
and the damned – where none of the rules and laws (not even
the law of gravity) holds good, there is any amount of scope for
back-chat and funny cracks.[26]*

And in a passage omitted from the book he wrote:

*Hell goes round and round. In shape it is circular, and by nature
it is interminable, repetitive, and nearly unbearable.*

Beckett's Godot

A very similar, but far more sinister, variation on this theme can
be found in Samuel Beckett's play *Waiting for Godot*. It is clear that
the hell that O'Nolan's narrator finds himself in is echoed by that
of Beckett's character Vladimir.

In *Waiting for Godot*, two tramp characters, Vladimir and Estragon,
await the arrival of a possibly mythical 'Godot'. As one reads the
work the theme of Eternal Return becomes clearer, but Beckett
presents it in a subtle rather than overt way. As the first act is
concluded, a boy turns up to explain that Godot 'will not come
this evening but surely tomorrow'. This triggers a sensation of *déjà
vu* in the mind of Vladimir who asks the boy if he has seen him
before. The boy says he does not know the tramp, which causes
confusion in Vladimir's mind. 'It wasn't you who came yesterday?'
he asks, and again receives a negative response. 'This is your first
time?' he asks. The boy confirms that, as far as he is concerned,
it is. There is then a moment of silence which is broken by Vladimir
simply stating 'words, words'. Beckett reinforces this ill-at-ease
feeling of recurrence by making the second act, for the most part,
a repeat of the first. The only change is the condition of the two
other main characters, Lucky and Pozzo. In the first act Pozzo is
dumb and Lucky is blind. In the second act the disabilities are

reversed with Pozzo now being sightless and Lucky unable to speak. This suggests to me that Beckett is not proposing a literal Eternal Return. The framework is the same, for example the dialogue is virtually identical, but with differences. Only Vladimir seems to appreciate that they are caught in a temporal trap. The others seem blissfully unaware of the circularity. In many ways this reminds me of the movie *Groundhog Day*, which we will be discussing later. In this film it is only the central character, Phil Conners, who is magically aware that the same day is repeating. This suggests that in some way the day is an illusion observed solely from the viewpoint of the person aware of the situation. The other characters simply respond to the actions of this central character. In *Waiting for Godot* it is Vladimir who is trapped even though he seems to have the freedom of choice given to him by his awareness. Yet Vladimir is doomed by his nature to follow the same road.

When Pozzo is asked what happened to him and Lucky he responds in frustration:

> *Have you not done tormenting me with your accursed time! It's abominable! When! When! One day, is that not enough for you, one day he went dumb, one day I went blind, one day we'll go deaf, one day we were born, one day we shall die, the same day, the same second, is that not enough for you?*
> *They give birth astride of a grave, the light gleams an instant, then it's night once more.*

Clearly Pozzo has some subliminal understanding of the situation but simply will not face up to it. Later, when Lucky and Pozzo leave, presumably to return the next day, Vladimir begins to realize the strength of his position. Like Phil Conners, he comprehends that within this world he may be a demigod with powers of perception denied the other characters. In a chilling soliloquy we hear the inner musings of Vladimir's mind:

He'll know nothing. He'll tell me about the blows he received and I'll give him a carrot. (Pause) Astride of a grave and a difficult birth. Down in the hole, lingeringly, the grave-digger puts on the forceps. We have time to grow old. The air is full of our cries. (He listens) *But habit is a great deadener.* (He looks again at the sleeping Estragon) *At me too someone is looking, of me too someone is saying, He is sleeping, he knows nothing, let him sleep on.* (Pause) *I can't go on!*

The similarities between *Waiting for Godot* and *The Third Policeman* are stark. Both titles contain the identity of a much awaited eponymous character whose nature and purpose the other protagonists discuss in great detail. The location is also a setting of rural anonymity, a place by a road, detached somehow from modernity and history. As O'Nolan's tale was published in 1966, nearly 13 years after *Waiting for Godot* premièred at the Théâtre de Babylone, Paris, it is highly unlikely that the plot device of *The Third Policeman* would have influenced Beckett. So one can reasonably assume that both writers may have taken their inspiration from Joyce.

This idea of being caught in some kind of temporal trap in which the central character repeats the same general course of action is now a staple plot device in many late 20th- and early 21st-century film scripts. However, it has long been recognized that one of the most effective novels to use the idea of going back to live one's life with prior knowledge gleaned from another run of the Eternal Return is called *The Strange Life of Ivan Osokin*. Unusually, this novel was not written as a fiction but as a way of getting across to the general public a concept that the author strongly believed in. The author in question was one of the greatest thinkers of the 20th century, the enigmatic, sometimes frustrating but always inspiring Peter Ouspensky. It is to this iconoclastic thinker that we now turn our attention.

CHAPTER 3

OUSPENSKY & 'SELF-REMEMBERING'

Old souls

Peter (Pyotr) Demianovich Ouspensky was born on 5 March 1878. His family had a tradition of calling each generation of sons either Pyotr or Demian. As each generation of the male line of the Ouspensky family alternated between Pyotr and Demian so each male had both names, alternating between Pyotr Demianovich and Demian Pyotrovich. (The suffix 'ovich' is simply a patronym, denoting the name of a male person's father.)

I am intrigued by the odd similarity between my use of the word 'Daemon' (as featured in my previous book *The Daemon – A Guide to Your Extraordinary Secret Self*) and how the name of one of the major writers on the subject of the Eternal Return came to be called 'Demian', a name that originates from the Greek word 'δαμάζω' (damazo), meaning 'to conquer, master, overcome or tame'.

According to Ouspensky's recent biographer, Gary Lachman, the Ouspensky family tradition stated that those with the name Pyotr (Peter) were outgoing, social individuals whereas the Demians were inward-looking mystics. This again resonates with the idea of personal duality, specifically as Ouspensky showed both traits.

Many years later Ouspensky was to tell one of his students, Maurice Nicoll (see page 77–80) that he was an unusual child in that he was extremely serious. Indeed, he stated that from infancy he had seen 'what life was really like'. He explained that this was because he had remembered his previous life. It is important to understand that by this Ouspensky was not suggesting reincarnation. He was not remembering a life as another person but his own life, a life that was, in this incarnation, out there in the future. Ouspensky believed that we all live the same life over and over again. In this discussion with his student, Ouspensky explained that Nicoll's own childhood was different. In Ouspensky's opinion, Nicoll was a 'young soul' who had had few, if any, 'turns on the wheel'. This is why, unlike Ouspensky, Nicoll could not recall his very early childhood memories in any detail. This was not the case with Ouspensky who could remember in great detail many events of his infancy.

It seems that Ouspensky had this ability to 'remember' from a very early age. He mentions in an autobiographical fragment (*A Further Record*) that he could recall himself quite clearly at the age of 4. 'I remember the exhibition of 1882 in Moscow and the coronation of Alexander III in 1883, chiefly in illuminations,' he wrote. Clearly this is not a memory of being here before, simply an unusually early childhood memory. But it may also suggest that Ouspensky had carried forward highly developed observational abilities from his previous life.

He claims that he began experiencing *déjà vu* very early in his life. He tells that, at the age of 6, while visiting a location near Moscow, he felt that it was not as he had remembered it before. His 6-year-old mind then showed considerable maturity by realizing that he had never been to this place before in this life and so the memory was not from this lifetime. This past-recall was to prove quite useful when, later on, his mother was taking him to a new school. She had never been to the location before and became hopelessly lost. But the young Peter 'recalled' the layout of the building and was able to assist his mother in finding her way out.

Clearly Ouspensky was suggesting that 'old souls' such as he carried through their lives an adult's ability to retain memory, even during their early childhood. This is because, for individuals such as Ouspensky, their early childhood is simply an extension of the last years of their previous life. In notes of his meetings he was recorded as stating that ['old souls' like him] 'would remember themselves such as they were grown-up. They are not children at all'.

Ouspensky was sure that this could be proven and he suggested that 'the study of recurrence must begin with the study of children's minds, and particularly before they begin to speak'. It is somewhat unclear as to how this could be done, as an infant would have to be able to describe their memories verbally. However, this is still an intriguing observation. Indeed, Ouspensky was adamant that in order for this experiment to be effective it had to be done before the child learned to speak.

Towards the end of his life, Ouspensky would always announce the ending of a meeting of his group with the Russian term *ne zabuyvayte*, which means 'don't forget'. This was an instruction to his followers that it is only by 'not forgetting' that any advantage can be gained from living one's life over and over again.

He believed that his knowledge of his 'last time round' could be shown by his childhood ability to foresee the immediate future. This skill was shared by his sister. They would test this out and, he writes, were successful. Unfortunately we have no way of knowing what he meant by this.

He claimed that at the age of 6 he read Mikhail Lermontov's 1840 novel *A Hero of Our Time*. When he described this reading many years later in his *New Model of the Universe* he recalled that this novel gave him the idea that events repeat themselves. He describes that throughout the novel Lermontov is preoccupied with precognitions and has the characters sense what is about to take place. Certain situations were remembered as if they had occurred in some unknown past. He also mentioned Lermontov's novel *The Fatalist*, which he considered was 'practically written on the theme of repetition and of remembering that which seems to have happened in some unknown past'.[27] In his book *Don't Forget: P.D. Ouspensky's Life of Self-remembering*, Australian writer Bob Hunter suggests that Ouspensky may have embroidered these early memories.[28] He thinks it is somewhat unlikely that a child of 6 would be able to interpret the idea of a 'return' from Lermontov's verse:

Would it not be better to finish the path of life in self-forgetting/
And to fall into an unending sleep/Looking for a new awakening.[29]

I have to agree with this observation. However, it can be argued
that if Ouspensky was 'self-remembering his previous life' then
this would have involved him carrying into that life all the
analytical abilities of his previous 71 years of life, including a
'remembrance' of that particular verse.

In Ouspensky's novel *Ivan Osokin*, the magician tells Ivan that
as soon as somebody becomes aware of what he terms 'the great
secret' they will only have a few more lives to live and so must
make the best of them. This is intriguing because it suggests that
by becoming aware of this secret, which is, of course, the Eternal
Return, we have somehow advanced our lives in such a way that
the ending is in sight. In the great Eternal Return movie *Groundhog
Day*, the central character, Phil Conners, lives the same day over
and over and in doing so he becomes a better human being. Only
then is Conners allowed to move on to the next day. Why this
occurs and who is the judge of this is not explained. However,
Ouspensky is suggesting that to bring the circle to an end you
only need to become aware that the circle exists. Osokin finds that
he makes the same mistakes as he did in his previous life, the
implication being that he has not progressed. Yet he still seems
to believe he is near the end. This implies that Ouspensky's returns
can be brought to an end by simply 'awakening' to the fact that
one is living within the 'Eternal Recurrence'.

Ouspensky's idea of the Eternal Return was developed from his
fascination with geometry. He noted that ideas regarding the
material form of space had usually been based on Euclid's model.
Here, space is conceptualized as a three-dimensional infinite
sphere. To construct this sphere, a line is rotated on its axis through
360 degrees. This line is then bisected by another line that is
perpendicular to the first. This second line is, in turn, rotated
through 360 degrees. From this is created a sphere in which any

convergent set of coordinates constitutes a point in space. Starting from the concept of a 'point', the three dimensions of space can be constructed by the infinite repetition of the one below. For example, a line contains an infinite number of points, a plane has an infinite number of lines and a solid has an infinite number of planes. This suggests that the fourth dimension, time, will contain an infinite number of solids. Indeed, Ouspensky felt that humanity restricted itself by simply accepting that the three dimensions of height, width and breadth were all that there could be. When he experienced higher states of consciousness, he became convinced that there are more dimensions, and these dimensions have the same relationship to the ones below as we have seen with regard to the three perceived dimensions. Obviously, Ouspensky considered time to be the fourth dimension. But, unlike Kant, he did not consider infinity to be the infinite extension of time but another dimension perpendicular to it.

Ouspensky further observed that we measure space by applying linear concepts. We do not measure space by using cubes, even though logic suggests that we should. After all, space exists in three dimensions, not two. However, such a linear measurement makes sense simply because, when we are on the surface of the earth, two coordinates (width and breadth) are all that are needed to plot locations on the plane. We extrapolate this model to time. We measure it in a linear fashion, with time running in a line from the future to the present moment and then into the past. Indeed, what we really measure with regard to time is duration and speed. We cannot measure its direction because this seems to be an absolute; time's arrow has but one direction: from the past and into the future.

But as we have seen, Ouspensky considered that time also has three dimensions because he felt it was important to include direction. In effect this gives 'reality' six dimensions; three of space and three of time.

Any 'point of three-dimensional space' exists as a moment of time. But each moment, when in isolation, has no movement in space. It needs other points to isolate its movement. The same can be said for the time aspects of each moment. In order for time to proceed, each point moment needs other point moments in which to gauge its temporal velocity. Objects in space are simply extensions of points moving in time. Indeed, because of the limits of our senses we can only ever be aware of a small 'section' of reality as it exists in four dimensions. We perceive movement of an object as movement through time, but a time that consists of a series of 'nows'. What creates the illusion of movement is how our memories merge into the present moment.

Life in six dimensions

For Ouspensky, objects observed from a position within the fourth dimension will need to be perceived for their whole duration in time. In other words, a person will be perceived not as a body at a given 'now' but as a 'long body' in which both birth and death exist in a permanent 'now'. This body will be static, never changing, complete and non-evolving. It will just 'be'.

This 'fourth-dimensional' body will extend in breadth, width, height and time much in the way that a time-lapse photograph shows individuals moving around a room as long, snake-like extensions. Each moment is, in effect, a slice of this extended four-dimensional figure.

We perceive the world through our senses, such as touch and vision. These are designed to perceive a world consisting of just three dimensions. Therefore our senses present to consciousness every six-dimensional object as something that exists as a three-dimensional body. Indeed, we have a vague idea about the fourth dimension, time, but this is a very ill-defined sense that has defied philosophers for centuries. All we can perceive of time is its direction. We sense that either time is passing us by or that we are travelling through it. The other two dimensions of time cannot be comprehended by our senses, but they still exist.

For Ouspensky, the fifth dimension of space-time is a line that runs perpendicular to the always-perceived linear time-line running from the future through now and into the past. But this is not one line but many. At every 'now' point there will be an alternative, fifth-dimensional time that moves at 90 degrees from the perceived time-line. These fifth-dimensional 'nows' exist in a perpetual present or, more accurately, within an eternity outside linear time.

So what is the sixth dimension of space-time? Well, this is where Ouspensky starts to echo elements of modern quantum mechanics, specifically the fascinating theory of Hawking and Hertog (which we will discuss in detail in Chapter 12). Ouspensky suggests that the sixth dimension contains all the potential outcomes and possibilities of each action that is taken in the lower three dimensions. It is worth focusing on this. When we make a decision, say to get up and make a cup of coffee, what we do is actualize that intention into a manifested outcome.

We get up, cross the room and turn on the coffee machine, so that the intention is turned into a reality. However, there are numerous other actions that could have been brought into existence if we had decided to do something different, such as check our emails or read a newspaper.

Each of these actions remains only a possibility within our four-dimensional world. But Ouspensky suggests that these potentialities are actualized within the sixth dimension. So, within the time-line of the fifth dimension will be found a series of events, each one of which brings into existence one outcome of that event. However, within the sixth dimension all outcomes of every action exist.

Now this is where it becomes fascinating. The sixth dimension exists in a permanent 'now' so all actions and all outcomes co-exist in a never-ending moment. We exist in a far more complex and fascinating universe than our senses tell us. Ouspensky described it in this way:

We are one-dimensional beings in relation to time. Because of this we do not see parallel times... we do not see the angles and turns of time, but see time as a straight line.[30]

In many ways Ouspensky's model, in which all outcomes are contained within the sixth dimension, reminds me of the Eastern concept of the Akashic Record, which has recently been placed on a scientific footing by the work of the Hungarian-born philosopher of science Ervin László (1932–) and his concept of the 'Zero Point Field' (discussed in more detail in Chapter 12).

However, Ouspensky had another card up his sleeve by proposing that time does not exist as a straight line but as a curve of the fourth dimension. As we have seen, motion itself has three dimensions: duration, speed and direction. To expand upon this he observed that:

Time is the measure of motion. If we represent time by a line, then the only line which will satisfy all the demands of time will be a spiral. A spiral is a 'three-dimensional line' so to speak...[31]

Indeed, he gives as an example of this the motions of the planets. When we look at the moon we see it as a cross-section of how it is perceived at any one moment. However, the moon in its extended form, perceived from the fourth dimension is, in fact, a spiral band brought about by the fact that, as it revolves around the earth, our planet, in turn, revolves around the sun. Although the moon seems to follow an elliptical orbit around the earth it never actually returns to its initial position relative to space because the earth itself has moved along its orbit around the sun during that lunar month. To complicate things even further, the sun itself moves in space.

The Strange Life of Ivan Osokin

A Russian migrant by the name of Nicholas Bessarabof took a copy of Ouspensky's second published work, *Tertium Organum*, to America and gave it to the architect Claude Bragdon. Bragdon could read Russian and so he was able to study this book in its original form – a version that was, at the time, virtually unknown in the West. Bragdon was so fascinated by Ouspensky's concept of the fourth dimension that he incorporated it into his own design of the Rochester Chamber of Commerce Building, completed in 1916. This design was, in fact, a 'hypercube' or 'tesseract'.

As Ouspensky grew older he began to focus increasingly on what would happen when he died. He became very aware of the fact that at the moment of his death he would return to the moment of his birth and live his life over again. As a consequence, the concept of the Eternal Return became a major preoccupation for the ageing Ouspensky. He believed that the way to put right any wrongs that were found in the present would be to, in effect, correct the decision or decisions made in the past that had brought them about. His philosophy was both simple and profound; any negative outcomes can be avoided by not starting the course of cause-and-effect that led to such negative situations. In his writings, he proposes that we live our own life again and in so doing we can, with great effort, realize that our actions will have outcomes. This suggests an extreme solipsism whereby other people are simply players in a huge drama that evolves from actions made by the 'observer' consciousness. However, what Ouspensky fails to explain is the mechanism by which this 'remembering' works. If each of us will, after death, be reincarnated into the past to live our lives again, what can be the agent of change? If we are ignorant of the fact that we are living our life again, how can we possibly change anything? All the other 'minds' that we encounter will blindly follow the same plot as they did the previous time. It is as if we are doomed to act a role in the same extended 'formation novel', or 'bildungsroman' as described in German literature. We are ignorant of the fact that this is a 're-run' and so will react in the same way to the lines as they are fed to us by the other 'actors' in the drama.

Ouspensky recognized how this would involve a genuine repetition of events as described by the Stoics; a simple re-run of a life as unchanging as the storyline of a movie on a DVD. He described this life by using the Russian term *byt*. This word is difficult to translate but broadly means living a habitual lifestyle, such as a peasant life, a merchant-life, living in a rut and so on. Ouspensky considers such people to be caught in a deeply routine world where nothing changes. They do not move far and probably die in the house they were born in. Ouspensky described this as a 'deeply rooted, petrified, routine life'. In a statement that is somewhat brutal and elitist, he states that natural calamities wipe out thousands of these people at a time, suggesting that they are somehow expendable or worthless. For *byt* people, repetition is all they really know in this life and so it will be in the next. They are trapped in a circle turning back upon itself. For Ouspensky, this was the lot of the vast majority of humanity.

However, Ouspensky believed that certain 'advanced' human beings can break out of this mindless repetition. By a process that he never explains, these people become aware of the fact that they are living their lives again. Indeed, not only this but they remember what happened last time. In this way they can correct any errors they made last time and follow that outcome to its conclusion. This theme of 'self-awareness' is central to his 1905 novel *Kinemadrama* and its subsequent rewritten form, the already referenced *The Strange Life of Ivan Osokin*.

The novel opens in April 1902 where a 26-year-old Ivan Osokin is bidding goodbye to his girlfriend, Zinaida, at Moscow's Kursk Station. Zinaida and her mother are travelling south to the Crimea. The atmosphere is not at all positive. Zinaida had hoped that Ivan would be accompanying her but he is remaining in Moscow. She feels that it is because he is not interested in her, but the simple fact is that he is too poor to travel with her and too proud to tell her. As the train draws out of the station, Ivan has an overwhelming feeling of *déjà vu* – that he has already lived this moment at some time in his past. Over the next two months, he receives three letters from Zinaida and then hears nothing. Soon afterwards he receives the unwelcome news that she is to marry.

Ivan cannot envisage a life without his love so he decides to end it all with a revolver. However, it is clear that he is not too sure about this course of action and so decides to delay his suicide to allow himself one last night of hedonism and pleasure. Ivan knows of a local magician who has a taste for the finer things of life and decides to pay him a visit. On arrival at the magician's sumptuous apartment, Ivan spots an hourglass. He realizes that this symbolizes how he is trapped in time and that all his woes are tied up in the inexorable flow of this fourth dimension. He cries out to the magician: 'If only I could bring back a few years of this miserable time which does not even exist, if only I could do things differently.' The magician tells Ivan that he can grant this request and promises to send him back to relive the previous 12 years of his life. However, as the magician explains, these 12 years will be different because Ivan will remember what happened to him in his previous journey through these years. Here, Ouspensky is allowing his central character to break out of the *byt* life and time through the eyes of an adept.

Ivan awakes and finds himself back in his dormitory at school. He is 14 years of age but with the mind of a 26-year-old. He knows exactly what effect each decision he will make in the next 12 years will have on him and those around him. This should give the young Ivan a wonderful opportunity to put right all the errors of his previous life. But this is not to be. He makes the same decisions and falls into the same traps. By the time he has met Zinaida his life has followed such a predictable path that he has even forgotten that he is living his life again. Indeed, this may be Ouspensky weaving into his novel his belief that even non-*byt* people, as they age, forget their 'past-life' memories.

Such is the inexorable unfolding of Ivan's life that, at 26, he finds himself again standing at Kursk Station waving Zinaida goodbye. He again feels the sense of *déjà vu*. This time the reader knows why he has such a feeling. However, and this is the crux of the novel, Ivan had the self-same feeling of recognition at the start of the novel. The implication of this is clear; Ivan has followed this path many times before.

Returning to the magician, who has clearly been expecting him – as he was last time – Ivan is keen to be given a 'second' chance to put right his mistakes. As the magician responds with his offer Ivan suddenly remembers that he has done this before. He then realizes that he is caught in some kind of temporal trap. He points this out to the magician:

> *'But this is simply turning round on a wheel!' says Osokin. 'It is a trap!' The old man smiles. 'My dear friend,' he says, 'this trap is called life. . . You must realize that you yourself can change nothing and that you must seek help. . . And to live with this realization means to sacrifice something big for it. . . A man can be given only what he can use; and he can use only that for which he has sacrificed something. . . This is the law of human nature.'*[32]

To many people, the name Peter Ouspensky will forever be linked with that of another fascinating character, the Georgian-Greek mystic George Ivanovich Gurdjieff (1866–1949). For many years the two men were inseparable. Ouspensky became a pupil of Gurdjieff in 1916, but within a few years it was clear that the two men had differing viewpoints about certain things, specifically that of the reality of the Eternal Return (or Eternal Recurrence). In his book *In Search of the Miraculous*, Ouspensky describes a dialogue he had with Gurdjieff regarding this contentious subject:

> *'. . . You never answer any questions I ask.'*
> *'Very well,' said G., laughing. 'I promise to answer now any question you care to ask, as it happens in fairy tales.'*

I felt he wanted to draw me out of my bad mood and I was inwardly grateful to him, although something in me refused to be mollified.

And suddenly I remembered that I wanted above all to know what G. thought about 'eternal recurrence', about the repetition of lives, as I understood it. I had many times tried to start a conversation about this and to tell G. my views. But these conversations had always remained almost monologues. G. had listened in silence and then begun to talk of something else.

'Very well,' I said, 'tell me what you think of recurrence. Is there any truth in this, or none at all. What I mean is: Do we live only this once and disappear, or does everything repeat and repeat itself, perhaps an endless number of times, only we do not know and do not remember it?'

'This idea of repetition,' said G., 'is not the full and absolute truth, but is the nearest possible approximation of the truth. In this case truth cannot be expressed in words. But what you say is very near to it. And if you understand why I do not speak of this, you will be still nearer to it. What is the use of a man knowing about recurrence if he is not conscious of it and if he himself does not change? . . . Why should he make any efforts today when there is so much time and so many possibilities ahead – the whole of eternity?'

Further on Ouspensky continues:

. . . My bad mood vanished, I did not even notice when.
G. sat there smiling.

'You see how easy it is to turn you; but perhaps I was merely romancing to you, perhaps there is no recurrence at all. What pleasure is it when sulky Ouspensky sits there, does not eat, does not drink. "Let us try to cheer him up," I think to myself. And how is one to cheer a person up? One likes funny stories. For

another, you must find his hobby. And I know that Ouspensky has this hobby – "eternal recurrence". So I offered to answer any question of his. I knew what he would ask.'

Further:

The future showed that I was right, for although G. did not introduce the idea of recurrence into his exposition of the system, he referred several times to the idea of recurrence, chiefly in speaking of the lost possibilities of people who had approached the system and then had drawn away from it.[33]

Clearly, the two men had very different opinions on the subject of Recurrence. As he grew older, Ouspensky became more and more preoccupied with what he called 'self-remembering'. Ironically enough, this had been a technique that had been introduced to him by, of all people, Gurdjieff himself. This was a crucial ability that had to be nurtured during this life if one was to gain anything from existence in the next. In order to change our lives we have to carry some knowledge forward from one life to the other. In contradiction of what he described in *The Strange Life of Ivan Osokin*, in which the eponymous hero, despite knowing the outcomes of his actions, still fails to avoid all the errors he had made the first time, Ouspensky believed that some people can turn the circle into a spiral. In many ways this echoes what Phil Conners does in the hugely Ouspenskian movie *Groundhog Day* (see page 273–6) by carrying his knowledge forward from day to day while all those around him start each day afresh. In this way Conners is able to fulfil all his ambitions and dreams in one, recurring 24-hour period.

For Ouspensky, 'self-remembering' could be developed by 'stopping thought' so that old memories flood in to fill the vacuum. He proposed that one technique to use was by becoming fully self-aware.

However, he pointed out that:

> *Thinking of nothing will not produce self-remembering in a person*
> *who knows nothing about self-remembering. Practice without theory*
> *does not work any better than theory without practice.*[34]

Ouspensky remained certain that eternal life was available not only to all people but also to everything that exists, but that the way this eternal life is perceived is of utmost importance. It is only by knowing what is taking place that we can escape repetition. He explained this in a section of *New Model* when he wrote:

> *'Eternal life' is a term that has several meanings. . . on the one*
> *hand eternal life belongs not only to all people but even to*
> *everything that exists, while on the other hand it is necessary to*
> *be born again in order to obtain it. This contradiction would be*
> *inexplicable, if the difference between the fifth and sixth*
> *dimensions had not been previously established. Both the one and*
> *the other are eternity. But one is unalterable repetition, always*
> *with the same end, and the other is escape from this repetition.*[35]

And this is how Ouspensky spent the last few months of his life, by trying hard to self-remember so that he would become self-aware in his next incarnation. Ouspensky passed over into another dimension of time in 1947, leaving a handful of very enthusiastic supporters keen to carry on his life's work. It is to this group we now turn.

CHAPTER 4
AFTER OUSPENSKY

Maurice Nicoll

One of Ouspensky's earliest followers was the Cambridge-educated psychiatrist and author Maurice Nicoll (1884–1953). Nicoll first heard Ouspensky lecture in London in 1921. At that time Nicoll was heavily involved in the work of the Swiss psychiatrist and founder of analytical psychology Carl Gustav Jung (1875–1961) and was even considering becoming Jung's representative in London. This grounding in Jungian thinking was to make Ouspensky's ideas particularly attractive to him. The following year Nicoll heard Gurdjieff speak and such was the effect that he relinquished his medical consultancy and joined Gurdjieff at his Institute for the Harmonious Development of Man in France. Unfortunately, within a year, Gurdjieff had closed the Institute. On their return to London, Nicoll and his wife, Catherine, joined Ouspensky's group. It seems that his relationship with Ouspensky was somewhat different from the other followers in that Nicoll often made the usually dour Russian intellectual laugh out loud. Indeed, Ouspensky regularly sought out Nicoll's companionship and he sometimes visited the Nicolls at their country cottage.

In 1929, Nicoll wrote *Living Time*. Although not actually published until 1952, this work has become a classic within the tradition of 'The Work', the term given to Gurdjieff and Ouspensky's underlying philosophy (also called 'The Fourth Way'). In her biography of Nicoll, his personal secretary Beryl Pogson described how he undertook this book by collecting 'all the thoughts about Time and Eternity that had come to him from Hermetic literature, from the Greeks, the neo-Platonists, from the mystics throughout the ages, and from Ouspensky, whose "Theory of Eternal Return" was not part of Gurdjieff's system.'[36] It is clear that Nicoll's extensive knowledge of Jungian philosophy was to add an intriguing new angle to our understanding of subjective time.

Indeed, this is why Nicoll's work is of such significance with regard to Ouspensky's philosophy of the Return/Recurrence. For him, this was a reality, a form of reincarnation in which a person's essence returns to visible life. However, Nicoll also believed that as one advanced through many lives one could reach a higher level of being and in doing so could relate to other people earlier than in previous existences. In order for this to take place, Nicoll proposed that an invisible guiding presence that existed outside of the world must assist in this development. He spoke of the universe itself as being an 'infinite response' that has its own intelligence. Many commentators have described Nicoll's model as an amalgamation of Ouspensky's ideas on the Recurrence with Nietzsche's far more rigid model.

In *Living Time*, Nicoll is sympathetic to the idea of Recurrence but places it within a much broader exploration of the concept of time. For him, there is an eternal place that is outside of time and space. This is similar to the Gnostic concept of 'Aeon', a world behind the perceived world of the senses.

Nicoll was willing to open himself up to alternative ways of understanding the nature of time and the Eternal Return. In a series of personal experiments with ether, he reported experiencing various changes in the subjective duration of time. During these encounters with the Aeonic, he felt both a sensation of the 'Eternal Present' and also an experience in which events recurred. Intriguingly, he also felt that his mind was functioning outside of his body.

From these experiences, he concluded that we inhabit a small portion of a greater reality that he calls 'living time'. As we have encountered many times in this book, it is the sense of 'now' that is central to our understanding of the true nature of 'living time'. Nicoll argues that the part of us that lives in time – the 'time-man' – is always so preoccupied with preparing for the future that he never perceives the 'now'. He is always anticipating what is about to happen and in doing so misses the true nature of reality. Nicoll writes:

> We must understand that what we call the present moment is not now, for the present moment is on the horizontal line of time, and the now is vertical to this and incommensurable with it. . . . If we could awaken, if we could ascend in the scale of reality concealed within us, we would understand the meaning of the 'future' world. Our true future is our own growth in now, not in the tomorrow of passing time.[37]

I am surprised by how similar Nicoll's model is to that of the concept of 'orthogonal time' proposed by the great speculative fiction writer Philip K. Dick (1928–82). In the autumn of 1977, Dick was invited to give a speech at a large festival in Metz, France. The evening before the speech, Dick agreed to be interviewed by two German journalists, Uwe Anton and Werner Fuchs. In this interview, Dick outlined how he had been experimenting with methods of synchronizing the firing of his neurons in such a way that he could, as he put it, 'catch up with time'. These methods involved consuming a particular formula of vitamins. He claimed that this meant he was able to allow time to accelerate past him and then, in effect, view the past. He tried to explain how this may have worked:

> The speech I'm going to give tomorrow is on orthogonal time which is not my invention. They do think that maybe there is another form of time, maybe at right angles to linear time, and this might account for my experience because there seemed to be a time flow within the linear time flow, maybe in an opposite or orthogonal direction from linear time. And it is in transformations around us.[38]

I suspect that both Nicoll and Dick were using similar Gnostic sources for this intriguing model of time. This is something I would like to return to later.

In many ways, Nicoll's views are the closest I have encountered to my own thoughts on the matter of the Eternal Return. Indeed, in this section his analysis is very similar to my own:

> It is difficult to reconcile oneself to the view that a single life determines our lot. We seem to come toward the end of our life just when we begin to get some insight. The illusion of passing-time makes us think that we cannot change the past and that it is not worth trying to change anything now. . . It is surely here that the idea of the repetition of the life necessarily comes in. . . Remember that we do not live only in this little visible moment but in a WORLD extended in every direction, visible and invisible.[39]

In his book *Don't Forget: P.D. Ouspensky's Life of Self-remembering*, Bob Hunter describes how Ouspensky once asked Nicoll what he would wish to do had he the opportunity to relive his life. Nicoll replied that he would like to have the power to feel meaning in all his experiences. It seems that this was of great importance to Nicoll. In her biography of Nicoll, Beryl Pogson described how, between the years of 1946 and 1953, Nicoll had tried very hard to become self-conscious and aware that he was reliving his life again. Indeed, in a letter to the author J.B. Priestley, famous for writing plays that explore the nature of time, Nicoll suggested the following idea to him:

> Now, could you write a play of a man, say of sixty, visiting 'himself' as he was (say) a lad of twenty at Cambridge and seeing what he could advise this lad to do? To move through 'time-body' was one of the exercises I was taught by Gurdjieff. Only you, with your fine dramatic sense, could do this play.[40]

Rodney Collin

As we shall discover in Chapter 11, J.B. Priestley was a great admirer of Ouspensky and did indeed write one play based upon the concept of the Eternal Return. Entitled *I Have Been Here Before*, this play even features a mysterious Eastern European character called Dr Görtler who is clearly based upon Ouspensky himself. Unfortunately, Priestley did not take up Nicoll's suggestion.

However, in another interesting parallel between Nicoll and Philip K. Dick, a similar situation was reported by the American writer in an interview with the science fiction author Richard Lupoff.

> *Back at the time I was starting to write science fiction, I was asleep one night and I woke up and there was a figure standing at the edge of the bed, looking down at me. I grunted in amazement and all of a sudden my wife woke up and started screaming a line of verse because she could see it too. She started screaming, but I recognized it and I started reassuring her, saying that it was me that was there and not to be afraid. Within the last two years – let's say that was in 1951 – I've dreamed almost every night that I was back in that house, and I have a strong feeling that back then in 1951 or '52 that I saw my future self, who had somehow, in some way we don't understand – I wouldn't call it occult – passed backward during one of my dreams now of that house, going back there and seeing myself again. So there really are some strange things. . .*[41]

After Ouspensky's death, other followers were equally keen to continue with his work. One of the most determined of this group was Rodney Collin (1909–56), who was born in Brighton. Originally called Rodney Collin Smith, he was to change his name to Rodney Collin in his teens. He attended the London School of Economics and then became a journalist, writer and traveller. He had read Ouspensky's *New Model* when it was first published and, although he felt that he was not quite ready for its message at that time, he attended some of Nicoll's groups and found that, with Nicoll's assistance, he began to understand what Ouspensky's philosophy really signified. Fortunately, Collin's wife, Janet, who was independently wealthy, shared his enthusiasm for Ouspensky's teachings and this allowed him to pursue his interests with vigour. Unusually for those in Ouspensky's circle, Collin had no great interest in the teachings of Gurdjieff and considered that Ouspensky was the true teacher.

From his earliest encounters with Ouspensky, Collin became his greatest supporter and admirer. Although this enthusiasm was not always reciprocated, Collin continued to be involved with Ouspensky to the end. Indeed, after Ouspensky's body had been removed for burial at Lyne Church in October 1947, Collin locked himself inside his master's bedroom and refused to leave. He stayed in the room for six days without food. When he eventually came out he was unshaven and dishevelled but carried with him an air of mysticism. He claimed that he had been in telepathic contact with Ouspensky and that his master had informed him that he had, at last, escaped from Recurrence.

In 1948, Rodney and Janet left England and moved to Tlalpam, in Mexico, where they set up 'Work Groups' to spread Ouspensky's ideas ('The Work'). It was here that Collin began writing his first major book, *The Theory of Eternal Life.* This book was published anonymously in 1949. In 1954, his most famous book, *The Theory of Celestial Influence,* was published in Spanish. An English language version was soon to follow. In honour of his influential teacher, Collin dedicated the book to: '*MAGISTRO MEO. Qui Sol Fuit Est Et Erit'.* This translates as, 'My Master, Who Was, Is, and Will Be the Sun.' It was clear that, for Collin, his book was simply a reflection of the work of Ouspensky. This book is Collin's most lasting legacy.

In 1955, Collin's path took a strongly spiritual turn. He converted to Roman Catholicism and travelled extensively in South America and Asia in search of further evidence of the 'Fourth Way'. During this time, he believed that he was being guided by an inner voice that he identified as that of his 'Master', Ouspensky. In 1956 he visited Peru. Tragically he experienced a heart attack while climbing a bell tower in Cuzco and died after falling from the tower into the street below.

Collin had taken Ouspensky's ideas and updated them with his own particular interest – the perception of time. Much of what Collin wrote is quite fascinating and he makes some very interesting observations. Unfortunately, Collin was more of a philosopher than a scientist. As such, he tends to come to conclusions via introspection rather than empirical study. This is in no way a criticism but in my opinion his willingness to do this without searching out scientific support for his assumptions sometimes led him down blind alleyways.

Central to Collin's belief system is that all of nature, from the infinitely small to the unimaginably huge, is linked by dimensions of time and space, with each 'level' functioning within its own space and time and touching the levels above and below along only one plane of its dimension. In this way, Collin applies Ouspensky's model of dimensions of time and space to a cosmological viewpoint.

The scales of perception

If we go outside on a cloudless night and look up at the heavens we may see the faint trace of the Milky Way spanning the sky, appearing as a curved line or arc of light. Now, from our viewpoint we see a collection of stars we call the Milky Way. In reality, we are viewing our own spiral galaxy, as seen edge-on from a position towards the rim and looking in towards its centre. However, if we viewed this same group of stars from a nearby galaxy, say the Small Magellanic Cloud, we would see a swirling cloud of gas and stars shaped like a huge Catherine wheel. So to us on earth, the Milky Way is a curved line whereas to our observer in intergalactic space it is a disk. In due course we cease to see the Milky Way at all as our closest star, the sun, begins to rise in the east, spreading its light across the sky. We see this new object as a disk. As the sun illuminates the world around us, we see part of our planet, earth, spread in front of us as far as the eye can see. How do we see our home planet from our vantage point? We see it as a vast surface curving into the distance, a curved solid. So we now have three objects, the Milky Way, the sun, and the earth seen as an arc, or curved line, or disk, or curved plane and a surface, or curved solid respectively.

Now, the relationship between a curved solid, a curved plane and a curved line is the relationship between three dimensions, two dimensions and one dimension. It can be said that during our night's observations we perceived the Milky Way in one dimension, breadth, the sun in two dimensions, length and breadth, and our home planet in three dimensions, length, breadth and depth. Now, what is interesting about this is that with each ascent of scale we lose a dimension. On earth we perceive all three. As we look at the sun (and indeed the solar system) we lose depth. As we gaze further out at the Milky Way then length too falls out of the equation. Furthermore, when viewed from the sun, the earth is not just a solid ball but also a line of movement. In relation to the Milky Way, the sun is not only a disk but also a moving point.

But Collin does not stop at this. In relation to the galaxy our sun is like a single cell within the human body. This cell is surrounded by untold millions of objects similar to itself that make up the human body, just as the sun is like the millions of stars that make up the galaxy. In turn, this cell is like a 'galaxy' to its own atoms. Each object in this ever-decreasing world exists in its own set of dimensions, unaware of the dimensions above.

However, a further dimension has to be brought in to this view, that of time. Each 'object' discussed above – atom, cell, person, planet, star, galaxy – has its own time scale of existence.

This time scale of existence, a lifetime, moves in a fourth dimension, time.

All creatures are born, live and die in this fourth dimension. In order to measure the actual perception of time for the differing levels of life, Collin argued that he only needed to do this accurately for one dimension. It could then be back-calculated for all the other dimensions.

For Collin, the problem was in understanding the relationship between diameter and duration, between line and time. He considered that the crucial element was that:

Time is created by rotation about the vital centre of the greater world. As regards the planetary world, [the German astronomer] *Kepler both recognized and expressed this in his Third Law, in which he showed that the relation between distances from the sun (line) and periods of rotation about the sun (time) is the relation between square roots and cube roots. Since all cosmoses are built upon the same general plan, and since the relationship between cosmoses now appears similar to the relation between dimensions within a cosmos, we will be justified in trying to use this formula to establish that general relation between line and time, between space and duration, which we seek. Put simply, Kepler's Third Law appears to suggest that while linear space develops by cubes, duration develops by squares only. In order to demonstrate this without complicated calculation, we will make two parallel columns – one representing space, in which each stage is a multiplication by 31.8, the other representing time, in which the equivalent stage is a multiplication by 10. The left-hand column will represent radii and the right-hand column lifetimes. Our base will be man and for convenience we will take his life-time as 80 years and his radius (heart to fingertips) as one metre. Upon this table we will now place examples of general classes of beings, wherever they appear to fit, either by size or duration.*[42]

He then presents a chart, which I reproduce here:

Linear Space-Radii	Object-Being-Organism	Duration-Lifetime
1,000 million kilometres		8,000 million years
	Planets	
31.8 million kilometres		800 million years
1,000,000 kilometres		80 million years
	Whole world of Nature	
32.8 kilometres	Mountains and lakes	80,000 years
1 kilometre		8,000 years
	Towns	
3.18 metres	Large trees	800 years
	Large animals	
1 metre	Men	80 years
3.18 centimetres		8 years
	Small animals	
1 millimetre	Insects and plants	10 months
	Bacteria	
0.03 millimetres	Large cells	1 month
0.001 millimetres	Small cells	3 days

Collin moves on to show that the subjective passing of time itself is different within each dimension and also different for living creatures. He calculates that there are approximately 28,000 days in a normal man's lifetime. Collin is then interested in the minimum time for perception. He says that this is the time taken to receive, and digest, one single photographic image or impression. If the eye were a camera, this would be its fastest shutter speed. This is not just the time taken in perceiving light by the retina but also in recognizing the image given. Collin says that there is an impulse in the brain that can be measured at ten cycles per second and suggests that this is the minimum unit of recognition. He makes an interesting diversion to say that the Egyptian hieroglyph for this period of time, *anut*, usually called 'the twinkling of the eye' combines precisely the two signs for 'eye' and for 'wave' or 'vibration'. Indeed, he points out that by looking in the back of an open film camera and varying the shutter speed one cannot see an image at 1,000th of a second but one can perceive that the shutter has opened. At a 30th of a second an image can, with concentration, be perceived. This speed is confirmed by the fact that images run through a cinema projector give the illusion of movement as images blur into each other at speeds over a 30th of a second.

Collin makes, in my opinion, the correct assumption that the major thing that separates human perception from that of other living creatures is time. He takes as an example gnats, whose life-time is a single day. He argues that all lives are the same length, the variable being not time, but the inner perception of time. He points out that a gnat lives its life nearly 30,000 times faster than man does. This means that all vibrations reaching the gnat will also be reduced by 30,000 times, or about 15 octaves. Indeed, a gnat will perceive radiation in a totally different way to man. Radio waves will acquire the nature of magnetism, heat and light that of electricity. Light in turn would be represented by gamma rays. Sound travelling at around 1,100 feet per second (340 metres per second) for man will cover no more than one third of an inch per second (7.6 mm) for a gnat.[43]

However, I have to disagree with Collin here in that he is missing the logical conclusion of his theory. Time is relative and as such each animal or insect perceives time in its own way. A gnat fits in 75 years of life relative to him in the one day of our life scale. This is well put by the naturalist Oliver Pearson, quoted by Collin. In an article published in *Scientific American* in 1953, Pearson made the following observation:

> The living rate of an animal depends upon its size; the smaller the animal, the faster it lives. Pound for pound the more diminutive animal eats more food, it consumes more oxygen, produces more energy – in short, has a higher rate of metabolism. The humming-bird has the highest rate of metabolism of any bird or animal.

Each gram of its tissue metabolises 15 times as fast as a gram of pigeon and more than 100 times as fast as a gram of elephant.[44]

Collin argues that nature exists in many different levels of perception. Living creatures inhabit one, and only one, level. As such the subjective passing of time itself is different within each perception level and therefore also different for living creatures. He comments on the observation made above by Pearson in relation to the hummingbird. He says that in order to live at this speed the hummingbird has to eat every ten or 15 minutes, that is, about sixty times a day to man's three times. In addition, it must hibernate every night in the same way and for the same reason that higher animals hibernate for the winter, simply because it cannot get any food to maintain its expenditure of energy. As he rightly says:

Watching the almost invisible buzzing of its wings, the ceaseless darting of its flight, we indeed get a vivid impression of a creature living a hundred times faster than man.[45]

It's all relative

Indeed, if we take the fact that certain animals move at a faster rate than ourselves and are therefore perceiving time at a much faster rate, is it not then consistent to apply this the other way. Plants, particularly trees, can be extremely long-lived. The bristlecone pine of the western USA is an example. A stand of bristlecones in Wheeler Peak, Nevada, is known to contain several trees over 3,000 years old, and one of them is thought to be about 4,900 years old. Perception of time, if indeed one can consider a tree to have any form of perception, for these life forms will be exceedingly slow. In his book *The Voices of Time*, Roland Fischer states:

The relativity of our reference point can be demonstrated by taking a moving picture of a plant at one frame per minute, and then

speeding it up to thirty frames a second. The plant will appear to
behave like an animal, clearly perceiving stimuli and reacting to
them. Why then, do we call it unconscious? To organisms that react
1,800 times as quickly as we react we might appear to be
unconscious. They would in fact be justified in calling us unconscious
since we would not normally be conscious of their behaviour.[46]

However, Collin's major interest is man's concept of internal time. He is particularly interested in trying to explain why life runs at different speeds as life progresses.

Collin suggests that in order to put a human lifetime into perspective it must be broken down into 1,000 equal segments, each of which is roughly equal to a month. Collin adds that these thousand 'bits' must be divided by a logarithmic scale (increasing by multiples of ten) rather than an arithmetical scale. As such, the crucial numbers between one and a thousand would be 1, 10, 100 and 1,000 months. This is where things become interesting. Collin then proposes that we look at what occurs in a normal human lifetime at each of these points. We take the first point to be the moment of conception. Man is then born 10 lunar months after his conception, thus giving us the end of the first period. The second period comes to an end after 100 months and coincides with the end of childhood. Between 100 months and 1,000 months is maturity and old age. So, in effect, there are three equal parts to a full-term human life – gestation, childhood and maturity.

Collin then decides to split each of the three periods into three crucial milestones, which he terms 'life-points'. These are at 2, 4½, 10, 20, 44, 100, 200, 440 and 1,000 months from conception. That is, at the first 2 and 4½ months of pre-natal life, then at birth, and then at 10 months, 2¾ years, and at 7, 15, 35 and 76 years. The periods between these milestones are, according to Collin, of equal duration in his scale of organic time. So what does happen at these points? The first two months of pre-natal existence sees the foetus become fully human in form and structure, with the various organs and parts clearly defined. At four and a half months 'quickening' occurs, and the foetus acquires involuntary movement and individual blood circulation. At birth the baby begins to breathe.

Ten months witnesses the child beginning to crawl and gain control over its voluntary movements. At two and a half years the child begins to talk and complete sentences, to refer to itself as 'I', and develop simple intellectual processes. By 7 the child attains the 'age of reason'. By 15 years, puberty is reached and by 35 our initial embryo is in the prime of life, the point marked with a momentary balance of all powers.

From then on it starts to go downhill until, at 76, the average person is approaching the end of the normal life term and is preparing for the next stage.

Whatever the reader feels about Collin's methodology in coming to these life-points, one cannot avoid the suspicion that in some way or other he may have hit on something. As we get into our thirties we can look back and say that our perception of time has quickened as we have become older, and as we age this perception becomes faster and faster.

This perception of time speeding up as we get older is experienced by us all as we age. This can be confirmed by talking to any senior citizen who describes their experiences in the Second World War as if it were yesterday. In their perception it was very recent and, in addition, the five years of the war occurred when they were much younger and time would have passed more slowly. So not only does the war seem closer in time but also the events that occurred to the person seemed to last much longer than events in the last ten or twenty years may have done. Indeed, notice how memory works with these older people. They can recall in great detail what happened in, say, 1945, but cannot tell you what occurred to them last week. That is because from last week to today seems like only a few minutes compared to the time scales they remember in the 1940s.

However, this speeding up of psychological time can be affected by a change of mood or some form of external stimulus. Great feelings of joy, pain or wonderment can make time slow right down. Lying in bed with the flu is an example. Whatever age you are the minutes slowly drag into hours. A wonderful example of this effect was a comment made by Einstein when asked about 'psychological time'. He replied: 'When a man sits with a pretty girl for an hour, it seems like a minute. But let him sit on a hot stove for a minute and it's longer than any hour.'

The Bentov technique

In addition, certain drugs can affect perception to such an extent that time can slow down to a snail's pace. Examples can be found of people who have taken drugs such as 'speed' where their perception seems to run much faster than the external world to the extent that they can 'watch' water being poured out of a jug as if viewing it in slow motion. When people talk to them the words are heard with long gaps between them. Obviously, the external world has not slowed down because it runs on astronomical time, but the speed of that incoming stimulus is processed by the brain as accelerated perception. In his book *Stalking the Wild Pendulum*, the Czech-born scientist and writer Itzhak Bentov (1929–79) suggested the following experiment, which can be performed by anybody. All that is needed is a clock with a second hand, or a wrist watch with a fairly large dial and an easily visible second hand. You then follow these instructions:

Step 1: *Relax. Position the watch in front of you on a table so that it will be easily visible without any effort through half-closed eyes. Lean with your elbows on the table if you wish.*

Step 2: *Look at the watch in a relaxed way and follow the second hand. Try to absorb and remember the rhythm at which it moves. All this has to be done quite effortlessly.*

Step 3: *This is the crucial step in the experiment. Close your eyes and visualize yourself engaged in your favourite activity. For instance, if you visualize yourself on a beach in the sun, you have to be there – all of you. Don't just think you are there, but feel the warmth of the sun and the texture of the sand; hear the sound of the waves; use all your senses. The result will be better if you choose a relaxing activity rather than a hectic one.*

Step 4: *When you feel that you have stabilized this visualization, slowly open your eyes just a bit. Do not focus on the watch, just let your gaze fall on the dial as if you were a disinterested observer of this whole affair. If you have followed the instructions properly, you may see the second hand stick in a few places, slow down, and hover for a while. If you are very successful, you'll be able to stop the second hand for quite a while.*[47]

What is important to realize in this experiment, and I believe that realization of this fact is crucial to the understanding of the concepts of this book, is that you have not actually stopped the second hand in the 'real world'. Somebody standing next to you would not see the second hand slow down or stop. To them it continues moving at its normal speed. It is your perception of time that has slowed down. After all, a second hand is not actually measuring time in an objective sense like a set of scales weighs a pound of flour, the second hand is just moving around a clock face. You are seeing 'motion', not 'time'. Time cannot be seen or quantified in any objective way. It cannot be packaged in ten-minute-sized boxes.

Take a little 'time' out now to ponder the next few lines – make yourself a cup of coffee and just think about what I am actually saying:

How long does ten minutes take?

The obvious answer, indeed the only possible answer, is ten minutes. However, a pound of flour is exactly that – an amount of flour (subject) weighing one pound (term of measurement). Time is the only thing that we measure against itself. There is no other way. That person is six feet tall. There has to be six feet of something; six feet only exists when it is measuring something.

The great Russian writer Leo Tolstoy (1828–1910) realized, at a later stage in his life, that he only had four remembered events that took place before he was 5 years old. He said that he found this both 'strange and terrible' because looking back from his age then (50) to being 5 years old:

> There was only one step, but from a new-born infant to a 5-year-old is a terrifying distance.[48]

If it is the case that metabolism is the main factor controlling the perception of time then the idea that children perceive time at a slower rate than adults is not at all surprising. We know that a child's metabolism does indeed run faster, and burns energy at a much greater rate than an adult's. As we progress through our lives this rate runs slower and slower. As such, Collin's belief that time runs much faster for a 60-year-old than for a 6-year-old has a basis in scientific fact.

Age and time

In 1877, the French psychologist Paul Janet (1823–99) suggested something he termed the 'Proportional Theory'. In simple terms, Janet argued that as we get older each time period constitutes a smaller fraction of our total life. For example, at the age of 5 a year constitutes one fifth of one's life; at 10 years of age a year's duration has decreased to a tenth. By the time we are 50 that year is only one fiftieth of one's lifetime. Therefore, at 10 years of age that six-week summer holiday is a much larger proportion of life-experience than at 30.

The American writer Gay Gaer Luce (1930–) proposed one explanation as to why this may be. She was of the opinion that a child's additional sensitivity to other external stimuli reflected this higher level of metabolism. In the progression from childhood to maturity there is a decline in the rate at which one consumes oxygen, and therefore a slowing of the metabolism. She wrote:

Our brains must respond at certain times to hear sounds of certain frequencies. A young person hears higher sounds than an old person, suggesting that his brain responses are faster. However humans do not have receptors that respond as fast as those of a dog, which means that our pets can hear ultra-high sounds that we cannot. We can see certain colours, but others are beyond our vision. We can see discrete movement until it becomes so fast that our brains no longer separate the frames of a moving picture but instead see continuous motion; when flashes of light occur swiftly we perceive only a beam.[49]

The idea that metabolic rates within the body influence our perception of time was first suggested by French psychologist M. François in the late 1920s.[50] However, it was a curious event noted by an American kidney specialist a few years later that was to focus research on to the role of metabolic rates and subjective time perception.

In the early 1930s a doctor by the name of Hudson Hoagland was treating his wife Anna at home for a bout of influenza. He left her for twenty minutes in order to visit a local drugstore on her behalf and on his return noticed that she was agitated. On asking her the reason for her concern, she replied that as far as she was concerned he had been away for over an hour and that she was worried about him. This intrigued the kidney specialist and, with his wife's agreement, he tested her subjective time perception at different times during her fever. He asked her to count to 60 at what she believed to be one-second intervals. Using a stopwatch, he noted precisely what number she had reached when one minute of stopwatch time had elapsed. He repeated this exercise as her temperature fluctuated. The results intrigued him. He found, for example, that when her temperature was at 97.4°F (36.3°C) her count to 60 took 52 seconds. But when her fever rose to 103°F (39.4°C) she counted to 60 in just 34 seconds. He plotted these results and found a direct correlation between increased temperature and accelerated subjective time duration. He discovered that as her temperature increased she reached the count of 60 in shorter and shorter objective time.

Hoagland was keen to follow up his findings under laboratory conditions and over a period of years he tested various volunteers under extreme temperature conditions. While in these states, Hoagland had his subjects describe their subjective sensations of time duration. He discovered that raising a person's temperature can slow down their sense of time flow by as much as 20 per cent. Hoagland concluded that there is some form of chemical pacemaker in the brain that governs our subjective sense of the rate at which time is being recorded by the brain.[51]

Put simply, the Hoagland Theory states that we all have an internal chemical clock that can be speeded up by a rise in body temperature. This causes objective time to appear to go more slowly, since clock time would pass in the same interval of objective time.

In many ways the work of Hoagland vindicated the ideas of Rodney Collin. All small, warm-blooded animals dart around at great speed. An example of this is a mouse.

We have all, I am sure, attempted to catch a mouse if it is found in our home. The small creature's speed of movement and reaction is simply amazing. It also lives a very short time. It is not therefore unreasonable to conclude that it also perceives its environment in a radically different way from man.

Time for the mouse must be far slower to take into account its much higher metabolic rate. Is it not beyond imagination that a day in the life of this creature could be the equivalent of weeks, or even months, in the way it perceives the temporal flow? To a mouse, we must seem not only huge but very slow-moving and clumsy. It is therefore no surprise to me, and fits in well with the overall position of this book, that a man can never catch a mouse because, to a mouse, man's movements are extremely slow and easy to avoid. This position can be extended to insects.

Although cold-blooded, their energy processing works differently from ours and so have much quicker rates of perception than man. Try to hit a fly with your hand, or catch one in flight. It is virtually impossible.

John G. Bennett and 'hyparxis'

Another of Gurdjieff's early students was John G. Bennett (1897–1974). In many ways, Bennett was a very different kind of thinker from Nicoll or Collin. He was a mathematician and technologist and his interest in the true nature of time is coloured by this way of thinking. In his model, he posits a six-dimensional universe consisting of three spatial dimensions and three time-like dimensions. The three time dimensions he called 'time', 'eternity' and 'hyparxis'. In his hugely ambitious four-volume series of books, *The Dramatic Universe*, he describes in great detail exactly what he means by these concepts.

Bennett explains that normal 'time' ensures that we perceive events as successive. From this we perceive the concepts of 'before' and 'after'. The present exists but the past and the future do not. Eternity, on the other hand, is another word for persistence. It is persistence that facilitates change, because without change we would exist in a meaningless, and totally static, present. Bennett calls eternity the 'storehouse of potentialities'. By this he means that there can be many lines of successive time simultaneously present in eternity. So far in this book we have already encountered very similar definitions by other writers. However, with his third concept, 'hyparxis', Bennett introduces something quite new. He argues that successive time does not allow for choice. Conversely, eternity presents us with choice but gives us no latitude to exercise that choice. In order to connect potential and actual action we need another form of time. This is what Bennett termed 'hyparxis'. In T.S. Eliot's *Four Quartets*, the meditation on the nature of psychological time that we have already discussed in relation to the Eternal Return, we encounter a line of verse that states:

> *Men's curiosity searches past and future/And clings to that dimension. But to apprehend/The point of intersection of the time-less/with time, is an occupation for the saint.*[52]

The line 'the point of intersection of the timeless with time' is hyparxis. Bennett defined this as 'ableness-to-be'. It combines what is actual with what is virtual and in so doing defines that mystical concept we perceive as the 'present moment'. We all have this feeling that the present moment is an instant but sitting behind it is a sense of permanence. Bennett stated that hyparxis can be:

> *Traced throughout all levels of existence from atoms through the simplest living forms up to man and it is this factor that entitles us to look beyond man to the attainment of superhuman levels. Without this factor everything would be compelled to remain wholly determined by its own eternal pattern.*[53]

In many ways, Bennett's model represents the curious timelessness of sub-atomic particles and the mysteries of the quantum world. It is to the science of time that we now turn our attention.

CHAPTER 5

THE PHYSICS OF TIME

The twin slits

For the modern physicist, time is one of the basic tools of her trade. She will use it to measure the relationships between differing physical substances. Super-accurate chronographs are used to calculate to the finest degree how chemical processes occur. Her associates in the fields of cosmology and astronomy use 'light years' as a way of measuring the distances between stars and galaxies. Time is everywhere in science, and yet it is the greatest mystery. Indeed, when discussing the true nature of time with scientists we quickly find ourselves straying into the areas of philosophy we discussed earlier. Time may be the framework by which science is done, but it remains a mystery to the very scientists that uses it to such effect.

Indeed, to appreciate just how totally odd the science of time is, we have first to discuss perhaps the greatest mystery of quantum physics – the true nature of something called electromagnetic energy. To understand what it is we need to go back over a hundred years. Up until 1905 and the publication of a world-changing paper by a little-known physicist living in Switzerland, electro-magnetic energy (of which light is the visible portion) was thought to behave as a wave in a process similar to sound and water waves. Repeated experiments had shown this to be the case.

It was in 1800 that Thomas Young first proved that light functions as a wave by performing what was called the 'twin-slit' experiment. Imagine dropping a pebble into a pond. The waves form a series of ripples moving out from the point where the pebble entered the water. Now imagine what would happen if a barrier was placed across the pond. As the waves hit the barrier they bounce back in the direction they came from. Now we place two holes in the barrier, both much smaller than the wavelength of the ripples. On the other side of the barrier two sets of waves, starting at each hole, spread out as if two new pebbles had been dropped into the water. As the two new sets of ripples move out they begin to 'interfere' with each other. In some places the two sets of ripples add up to make extra-large ripples; in other places, the two sets of ripples cancel each other out, leaving no wave motion in the water.

Young performed this same exercise with light in his 'twin-slit' experiment. Here, light is shone through a single slit in a barrier. As the light flows out it encounters a second barrier, this time with two slits. The light acts like a wave in that each slit then marks the start of a new wave pattern on the other side of the second barrier. Immediately the two waves start to interfere with each other. If a screen is set up after the second barrier, when the light from the two slits hits this screen there appears a pattern of light and dark stripes. These stripes are called 'interference fringes'. They correspond to where the light waves add together ('constructive interference') and where the waves cancel each other out ('destructive interference').

However, there was one huge problem with the wave theory of light. Waves do not have independent existence over and above the medium that is doing the waving. We can simulate a wave by using a skipping rope. If we flick our wrist a wave is seen to go from one end of the rope to the other. Imagine doing this without a skipping rope. You flick your wrist but nothing happens. This is because without the rope the wave does not have existence. A wave can only move by 'waving' through something else.

Now, if electromagnetic energy travels as a wave, how does light travel across the average 93 million miles (150 million kilometres) of space that separates the sun from the earth? It is important at this point to realize that space is called 'space' because it is empty. It is a complete vacuum. So what is doing the waving that transmits the energy of the sun to the earth? This was a huge problem for science at the time. A hypothetical solution had been proposed many years before and this suggested the existence of a medium called the 'luminiferous ether'. This elastic, inert substance was believed to fill up space. As light can be polarized it was similarly suggested that this substance must be a solid, not a fluid (because transverse waves are not possible in a fluid, only in a solid). And so there arose the scientific belief that this 'quasi-rigid' ether filled the vacuum of space. There was only one problem. There was absolutely no evidence that such a substance existed. Try as they might, the scientists of the mid-19th century could not isolate it. But it had to exist because otherwise the propagation of electromagnetic waves across space was inexplicable.

The mysterious photon

In 1887, at the Adelbert Dormitory of Western Reserve University in Cleveland, Ohio, two American scientists, Edward Morley and Albert Michelson, set up an elaborate experiment that failed to find any evidence for this substance. Science had to face up to a massive problem; if luminiferous ether did not exist then the propagation of light across space was, indeed, an absolute impossibility. Of course there was a solution, and that was that electromagnetic radiation was not made up of waves but something far more practical, tiny particles. If this was the case then there was no need for ether or any other medium. The particles were simply ejected from the surface of the sun and some arrived on earth.

This idea that light was particulate was not new. Isaac Newton himself had suggested this to be the case. However, the overpowering evidence from observation and experimentation suggested that light could only be a wave. Something radical was needed to get physics out of this impasse. In 1901 researcher Max Planck (1858–1947) refined Newton's idea, suggesting that energy existed in discrete packets or 'quanta'. And in 1905, a young patents clerk in Zurich also took up this idea, publishing a paper that proposed that light was, indeed, made up of tiny particles. This young man was Albert Einstein (1879–1955) and, in one fell swoop, the particulate nature of light – and the rest of the electromagnetic spectrum – had been proven, or had it? In 1926, chemist Gilbert Lewis gave this particle of light a proper name, calling it a photon. But giving it a name was one thing, identifying exactly what it is was another thing altogether. The photon was found to be massless, with no electric charge, and it still had the annoying habit of acting like a wave in certain circumstances and like a particle in others. In what came to be known as Einstein's 'annus mirabilis' (or 'miracle year'), 1905 saw the publication of five groundbreaking papers by the young physicist. In the first of these (called 'On a Heuristic viewpoint Concerning the Production and Transformation of light'), Einstein explained a phenomenon that had been a particular puzzle for early 20th-century science. It was observed that when light was shone on a metallic object it seemed to generate an electric current. This phenomenon, known as the 'photoelectric effect', could not be explained by the wave theory of light. However, Einstein said in his first 1905 paper, if light is made up of individual particles then this would explain the effect. As the particles hit the surface they would knock out electrons, producing the current that had been identified. This supposition was later supported by experimentation and in recognition of this discovery Einstein was awarded the Nobel Prize for physics. One problem solved, but many more revealed. If light was also made up of discrete packets how can this be squared with the fact that light is also a wave? This dual nature of light (or 'wave-particle duality', as it is known) was to cause a radical review of our perception of electromagnetic radiation. To understand this we need to revisit Young's 'twin-slit' experiment, but this time thinking about light as a particle rather than a wave.

Imagine that a single photon is fired at the barrier. The photon, in order to get to the other side, has to go through one or other of the two slits. Recording such a small particle of light needs a super-sensitive photographic plate and this is set up on the other side of the barrier. Each photon, as it arrives, registers on the photographic plate as a single white spot. As billions, then trillions of photons arrive at the plate a pattern begins to emerge. Common sense would lead you to assume that there would be two circles of white light coinciding with the trajectory of each photon through whichever hole it passed through. However, we are dealing with the quantum world where common sense does not seem to exist because, as we have already seen, we get an interference pattern of light and dark stripes.

Now think about this; each particle passes through one hole on its own, yet something seems to affect it on the way in order to form the unexplained interference pattern. This seems to suggest that the photon starts out as a particle, and arrives as a particle, but en route it seems to go through both holes. In doing so it becomes a wave so it can interfere with itself (so to speak), and then becomes a particle again and works out exactly where to place itself on the photographic plate to ensure that ultimately, and with all its fellow photons, a perfect pattern of light and dark stripes is to be found. If so, how does the photon manage to go through both holes at the same time, and having done that how does it 'know' where to place itself on the photographic plate?

This duality of light certainly is a puzzle but light is strange anyway. It travels at a huge speed (either as a wave or a photon) and seems to be constant in a vacuum. This speed of light, approximately 186,000 miles per second (around 300,000 kilometres per second) is the fastest anything can possibly travel, according to current laws of physics. Okay, so what if I am sitting on a train travelling at 100 miles per hour (160 kph) and I switch on my torch in the direction of travel? Surely those light waves (photons) will now be travelling faster than the speed of light once the speed of the train is added, at 186,000.0277 miles per second? Actually no, they are still travelling at 186,000 miles per second relative to you and the train. Perhaps relative to somebody on the platform of the station you have just travelled through the speed of light has been exceeded by 100 miles per hour? No, and this is another curiosity of modern physics. Einstein argued that even relative to the observer on the station the speed of light remained constant. So what has given way? Einstein says that time itself slows down (or speeds up) to accommodate the anomaly. So, for you on the train time was passing more slowly than for those on the platform. At greater speeds the relative time differences become greater until at nearly the speed of light time almost stops.

Observer-based reality

So, light is weird, but at least atoms, however empty they may be, are, in the final analysis, solid and do not suffer the wave-particle schizophrenia of light. Imagine, however, if it were shown that electrons and even, heaven forbid, atoms themselves had this same problem. Well I am sorry to inform you that heaven was not very effective in its veto. In 1987 teams from Hitachi research laboratories and Gakushuin University in Tokyo found that electrons have the same wave-particle duality. They are some-times solid particles and sometimes non-physical waves. Problematic, yes, but electrons are still incredibly small and nobody has ever seen or photographed one. Atoms, now, are different. We can photograph the larger types so they are 'solid' in a very real sense. However, at the beginning of the 1990s, a team from the University of Konstanz, in Germany, proved the impossible; atoms also travel as a wave and arrive as a particle. Your chair is not only made up of vast areas of empty space, but what solidity it has depends upon whether the atoms choose to be solid particles or non-solid waves. The question is, what causes them to make this choice? The answer is simple but hair-raising. The factor that turns the atom from a non-physical wave to a solid point of matter is your mind. The act of observation by a thinking being brings matter into physical existence!

As we have seen, when the twin-slit experiment is performed with light it results in an interference pattern. These experiments have now been repeated with a stream of electrons and exactly the same interference pattern is seen on the screen. This is not only fascinating in itself, as photons and electrons are quite different things, but it also allows the researchers to take a 'peek' as to what is actually happening as each particle approaches one or other of the slits, in a process now known as 'Quantum Eavesdropping'. At each slit the experimenters have placed a detector that illuminates the entrance with photons of sufficient energy to discern which slit each electron passes through. The detector then registers whether or not the electron has gone through its respective slit.

The experimenters were sure that this would solve the problem once and for all. And it did, but the result was far weirder than they can ever have imagined. The detectors showed that each individual photon did indeed go through one or other of the slits. This is exactly how Newtonian science would have expected it to behave. A single electron is fired from a gun and goes through one or other of the slits and arrives at the screen as a particle. It never changes its physical reality. Once a particle, always a particle.

When the detectors were placed in position and measured the passage of each electron a very strange thing happened. The 'observed' electrons arrived at the screen as if they had remained as particles and created two discrete bands. The interference pattern was not produced. However, and you really need to consider the implications of this, when the detectors were removed the interference pattern magically reappeared on the screen. This happens every time this experiment is done. The conclusion is clear; if the electrons are 'observed' they behave as particles and if they are not 'observed' they act as waves.

The implications of this result cannot be underestimated. The act of measurement makes the electron decide to be 'particulate'. It is important that we reiterate a fact stated earlier: a 'particle' is something that has physical reality. It has location and mass (or momentum, in the case of a photon). It exists as a point in space.

As we have already discovered, a wave has no physical presence in itself. Consider an ocean wave. Now take away the water and what do you have? Nothing. The same thing applies to a sound wave. Take away the air and what do you have? Nothing. So if the electron is a 'wave' when it is not being observed what exactly is it? Or, of more relevance, what is doing the 'waving'? So we have 'nothing' that becomes 'something' by the act of measurement. The implication is that an electron, photon or atom has no physical reality until it is measured. And, of course, a measurement is of no significance unless it has an 'observer' to observe it. This suggests that all the basic building blocks of our 'reality' are brought into existence by the 'act of observation'.

This stunning conclusion was first made by a group of scientists working in Copenhagen in the 1920s. Under the leadership of the great Danish physicist Neils Bohr (1885–1962) these dedicated researchers devised a model of reality in which sub-atomic particles have a statistical 'reality' that only becomes actual when they are being observed.

This is known as 'wave function collapse' – reducing all the physically possible outcomes (the wave function) of an event to a single one of those possibilities. This means that until the event is observed, all outcomes are possible. This model has become known as the 'Copenhagen Interpretation'. Such is the power of this statistical model that over the years it has become the most successful theory known to science. Not one of its predictions has been seen to be in error. It may be counter-intuitive and fly in the face of common sense, but it seems to be an accurate reflection of how the universe actually works.

So, from this it is reasonable to conclude that physical objects, which are made up of countless numbers of these mercurial entities, only exist when 'observed'. So the Copenhagen Interpretation suggests that physical objects are mind-created. However, things get stranger still when we apply the implications of 'momentum space', as proposed by the American theoretical physicist Lee

Smolin (1955–), which suggests that the space-time backdrop in which objects are located is similarly in need of an observer. This means that we must all carry around our own, absolutely unique, perceptions of what we loosely call 'consensual reality'. In an article published in *New Scientist* magazine, Amanda Gefter explained her understanding of this new model:

> *Smolin's hunch is that we will find ourselves in a place where space-time and momentum space meet; an eight-dimensional phase space that represents all possible values of position, time, energy and momentum. In relativity, what one observer views as space another views as time and vice versa, because ultimately they are two sides of a single coin. A unified space-time.*[54]

This suggests that each observer's own internally created temporal model echoes the collapsing of the wave function, as suggested by the Copenhagen Interpretation. This may not be as strange as it seems. For many years it has been thought that time itself may be quantum by its very nature. By this we mean that time, like energy, is not a continuum but a series of discrete 'bits' or 'quanta', just as matter is. Physicist David Finkelstein (1929–) has jokingly called these particles of time 'chronons'. Now could it be that 'chronons' have exactly the same wave-particle duality as electromagnetic energy? If this is the case, and after the discovery that atoms and molecules also share this peculiar duality, it is a perfectly reasonable extrapolation, then that means time exists as a superposition (or 'overlapping') of possibilities, a 'time wave', if you like. This time wave is collapsed into a point particle (a chronon) by the act of observation of a consciousness. Each of us creates our own time by attending to it and turning a potentiality into an actuality. This does rather reflect the model proposed by Smolin and his associates. This fits with the ideas of some of the philosophers we have already discussed that the 'now' is the instant that changes the potentialities of the future into the actualities of the present moment.

Curiouser and curiouser

Oddly enough, another American theoretical physicist, John Archibald Wheeler (1911–2008), suggested that not only does the act of observation bring into existence reality by turning the future into the present, but that by observing we can also bring the past, even the distant past, into existence. It is to this fascinating model of reality that we now turn.

In his famous *Rubáiyát* Persian poet Ghiyath al-Din Abu'l-Fath Umar ibn Ibrahim Al-Nishapuri al-Khayyami, otherwise known by his Westernized name of Omar Khayyám, wrote the following immortal lines:

The Moving Finger writes; and, having writ, Moves on: nor all thy Piety nor Wit Shall lure it back to cancel half a Line, Nor all thy Tears wash out a Word of it.

Written in the early 12th century, this sentiment reflects a totally common-sense viewpoint on the nature of time. The past is the past and once something has happened it can never be changed. What has been written cannot be erased and what has been done will always be done. Well, not quite. Modern science has presented us with many mind-blowing discoveries but one stands out above all others in this regard. Its implications are truly profound and possibly even paradigm-changing. It took place in 2007 and it remains little known.

The experiment in question was performed at the Ecole Normale Supérieure de Cachan, in France. A team led by Jean-François Roch shot photons one by one through a 'beam splitter'. This device, also known as a 'half-silvered mirror', is designed to reflect 50 per cent of the photons fired at it and let the remaining 50 per cent go straight through. Of course, being a quantum experiment, the chance of a photon either being reflected or going straight through is totally random and so completely unpredictable. It is only when large numbers of photons are fired at the beam splitter that the 50 per cent effect is most likely to be observed. It is important to recall that while in an 'unobserved' state the photons are acting not as point particles but as light waves that show all the attributes of a wave function, such as the ability to interfere with other electromagnetic waves. On arrival at the beam splitter, the photons – both those that are reflected and those that pass straight through – are sent, via a series of prisms and mirrors, on a route that directs them to a second beam splitter located 48 metres from the first. Here they are recombined and the normal interference patterns are observed. The experiment is designed in such a way that the experimenters can switch this second beam splitter on and off automatically at random (by means of an electronic random number generator), well after a photon had passed the first one.

If the second splitter is turned on, the two paths of photons are recombined and directed to a single detector, where they form an interference pattern. If the second beam splitter is turned off, the two paths cannot recombine, and are directed to two different detectors, with the result that there is no interference pattern.

In effect, by removing the second beam splitter the bullet-like photons take one path or the other. Leave it on and the photons behave as a wave that divides and then creates an interference pattern.

The implications of this experiment are absolutely stunning. The experimenter's decision affects something that has already taken place in the past, exactly what Wheeler predicted many years before. Roch was quite precise when he stated:

> The results proved that the photon does not decide whether to behave like a particle or a wave when it hits the first beam splitter, rather, the experimenter decides only later, when he decides whether to put in the second beam splitter. In a sense, at that moment, he chooses his reality.[55]

Here we have clear evidence that a decision made in the future can have a direct and predictable effect on something that happened in the past. Indeed, in an earlier 'thought experiment', Wheeler, not knowing that his proposition would ever be shown to be empirically correct, suggested that the implications of the twin-slit experiment could be shown to suggest that events from hundreds of millions of years ago can be brought into actuality by the act of observation taking place now.

For most of his career, Wheeler was a professor at Princeton University and is most famous for coining the terms 'black hole', 'quantum foam' and 'wormhole in space'. However, for me his most important contribution to modern science was a concept that has become known as the Participatory Anthropic Principle (PAP). By this he meant that consciousness is somehow responsible not only for the observed universe that we perceive now but also the universe as it was billions of years ago. In other words the 'act of observation' of a sentient intelligence is responsible for bringing into existence a universe that existed eons before that intelligence existed. This profoundly questions our concept of time as a linear process and, even more importantly, suggests that actions taking place now can have a direct effect on the past. Two years before his death in 2008, Wheeler appeared on the American TV series *Science Show*. Interviewed by science journalist Martin Redfern, he was asked to explain his position on PAP. This was his reply:

> *We are participators in bringing into being not only the near and here but the far away and long ago. We are in this sense, participators in bringing about something of the universe in the distant past and if we have one explanation for what's happening in the distant past why should we need more?*[56]

In 1983 Wheeler had suggested his truly stellar, or more literally, quasar, version of the twin-slit experiment could be attempted. Quasars are mysterious astronomical objects that generate huge amounts of electromagnetic energy, which means they can be observed from earth even though they are located vast distances away from us. I use the present tense here but this is a relative statement. These objects are so distant that the light by which we see them left the object billions of years ago. Indeed, it is likely that relative to our earth definition of 'now' these objects ceased to exist long ago. We are seeing them just a few billion years after the universe first formed. We are, in fact, looking back into deep time. Wheeler was sure that exactly the same outcome would be recorded as is seen every time detectors are placed in front of the twin slits. What Wheeler proposed was to use a phenomenon known as 'gravitational lensing' to influence the deep past and in doing so erase that which Omar Khayyám said could not be erased.

How the future creates the past

Gravitational lensing is an astronomical effect that was first predicted by Albert Einstein. He proposed that the gravity of any very massive body such as a galaxy will warp the space around it. As a result, the path of any light that passes close to this body has to follow a deflected course as it negotiates its way through the depression in space so created. In practice, this means that any source of bright light, such as a quasar, that is located directly behind the galaxy as viewed from earth (and so would otherwise be obscured) can still be seen from our planet as its light is bent around the massive body. This can give rise to a phenomenon known as the 'Einstein Cross' in which we see a galaxy with four star-like objects surrounding it. In actual fact there is only one source of the four 'stars' and this is a very distant single quasar. The quasar's light is bent around the galaxy so creating the illusion of four separate light sources.

In Wheeler's thought experiment, a group of earth-based astronomers decide to observe such a quasar. In this case their telescope plays the same role as the photon detector in the twin-slit experiment. If the astronomers point the telescope in the direction of one of two intervening galaxies they will see the photons from the quasar as they are deflected by that galaxy. If they point their telescope at the second galaxy they will get the same result. By carefully arranging mirrors, the astronomers can make the photons arriving from the two routes around both galaxies strike a single piece of photographic film. Alternating light and dark bands would then appear on the film, identical to the interference pattern created when photons passed through the two slits in Young's experiment.

Here's the odd part. The quasar could be very distant from earth, with light so faint that its photons hit the piece of film only one at a time. But the results of the experiment wouldn't change. The striped pattern would still show up, meaning that a lone photon not observed by the telescope travelled both paths towards earth, even if those paths were separated by many light years. And that's not all.

By the time the astronomers decide which measurement to make – whether to pin down the photon to one definite route or to have it follow both paths simultaneously – the photon could have already journeyed for billions of years, long before life first appeared on earth. The measurements made now, says Wheeler, determine the photon's past. In one case the astronomers create a past in which a photon took both possible routes from the quasar to earth. Alternatively, they retroactively force the photon to follow one straight trail toward their detector, even though the photon began its jaunt long before any detectors existed.

This thought experiment was astounding when it was first suggested by Wheeler. We now know from the results of the 2007 experiment at Ecole Normale Supérieure de Cachan that this is not just a hypothesis but actually the way the universe works.

Even more remarkably, there is an earth-based experiment that suggests that the act of observation can actually make time stop altogether. In a fascinating application of the 'observer' collapsing the wave function into a point particle, researchers have shown that by continually observing a quantum system that system can become trapped at a single moment in time. In effect the act of observation can freeze time.

A fundamental tenet of quantum theory is that it is possible for a quantum system (such as a sub-atomic particle) to be in all its potential states simultaneously until it is measured (this is known as 'quantum superposition'). These measurements are idealized as occurring in a discontinuous fashion. A quantum system such as an unstable atomic nucleus is glanced at for a single instant in time and then glanced at again at another instant in time. Two researchers at the University of Texas in the mid-1970s decided to turn this around by continually 'observing' an unstable nucleus to see what happens. The results were stunning. It seems that if an unstable nucleus is never allowed privacy from the observation of consciousness it never decays. It continues in its unstable state in defiance of all known physical laws.

The two researchers, Baidyanath Misra and George Sudershan, suggested that continuous measurement forces the unstable nucleus to remain in the undecayed state from which it cannot undergo a transition. Misra and Sudershan called this phenomenon the 'quantum Zeno effect' as they felt it reminded them of the Zeno paradox of the arrow in flight that we discussed in Chapter 1. You will recall that Zeno proposed that an arrow in flight is not actually moving at all. So it is with the unstable nucleus.

In 1989 a complex experiment took place at the National Institute of Standards in Boulder, Colorado, that was to give clear experimental support to the Misra and Sudershan model. The researchers observed the behaviour of 5,000 charged beryllium atoms trapped in a magnetic field. The atoms all started at one energy level, although they could be 'boiled' by exposure to a radio-frequency field for 256 thousandths of a second. After exposure to this field, the atoms all occupied a higher energy state – so long as no measurements were made in the interim. By probing with a laser at intermediate moments, the team found that the more often they recorded the state of the atoms, the fewer reached the higher energy level; with observations made every four-thousandths of a second, no atoms boiled at all. It seems that a watched quantum kettle never boils.

This suggests that the act of observation places the quantum state into a location that is outside normal time flow. If this is then the case, could this be evidence that consciousness itself in some way creates time and this is why it can manipulate it?

Many worlds and many times

Not surprisingly, many traditional physicists have profound problems with this model. The idea that consciousness is in some way crucial to bringing about the collapse of the wave function strikes many of mysticism disguised as science. For centuries, modern thinking has moved man away from the centre of things and placed him on the periphery of a fascinating, but ultimately mechanistic, universe. The introduction of consciousness into the equation presents an unnecessary complication. Those who hold close to the classical reductionist-materialist model look back with fondness to the pre-1901 world in which Newton's model explained everything.

Einstein himself felt very ill at ease with the direction Neils Bohr and his associates had taken his ideas and spent the last years of his life trying to find a model of reality that lay underneath the observer-driven Copenhagen Interpretation. He called this the 'Hidden Variables' model. Although he was to fail in this endeavour, he presented a series of challenges to Bohr and his associates, each one of which was an attempt to show the underlying illogicality of the Copenhagen Interpretation. Ironically one of these, the famous Einstein, Rosen and Podolsky (EPR) Paradox was to become the foundation of another mind-blowing quantum reality, a phenomenon known as 'quantum entanglement'. In effect, when two particles become entangled, if one is measured then whatever its value (such as direction of spin), the other will be found to have taken the complementary value (such as the opposite direction of spin) even though the two members of the entangled pair are far apart from each other. Einstein famously called this effect 'spooky action at a distance'. We will revisit this phenomenon in the last chapter. If you are interested in knowing more about this you will find a discussion about it in my first book.

Suffice to say that Einstein was sure that our understanding of the quantum world is, in some way, as he termed it in the original title of the EPR paper, 'incomplete'. He once famously stated: 'I like to think that the moon is there even if I am not looking at it.' This was a clear attack on Bohr's model. As we can see, this whole observer-based system creates some huge philosophical conundrums that are totally at odds with common sense.

Another scientist who was unhappy with Copenhagen was the Austrian physicist Erwin Schrödinger (1887–1961). He proposed a thought experiment that became known as 'Schrödinger's cat' to highlight what he saw as a paradox. A cat is locked in a box with a Geiger counter, a poison and a radioactive source. If the radioactive source releases a sub-atomic particle that is detected by the Geiger counter then the poison escapes and the cat dies. But it cannot be known whether the cat is alive or dead until the box is opened and the cat observed. As a sub-atomic particle can be in all its states until measured (quantum superposition), it means that until the box is opened the cat is both alive *and* dead.

In an attempt to offer an alternative to Copenhagen, the American graduate physicist Hugh Everett III (1930–82) presented as part of his 1957 PhD dissertation a paper that offered a solution. Everett suggested that the wave function is not 'collapsed' by an act of observation but continues through time unchanged. As such, Schrödinger's cat is not in a state of superposition of being alive and dead at the same time until the box is opened. This is because at the moment the box is opened there are two cats, and two boxes, and two observers. One observer sees a dead cat and another a live cat. This 'solution' to the paradox has become known as the Many-Worlds (or Many-Minds) Interpretation.

For many traditional physicists, Everett's solution is as crazy as the Bohr model it attempts to replace. They have yet to give up on their quest to bring rationality back to science and in 1986 Professor John G. Cramer proposed what has now become known as the 'Transactional Interpretation'. This model is intriguing in that it proposes a solution that involves the wave function moving backwards and forwards in time.

In order to work, Cramer's model has to accept that the philosophical concept called 'Eternalism' is a true model of reality. You will recall that in Chapter 1 we discussed this idea. It suggests that there is no such thing as the flow of time. This is a construct of the human mind. In its pure state reality is timeless. Everything that has been, is, and will be, exists in a permanent 'now' status. If this is accepted then we can postulate two forms of waves. These are 'retarded waves' (moving forwards in time) and 'advanced waves' (moving backwards in time). Because of our particular viewpoint, we only ever perceive retarded waves as we only sense time flowing in one direction. The future approaches us, becomes the 'now' and then disappears into the past. It is important to realize that in the Eternalism model these waves travel within an eternal present. In 1884, a schoolmaster named Edwin Abbott (1836–1926) wrote a famous satirical novel called *Flatland: A Romance in Many Dimensions* about a race of two-dimensional beings who are visited by a three-dimensional being. Lacking the ability to see three dimensions, they perceive the three-dimensional being from a two-dimensional viewpoint. So it is with us. As we have already seen, according to Lee Smolin, our four-dimensional space-time is simply an aspect of an eight-dimensional reality known as 'phase space'. Could Smolin's 'phase space' actually be the eternal 'now' suggested by the Eternalists and the backdrop crucial to Cramer's model?

As these two waves, the retarded and advanced, come into contact they create an interference pattern in the way that all waves do. It is the interaction of these waves that brings about the curious observed oddities discussed earlier when I introduced the twin-slit experiment. Each particle seems to interfere with itself simply because we cannot perceive or measure the advanced wave travelling backwards in time.

This model suggests that quantum waves do not follow time's arrow. They travel from past to future and back to past. All events, be they past or future, are connected with each other and settle down as a standing wave. This is a simply stunning idea and has huge implications for our understanding of the nature of reality. Suddenly what we consider to be observed reality is simply part of a greater reality involving multiple times flowing backwards and forwards and interacting every instant but still being invisible to our senses. However, Cramer's model may have support from another stunning, but little-known 20th-century scientific discovery, the existence of anti-matter.

When the term 'anti-matter' is mentioned in general conversation most people immediately think of science fiction books and movies. Indeed, it surprises me how many people are unaware that this 'substance' is not at all science fiction but very much part of science fact. But what is even stranger is that anti-matter may present something astounding: that objects can travel backwards in time as well as forwards. In order to appreciate this we need to revisit some basic, and some not so basic, science.

Atoms can generally be considered to be the basic building blocks of all matter. Atoms can combine to form molecules, which in turn are the smallest components of an element or a compound that can exist independently. However, the atom itself is made up of sub-atomic particles; the proton, the neutron and the electron. The protons and neutrons are concentrated together in the centre of the atom and together they make up the nucleus. Orbiting at huge speeds can be found various numbers of another sub-atomic particle called an electron. Each element differs in the number of protons they have. For example, gold has 79 protons in its nucleus whereas carbon has six. The proton carries a positive charge, the electron carries a negative charge and the neutron is neutral. Therefore an atom that has more electrons than protons will have a negative charge and one with fewer electrons than protons will have a positive charge. Such atoms are known as ions. Under ordinary circumstances, electrons are bound to the nucleus by the attraction of these opposite charges. This attraction is known as the electromagnetic force. However, electrons can also be found existing free within gas or a vacuum. These free electrons flow in a current and this effect is known as electricity.

Dirac's anti-particles

This is all nicely comforting. Most people understand the general structure of the atom and similarly most of us use electricity all the time. However, in the late 1920s the great British particle physicist Paul Dirac (1902–84) discovered a curious result when he applied his own quantum-mechanical equations to the energy content of electrons. He found that whatever way he calculated the equations they always predicted that for every electron of a given energy there was always another result that predicted an electron with an equal amount of negative energy. This was needed however large the energy was. The implications of this were startling and somewhat disturbing. All these negative states of energy should cause a catastrophic collapse of every atom into a bottomless pit of negative energy – and the universe to disappear in one huge blaze of radiation. Self-evidently the universe exists and so another answer had to be found to explain where this negative energy is located.

In a paper published in December 1929, Dirac suggested a solution. According to a theory known as Pauli's 'exclusion principle', no two electrons can occupy the same energy state. In the classical model of atomic structure this can be visualized as saying that no two electrons can share the same orbit around the nucleus. Dirac proposed that the electron could not collapse into ever lower energy states because those states were already occupied by other particles. He argued that these mysterious new particles filled all the negative energy 'orbits'.

In order for this model to work, these mysterious particles had to be positively charged. Not only that, but in order to exist in the way predicted, they would also need to have negative energy and negative mass. These were totally bizarre assumptions. Many years later the philosopher Arthur Koestler (1905–83) made the following observation:

> *Negative mass is of course beyond human imagination. If anything can be said of a particle of this kind it is that if you try to push it forward, it will go backward, and if you blow at it, it will be sucked into your lungs.*[57]

However totally odd Dirac's model seemed, the maths worked and, unusually for the time, his suggestion received a considerable amount of media attention. On 10 September 1930, the *New York Times* ran an article with the heading 'Scientists acclaim new atom theory'. All Dirac had done was to suggest that such a particle could exist. The challenge was to actually find one of these intriguing objects. At the time, physicists lacked the sophisticated equipment available to the modern scientist who can generate particles almost at will in such huge devices as CERN's Large Hadron Collider that straddles the Swiss–French border. In the early 1930s it was the universe itself that was the natural laboratory. Unfortunately, the universe cannot be controlled like the LHC. The physicists of the time had to look to the mysterious cosmic 'rays' that continually bombard the earth from deep space. These are called rays but this is a misnomer. They are actually charged particles rather than electromagnetic waves such as light or radio waves. Most of these particles are absorbed by the upper atmosphere but some do manage to get through and reach the surface. It was one such particle that made its way through to a cloud chamber at the California Institute of Technology one hot and sunny August day. This particular cloud chamber had been set up by research scientist Carl Anderson. Anderson was hoping that one of these elusive cosmic waves would act differently to the ones that occasionally showed their presence by leaving an ionization trail in the water vapour. Anderson had placed this particular cloud chamber in a magnetic field that diverted the particles in one direction or another depending on their electrical charge. In effect, he could tell by the direction the trail took whether the particle was negatively or positively charged. Up until that fateful day, a series of protons and electrons had indeed left their respective trails, each one following the expected direction. But that day was different. Anderson photographed a vapour trail of a particle with exactly the same mass as an electron. However, this particular electron-like particle had been deflected in the direction expected if it was positively charged. As we know, electrons are always negatively charged, but this one was different. For the first time a positively charged electron had been observed under laboratory conditions and Dirac's theoretical particle of anti-matter had been discovered. Anderson decided to call this new particle a 'positron' and in 1936 he was awarded the Nobel Prize for his discovery. Three years before, in 1933, Dirac had been similarly recognized for his theoretical model. By the 1950s scientists were able to create anti-matter at the Lawrence Berkeley Laboratory, in California, using a particle accelerator known as the Bevatron. What was, and for many still is, pure science fiction, has been a reality for many decades.

Feynman and 'time reversal'

It was left to another great intellect, that of the physicist Richard Feynman (1918–88), probably the greatest mind of the late 20th century, to carry forward the implications of Dirac's work. For Feynman it was a quest to understand exactly what happens when electromagnetic energy and matter interact. In doing so Feynman suggested something both profound and simple to explain the nature of this interaction. He proposed that everything would work if we accepted that Anderson's positron was nothing more than an electron *moving backwards in time*. Indeed, he further suggested that this may be the case for all anti-particles. He published a paper on this in 1949, for which he received the Albert Einstein medal in 1953 and – the ultimate recognition – the Nobel Prize in 1965. Such was the effect of Feynman's model of 'time reversal' that the philosopher of science Hans Reichenbach was to term it: 'The most serious blow to the concept of time ever received in physics.'[58]

A few years after Feynman's iconic paper, another anti-particle was detected. This was the equivalent of the proton and so was called, unsurprisingly, the 'anti-proton'. By this time physicists were able to use very powerful magnetic fields to increase the speed of the particles flying through their particle accelerators. This discovery made it clear that most, if not all, particles have their own anti-matter equivalents. The race was now on to create a full 'anti-atom'. In 1965 a heavy hydrogen anti-nucleus was created at Brookhaven Laboratory in the USA. This consisted of an anti-proton and an anti-neutron. Tagging on a positron (which you will recall is an anti-electron) to an anti-proton took a little longer but in 1995 this was also achieved to create a hydrogen 'anti-atom'. Surprisingly, anti-hydrogen behaves in exactly the same way as normal hydrogen.

For me the implications of this are simply stunning. If *all* normal particles have anti-matter equivalents this means that there will be anti-matter atoms, molecules, elements and equivalents of all things that can be built by these elements – in effect everything that exists in this universe, including you and me, will have anti-matter equivalents *travelling backwards in time*. From the viewpoint of an anti-matter being there will be nothing odd. I can only assume that entropy will also be reversed for these creatures so for them time flows exactly as it does for us, only in the totally opposite direction.

Indeed, we could exist as anti-matter beings and we would be none the wiser. Physics would still be the same and our arrow of time would, for us, still carry us into the future from the past. However, we would actually be travelling in totally the opposite direction from 'normal' time. For me this is analogous with driving south on a motorway, for example from Birmingham to London, and then later heading north, back to Birmingham again. When driving in either direction nothing feels odd or strange. Both are natural and both feel totally normal.

Many people envisage that time reversal is similar to the theme of the movie *The Curious Case of Benjamin Button* or as in Martin Amis' novel *Time's Arrow*. In both these examples the reverse flow of time is perceived as the 'correct flow'. The characters are born from death and live their lives in reverse.

According to the latest research, the Big Bang that brought the universe into being also created equal amounts of matter and anti-matter. The matter created the stars, galaxies and everything else we see. So the question is where is all the anti-matter? Under certain circumstances anti-matter is now routinely created on earth in the form of low energy positrons. In any one year the full worldwide production amounts to no more than a few millionths of a gram. But this is enough to be used across the world as part of a form of medical imaging known as Positron Emission Tomography (PET) Scanning. I wonder how many people are aware that when they have a PET scan they are having anti-matter injected into them? Indeed, with this knowledge would they be so keen to use such devices? How they work is fascinating. What happens is that a weakly radioactive positron-emitting tracer chemical is injected into the bloodstream. When the tracer reaches active areas of the body being scanned, such as the brain, the anti-matter positrons knock into their sub-atomic opposites, electrons. When matter and anti-matter particles collide they are both destroyed and gamma rays are generated. These rays are picked up by the scanner and are used to generate images.

The implications of this could be far-reaching. If we can create anti-hydrogen then it is clear that any element has its anti-element and by combining anti-elements using normal chemical processes anti-compounds can be created. In other words everything we perceive that makes up the material world has its mirror-image *going backwards in time*. Why this is not headline news in every paper in the world I have simply no idea.

So we have now found that objects can travel backwards and forwards in time. But this still fails to tell us exactly what science considers 'time' to be. It is to this great intellectual challenge that we now turn our attention.

The mystery of measurement

A little-known fact (well, for me anyway when I came across it) is that the ancient Egyptians recorded time by using images of baboons. For example, on the tomb of Tutankhamen, a day's duration is depicted by a picture showing 24 baboons. This is simply because the Egyptians believed that baboons urinate exactly once an hour. This may be an amusing piece of information but within it can be found a deeper truth about the nature of time. In order for early man to measure time flow he needed something that he could measure that time flow against. For example, if we could find a baboon that urinated exactly on the hour we would have a perfect time measure. We have our own version of a micturating baboon in the form of the caesium atom. Caesium is one of the most stable frequency generators under laboratory conditions. The Bureau International des Poids et Measures (International Bureau of Weights and Measures) or BIPM in France computes the frequency using 250 co-ordinated atomic (caesium) clocks, which in turn are used for the computation of what is known as Co-ordinated Universal Time.

According to the BIPM, one second is defined as the duration of 9,192,631,770 periods of the radiation corresponding to the transition between the two hyperfine levels of the ground state of the caesium 133 atom. Thus, 1 second = 9,192,631,770 cycles of the standard Cs-133 transition.

Any attempt to measure time in an objective way ends up facing the same problem. Indeed, be it philosophy or science, the enigma of time really does fulfil Augustine's observation that it is easy to state that we understand the nature of time when we consider it as a general concept.

As a philosophical or experiential concept, time seems to be something we all take for granted. It simply 'is'. But even that simple phrase becomes problematic in relation to our understanding of exactly what time is. We use the third person singular present form of the verb 'to be' to describe that time 'is'. But the word 'is' is based within time itself. 'To be' is to exist 'now'. However, time does not 'exist' at any point 'in time' because it is the thing in which everything else is, in some way, embedded. I am writing this book while in my study. I am located in the study; I am not the study itself. So in this way time exists outside of time.

Such logical and philosophical conundrums have caused problems for philosophers and logicians for thousands of years. However, these subjects are, by their very nature, woolly and somewhat imprecise. Modern science, however, is neither woolly nor imprecise. It is based on measurement and specific observations regarding the nature of the physical world. Indeed, it is by looking first at the nature of the physical world that we can truly appreciate the enigma of time in our modern scientific world view.

The first important observation that all people, scientists and laypeople alike, make about time is that it seems to flow from the future, becomes 'now' and then flows into the past. It has an arrow of direction. 'Now' seems to be the point where the multiple potentialities of the future are actualized and turned into a solid something that then disappears into the past. This then remains as a solidified picture that can never be altered and has become somehow lost to us. It is like an insect caught in amber, forever in the memory but totally unchanging as more potentialities join it in its captured but impossible-to-touch place in memory.

As far as our present scientific understanding goes, does time flow? If it does, what is actually doing the flowing? Does time flow past us or do we travel along with it? If there is an arrow of time is this the only direction possible, or can we travel back in time or, indeed, stop its flow altogether?

The time of our life

In his book *The Fabric of the Cosmos*, Brian Greene, Professor of Physics and Mathematics at Colombia University, USA, makes the interesting point that time may be analogous to a series of frames on a cine film. Each frame is illuminated for an instant, the next one is then illuminated and so on. This is what gives us our concept of time flowing. However, if this is the case, what is the source of the illumination and indeed, what exactly *is* this illumination? Is it literally a form of light or is it something more personal, possibly the conscious attention of the observer who is experiencing the time flow? Does each one of us, by illuminating each moment with our observation, bring time and its flow into existence?

One of the little-discussed implications of Einstein's work is that all times are equal. In other words there is nothing special about this 'now' rather than any other. As Greene states:

> We argue that every part of space-time exists on the same footing as every other suggesting, as Einstein believed, that reality embraces past, present and future equally and that the flow we envision bringing one section to light as another goes dark is illusory.[59]

We cannot escape from the beguiling image that 'now' consists of a snapshot of the entire universe at one specific moment in time. Everything that is happening across the world and, indeed, the universe, shares this moment with me.

All events are happening simultaneously. My 'now' contains them all. Excluded from this 'now' are things that are yet to happen and things that have already happened. In this model these locations in time, in a very real sense, do not exist in any way, shape or form.

But let us consider this belief. As I sit here at my desk there is nothing that I perceive around me that is sharing this 'now' with me. Even the light from my computer screen has taken a period of time to reach my eyes. What I see on the screen is already part of my past. The house across the road that I see is even further into the past, further into that non-existent state of things that have ceased to be. Whatever is taking place in the house across the road now is yet to be perceived by me and is therefore in my future, something again that from my point of view is an unrealized potential that is yet to be. I now look up into the sky and I look at the sun. I am seeing that as it was eight minutes ago. Myself and that bright golden orb that bathes me in heat through the glass of my window are existing in totally different versions of 'now'. If the sun suddenly disappeared, relative to its own perception of 'now', I would not be aware of this for eight minutes when the sun's disappearance would then become part of my 'now'.

But the idea of 'now' becomes even stranger when we apply it to the really distant objects that share our universe, specifically those strange objects already discussed known as quasars. These relatively small, star-sized objects that throw out as much energy as a galaxy are so far away from us that the mind simply cannot comprehend what the numbers mean. The closest are around three billion light years away but most are far more distant than that. For example, in July 2011 a quasar now known as ULAS J1120+0641 was discovered by the UK Infrared Telescope in Hawaii and has now been confirmed as the most distant quasar known. The light we receive from ULAS J1120+0641 has travelled 12.85 billion light years to get to earth. Therefore, we know that 12.85 billion years ago this was its location. However, quasars are all moving away from us at great speed brought about by the expansion of the universe. In recognition of this, astronomers use a term of measurement known as the 'comoving distance'. So, relative to the respective 'now' points of ULAS J1120+0641 and earth, the comoving distance has been calculated as 28.85 billion miles (46.43 billion kilometres).

However, this quasar is still not the farthest-known object in the heavens. On 26 January 2011, a small compact galaxy called UDFj-39546284 was discovered. Its light has taken 13.2 billion years to arrive at the Hubble Space Telescope, where it was imaged. It is now calculated that the universe is 13.7 billion years old. So the photons that landed on the sensors of the Hubble Space Telescope had started their journey at around 500 million years after the Big Bang. However, when we calculate the present comoving distance to this galaxy we find a mind-blowing figure of 31.7 billion years, more than twice the age of the universe.

But things become even odder when we focus in on the photons arriving at Hubble in January 2011. Imagine that we could hitch a ride on one of these particles of light. How long would the journey seem to be from this point of view? Surprising as it may seem, the journey would be instantaneous. In a very real sense each photon exists in a permanent 'now' that includes the leaving of the small galaxy and its arrival at Hubble. For the photon, the present moment encompasses all time both in the past, and even more surprisingly, all the future as well. For every single photon in the universe, from those that are bouncing off the pages of this book and entering your eyes, to the ones escaping in the first nanoseconds of the Big Bang, there is no time.

So what exactly is a photon? As we have seen, science text books will inform you that a photon is a 'particle' of electromagnetic energy. Now on hearing this most people will naturally visualize a tiny ball of solid matter and will then imagine trillions upon trillions of these tiny ball-like objects flying through space from a light source such as a star, and showering themselves over the surfaces of planets and other objects. To continue this analogy, billions of these particles hit a surface and some of them bounce off in all directions. Known as reflection, this effect illuminates the universe and gives objects their specific colour. For example, if the wavelength of the photons reflected is around 650 nanometres then the object is seen by us to be red in colour. If the wavelength is around 510 nanometres then the object is perceived to be green. Now here is the mystery. I used the term 'wavelength' to describe the state of photons that bring about the perception of the colours red and green. Surely I am wrong in using this description. A wavelength is used to describe movement in a medium such as water or air. A wave is smeared out over space. But we imagine a photon to be a point particle with a specific location. As we know, electromagnetic energy, of which visible light is just one small part, is both a particle and a wave. It decides what to be depending upon who is looking. We will return to this intriguing fact later in this chapter. For now all we need to be aware of is that to identify the base-line units as photons is not exactly correct but for the sake of this discussion let us accept that this is the case.

So what do we know about photons? Well, a fair amount. For example we know that they have zero mass. This is assumed because of another attribute they have and that is that they only travel at the speed of light. Indeed, they are light so therefore it is rather like saying that a cheetah can only run at the speed of a cheetah. It is a self-evident statement. According to Einstein's Special Theory of Relativity (described in another of his 1905 'annus mirabilis' papers, 'On the Electrodynamics of Moving Bodies'), the faster an object travels the greater its mass becomes. Another element of the Special Theory states that the faster an object travels the shorter it becomes as well. This is known as the Lorenz Contraction.

Imagine then an object accelerating towards the speed of light. As the object increases its speed so its mass also increases. As the mass increases the object needs more energy to continue accelerating. The closer it gets to the speed of light the greater its mass becomes so that at the speed of light the mass is, in effect, limitless. It is impossible for an object of such mass to be accelerated sufficiently to reach 186,000 miles per second (300,000 kilometres per second). Only an object with zero mass can reach the promised land of light speed. This is why it is known that photons have no mass whatsoever. Now mass is a fundamental measure of the amount of matter in an object so, by implication, a photon has no weight or displacement. As such it is reasonable to say that a photon does not 'exist' in any reasonable meaning of that word.

A photon cannot have a position in space because it fills no space. But things become even odder because Einstein's Special Theory also states that as an object approaches the speed of light time starts to dilate, or get stretched out – in effect, to slow down. This slowing down of time becomes greater and greater until, as the speed of light is reached, time grinds to a halt. So for any object travelling at this speed time ceases to exist. But we know that photons only travel at the speed of light so for them there is no time.

Let us go back to the photons leaving UDFj-39546284 13.2 billion years ago. What has the journey been like for them? Well, like nothing actually because from their viewpoint both locations exist at the same moment, the same 'now'. No time has passed for these mysterious things. Not only that but they have no actual 'location' within space-time anyway, so to say that the photon was leaving the surface of a star in UDFj-39546284 some 13.2 billion years ago has no meaning, and, in a similar way, to state that the photon arrived on earth on 26 January 2011 is similarly a meaningless statement.

But there are some objects in the universe that defy all logic and common sense. In the constellation of Cygnus is an X-ray source known as Cygnus X-3. X-rays are simply a very high-energy form of electromagnetic radiation. It is believed that this object is actually an imploding star. The cosmic ray particles reaching the earth from this object have shown a very strange ability. In their 35,000-light-year journey they have never been deflected from their straight-line course between Cygnus X-3 and the detectors based on the earth's surface. Any charged particle will be deflected by the electric field of any large object, such as a galaxy. However, even in their journey through our own galaxy no deflection has been detected. This suggests that these mysterious particles have no charge at all. So what exactly are they? A logical solution was that they were uncharged sub-atomic particles called neutrinos. There is a degree of debate as to whether neutrinos have any mass. If they were massless then they can attain full light speed. However, if they have a small amount of mass then they will have a velocity equivalent to the fastest known cosmic waves (which are, in fact, not waves at all, but particles) which has been calculated at 0.999999999999 times the speed of light.

However, if these mysterious objects were neutrinos this presents a huge problem. Neutrinos are comparatively short-lived particles. They usually decay in around 15 minutes. How could they exist for the more than 35,000 years they would need to cross vast areas of space to arrive on earth? Logic tells us that the farthest they could get would be less than 15 light *seconds* from the surface of Cygnus X-3. This is a distance of under 3 million miles (4.8 million kilometres), a vast distance by earthly standards but ridiculously small when compared to 35,000 light years. How did these objects arrive on earth?

The answer is a simple one. It is all down to the relativity of time. As we have seen in our example of photons travelling at light speed, the same set of circumstances apply to these neutrinos. From the 'relative' temporal viewpoint of a neutrino 15 minutes translates into 30,000 years across space before decaying. So if it were possible for me to hitch a ride with one of these neutrinos it would take me 15 of my minutes to travel 30,000 light years. Now, that is not only time dilation, but also science fiction disguised as science fact!

This information adds more to the suspicion that our

understanding of time is completely in error. If, for these cosmic rays, time can dilate to the extent it does and if the universe is 13.7 billion years old, whose 13.7 billion is this? To a super-charged particle, the universe is only a year old. From this add the fact that some galaxies are travelling away from the earth at speeds approaching light then time becomes totally confused and confusing. Put simply, time is a construct of man's mind – it does not exist 'out there'.

Faster than the speed of light?

In my first book, *Is There Life After Death? The Extraordinary Science of What Happens When We Die*, I give an example in which even the direction of time flow can be seemingly reversed by the observed behaviour of sub-atomic particles known as muons. I wrote:

Muons are heavy relatives of electrons – in fact, they are about 200 times heavier than an electron. When the energetic particles of cosmic radiation strike the nuclei of atoms in the upper atmosphere they produce showers of sub-atomic particles. Most of these promptly decay into electrons but among the longer-lived ones are those that go by the name of muons. Since they have a longer life, most of them make it to ground level. If a Geiger counter is placed anywhere on earth it will click fairly frequently and it is likely that some of these clicks will be caused by muons.

The interesting thing is that muons are inherently unstable and decay with a half-life of about two microseconds. Assuming that they are travelling at virtually the speed of light, the fastest a muon could travel in two microseconds is less than a kilometre. Light travels this distance in a few microseconds and as we know, it is impossible to travel at faster than the speed of light. In order for the muons to get from the upper atmosphere to the surface of the earth they have to be travelling many times faster than light. How can this be possible? The answer is that for the muon time dilates relative to our time.

It works like this. According to Einstein's theory of relativity, when a muon moves close to the speed of light its time becomes highly warped. In our time reference on earth the moving-muon time becomes considerably stretched out (dilated) – perhaps by a thousand times. Instead of decaying in a few earth-time microseconds the muon can live a lot longer. Long enough to reach the ground.[60]

In 1941 Bruno Rossi and David Hall of the University of Chicago devised an experiment that showed that faster muons existed for longer than slower ones. The researchers used a series of metal sheets of varying stopping powers. Underneath the sheets was a bank of connected Geiger counters. It was found that the particles that took longer to get through the thicker metal sheets decayed three times quicker than the fast ones. This was directly related to the speed as measured within our earth-based time frame.

However, it was in September 2011 that the real breakthrough was made. It was announced that a team of researchers at CERN had discovered that these very same muon-neutrinos that I discussed in my first book had been discovered travelling at faster than the speed of light. The researchers, led by Antonio Eridato of Berne University, had been running a series of experiments that involved firing muon-neutrinos from the CERN laboratories in Geneva towards a series of detectors at Gran Sasso in Italy. Over a period of three years the experimenters fired a total of 15,000 beams of particles the 500 miles (800 kilometres) from the source to the detector. Light would cover the distance in around 2.4 thousandths of a second. But it was found that the muon-neutrinos covered the distance 60 billionths of a second quicker than light would have taken. The results were officially announced at CERN on 23 September 2011. Ironically enough, this is the day I am writing these words, so clearly we are recording history as it happens.

The implications of this result cannot be overemphasized. By travelling at superluminal speeds these particles will, in effect, travel backwards in time. In 1974, two researchers, Roger Clay and

Philip Crouch, announced that they had discovered something similar. When analyzing cosmic waves Crouch and Clay noticed what they termed a 'precursor blip' before a neutrino impact was recorded. They suggested that this was evidence of a particle travelling backwards in time. This hypothetical particle was first suggested by George Sudershan in the 1960s. It was Sudershan who coined the term 'tachyon', from the Greek takhus (ταχύς), meaning 'swift'. For a time afterwards there was much discussion about the implications of such a discovery. For example, one debating point was known as the 'tachyonic antitelephone paradox'. If a message could be encoded on to a tachyon then that particle would carry the message into the past. A person could then send a message back to an earlier version of themselves and so advise a course of action that could change the future. This is clearly a paradox and one that may become a reality if Eridato's CERN results are confirmed. However, Everett's Many-Worlds Interpretation and, as we shall discover later, a new variation on this concept suggested by Stephen Hawking and Thomas Hertog, presents a solution in that the communication will be with a different universe and as such it can have no direct effect upon this one, which would have evolved along a different time-line.

Unfortunately, Clay and Crouch never repeated their one-off result and the event has languished in obscurity ever since. I suspect that the latest CERN announcement will resurrect interest in these fascinating particles.

However, what is even more stunning is that many of us wear evidence of time dilation very close to our bodies. Physicist Paul Davies explains:

A typical electron orbits a hydrogen atom at about 200 kilometres per second, one per cent of the speed of light. However the speed is much greater for heavier atoms on account of the greater electric charges on the nucleus. The inner electron within atoms such as gold, lead or uranium can whirl around the nucleus at an appreciable fraction of the speed of light. Consequently, the influence of time dilation and other relativity effects will modify the behaviour of these electrons in important ways.[61]

Unlike most other metals, gold has a distinctive colour and reflective capacity. Together with its comparative rarity, this has contributed to its value as a precious metal. Most other metals have a less reflective silver colour. It is the velocity of revolution of the inner electron within the atoms of gold that give it its glitter and colour. You may therefore be wearing a time-dilation device on your finger, in your ears or around your neck.

Entropy

We have now discussed how the actual 'flow' of time is relative to the observer in a similar way in which the observer has a crucial role in the creation of matter from waves of potentiality. But we still have not really addressed the ultimate question about the true nature of time itself. Why do we feel that it flows, and why does that flow seem always to be in one direction? This is to do with something called entropy.

If you discuss time with most scientists the word 'entropy' will crop up again and again. Entropy is defined as the state of disorder in a closed system. According to the Second Law of Thermodynamics, all closed systems move from a state of low entropy to a state of high entropy. By doing so, time's arrow moves forwards. From this it is generally believed that entropy increases as we move towards the future and therefore, by implication, it similarly decreases as we move to the past. In other words time's arrow is defined by this scientific truth. However, and this may come as a surprise to you, it is simply not true.

As we have already discovered, for Isaac Newton time was the backdrop for everything. You will recall that Newton's paradigm of science stated that any object can be located by four variables: its position in the three dimensions of space and its temporal location within time. With regard to an object's position in space all we need to know is three co-ordinates, or dimensions. These are defined as length, breadth and height. All objects have these co-ordinates as part of their own physical reality. For example, if I am flying in an aircraft over London my position can be known by my longitude, latitude and altitude. I am at so many degrees west and so many degrees north and at a height of 35,000 feet (say, 10,000 metres). This gives my precise location in space. However, we also need to know an object's position in the fourth dimension: time. The aircraft I am flying in is also moving through time and at each specific time it will be in one location and then at another time it will be at another location having moved within three-dimensional space. How far the aircraft moves in a given time is expressed as its velocity relative to the ground. So, at 10.30 am I will have one spatial location and at 10.31 am I will have another. Therefore time is the fourth dimension.

For Newton, and for most people, time is a different sort of dimension from the other three. One cannot arbitrarily decide on a location in time. One is caught up in its inexorable 'flow'. The pilot of my plane can decide to move his craft to another location in space but he has no real control with regards to time. He can accelerate and in doing so arrive at his destination 'earlier' but all he has really done is increased his speed in three-dimensional space. He may arrive at his destination at 11.00 am rather than 11.15 am but he has not had any influence on time's flow. External to the plane, time still flows at a minute every minute. By 'accelerating' it to an hour every hour makes absolutely no difference to the speed of time's duration. Newton believed that time was a kind of huge container in which everything takes place. This container is the same everywhere. The present moment in one location is the same as every other moment. Everything is simultaneous. The 'now' I perceive in my aircraft flying over London is the same 'now' that is taking place on the surface of the sun or on the star Arcturus. 'Now' is 'now'.

This 'common-sense' approach to time was the accepted model from the time of Newton until the iconic year of 1905. Indeed, this viewpoint is one that is still accepted by most people. In many ways this reminds me of the way in which for centuries we believed that the sun revolved around the earth. This is again common sense, a common sense that is presented to us by the act of simple observation. The sun rises in the east and sets in the west. We have no sensation that the earth is moving whereas simply waiting for a short period of time it becomes clear that the sun has changed location in the sky. However, Copernicus showed us that this common-sense position was completely wrong. The earth actually revolves round the sun and the ground beneath our feet is revolving around the earth's axis at up to 1,038 miles per hour (1,770 kilometres per hour). It may not seem that way but that is what is taking place. And so it is with time. Most people believe that we all share the same time frame irrespective of location. And just like the error of the sun moving round the earth this common-sense viewpoint is completely and utterly wrong.

Enter Einstein

It was in 1905 that the young Einstein, working as a patent clerk in Berne, published a paper in Berlin's prestigious science journal, *Annalen der Physik*. In this paper he suggested that the speed of light has a constant value. It travels away from the observer at approximately 186,000 miles per second (around 300,000 kilometres per second) irrespective of the location and speed of the observer. Imagine that you and I are sitting in a spaceship that can travel at 185,999 miles per second. At the front of this spaceship is a searchlight. At the same moment we switch on the searchlight and fire the spaceship into action. Common sense tells us that the leading edge of the light beam will be travelling away from us at one mile per hour faster than we are. As such we should find ourselves literally one mile away from the light beam. However, when we measure the speed of the light beam in front of us we will discover something very strange; the light beam is travelling away from us at exactly 186,000 miles per second. But we are travelling at 185,999 miles per second. We do a quick calculation. This suggests that relative to our friends watching from the ground the light beam must be travelling at 371,999 miles per second. We immediately send a message back to our friends on earth and ask them to measure the speed of the light beam (I know that this would be impossible as any message would have to use radio waves – just another form of light, but please bear with me as this is just a hypothetical example). We get a message back straight away.

Much to our surprise our friends cannot understand our excitement. For them the light beam is moving away from the surface at exactly 186,000 miles per second. We are stunned. This is the speed that, according to our measurement, the light beam is moving away from us. Common sense tells us that this is impossible. But common sense is, again, wrong.

Relative to us the speed of the light beam is the same as the relative speed of the light beam from the earth. This is why Einstein called his theory 'Relativity'. Einstein's new model of light was to change our concept of time totally. Newton's model of time had been destroyed. Time, it seems, travels at different speeds relative to each observer. Our time on the spaceship was a different time to that being experienced on the ground. Relative to our friends on earth, our time had dilated. Suddenly it was understood that time is not consistent. As anything approaches the speed of light, time itself becomes stretched out. Indeed, as we have already discovered, at the speed of light time stops altogether.

In one short paper Einstein had replaced the Newtonian four dimensions (three of space and one of time) into a unified singularity that has become known as 'space-time'. In a paper delivered in 1908, Einstein's tutor Hermann Minkowski (1864–1909) was to state:

Henceforth space by itself, and time by itself, are doomed to fade into mere shadows. Only a kind of union of the two will preserve an independent reality.[62]

In 1907 it was Minkowski who developed from Einstein's theory a concept known as 'Block-Time'. In this model Minkowski suggested a four-dimensional continuum in which the three dimensions of space, usually termed 'the Cartesian axes', are joined by time as the fourth axis or fourth dimension. In modern scientific jargon, time is conventionally called the 'zeroth dimension'. An event that occurs in space at a specific time can be thought of as a point in space-time. As this event moves along the zeroth dimension it traces out a path in space-time that Minkowski called a 'world-line'.

By introducing time as a dimension, Minkowski radically changed the way scientists perceive reality. So what do scientists actually mean when they talk about four dimensions? Look at a pencil and the shadow it casts on to a flat surface. In our three-dimensional world, the pencil has a defined length that you can measure with a ruler. This length is consistent at all times. However, if you change the angle of the pencil relative to the surface and watch its shadow, the shape and length of the pencil's shadow on the flat (or two-dimensional) surface changes. By changing the angle of the pencil you can make the shadow zero or as long as the pencil itself, or any length in between. The length of the shadow in two dimensions depends upon the orientation of the shadow in three dimensions.

Minkowski said that the pencil also has a fourth-dimensional length, which he termed its 'extension'. This extension, however, is not in space but in space-time. This is the pencil as it exists in time. As it progresses through time it follows what is termed its 'world-line'. For example, if I chose to take a photograph of the pencil using a slow shutter speed of, say, one tenth of a second, and I move the pencil backwards and forwards, the pencil, when photographed, will cease to be pencil-shaped but will appear oblong with a length corresponding to how far I moved the pencil from side to side. It will have a depth equivalent to the width of the pencil and it will be seen as a solid object. The photograph will show the time-line of the pencil in four dimensions. Imagine that you can actually hold this four-dimensional pencil. You could cut it laterally at any point and end up with a slice of the pencil as it was at any point in that tenth of a second period. According to Minkowski, all things really exist in this four-dimensional state, including you and me. We move through space-time perceiving reality as a slice of this fourth dimension. It is we who do the moving, not time. Past, present and future do not exist; they are introduced by human consciousness. The slice of space-time consciously perceived defines the present moment for the observer.

Earlier we found that Brian Greene (1963–) suggests in his book *The Fabric of the Cosmos* that each individual consciousness travels like a spotlight moving over a dark landscape. Those bits of the landscape that the spotlight has in view the observer terms 'his present'; those that it has already picked out he terms 'his past'; those that are yet to appear in the spotlight he terms 'his future'. The four-dimensional block universe is static and unchanging. However, consciousness is under the illusion that things 'happen' in the same way that a traveller on a night train journey sees an illuminated station platform rush past and disappear. To the traveller, the station was somewhere in the future, 'happened', and then disappeared into the past. In reality the station was static and has an ongoing, and unchanging, existence that will be 'perceived' by another traveller as it travels along its own time-line.

So for Minkowski, and his student, Einstein, space and time are not separate entities. They are a continuum of different aspects of the same fundamental 'something'. The ultimate interchangeability of space and time is, in many ways, equivalent to the similar relationship between matter and energy.

We move in our own little bubble of consciousness perceiving time in our own subjective way. We can therefore never 'share' somebody else's perception of time. The 'flow' is relative totally to what we feel it to be. According to Minkowski, your future exists now, it is just that you have yet to reach it.

Momentum space

The idea that your future is already out there waiting for you to arrive is a very disconcerting concept. Indeed, this idea can be expanded to assume that your own past, although experienced, is also, in a very real sense, still here. However, recent research suggests that Einstein and Minkowski, too, may be wrong. It is all to do with something called 'phase space'. In a curious echo of Ouspensky (see Chapter 3), phase space is regarded as an eight-dimensional world that merges our familiar four dimensions of space and time and a four-dimensional world called momentum space. You will recall that Ouspensky proposed that time existed perpendicular to space and that the zeroth actually consisted of three separate dimensions. But momentum space is both strange and familiar at the same time.

The world we perceive around us is odd in that the two elements of space-time, that is, self-evidently, space and time, are not accessible to our senses in the way normal physical objects are. An object exists in space but the space it occupies cannot itself be perceived. For example, even in an empty room there exist molecules, atoms and other, sub-atomic, particles. Even outer space cannot be perceived directly. If there were no planets, suns, quasars or other physical objects in space there would be nothing. Space is defined by its non-existence. It is simply the distance between physical objects. No objects, no space. The same can be said for time. As we have discussed many times in this book, clock time is not the same as external time. A clock measures the duration of time but not time itself. We have no physical sensation of travelling through time; we cannot feel it, touch it or taste it. We cannot weigh it. Indeed, it can be reasonably stated that time is not just a construct of the mind, it is analogous with the mind. Thoughts, like time, also have an effect on physical reality but they do not exist, have a location or a physical presence within consensual reality. So, if this is the case neither space nor time have any objective 'reality'. But two other observed effects do: energy and momentum. When we look at a watch to tell the time it is energy and momentum that we are actually measuring. The photons bounce off the watch and enter your retina. The reflection and the registering of the light are simply effects of that energy and momentum.

Physicist Lee Smolin of the Perimeter Institute for Theoretical Physics in Waterloo, Ontario, suggests that every scientific experiment that has ever been done involves the measurement of energy and momentum. For example, telescopes that show us the farthest reaches of the cosmos are simply using photons of electro-magnetic energy to detect the locations of stars, galaxies and quasars. Smolin puts this succinctly when he states: 'If you go by what we observe we don't live in space-time, we live in momentum space.'

The whole model mirrors the structure of the space-time axis. In the new model, the axis is energy and momentum. Indeed, just as the space axis consists of three components so, too, does momentum. Until recently, this idea has only been used as a mathematical model that seems to work well with observed reality. But Smolin and his associates believe that it is more than just a useful tool and that it is the true nature of reality. He points out that Max Planck's 1901 quantum model of energy was initially thought to be no more than a useful mathematical tool rather than a reflection of nature's true underlying structure. It was soon discovered that Planck's model was not just a reflection of reality, it *was* reality.

In 1938 the German physicist Max Born (1882–1970) noticed a curious similarity between space-time and momentum space. Several central equations worked just as well with both models.

He suggested that both concepts should be seen as totally inter-changeable. This theory became known as the 'Born Reciprocity' in his honour. From this comes one hugely remarkable consequence. If Einstein's 'space-time' can be curved by the mass of stars and galaxies then so can momentum space. The major problem with such a model is that nobody had any idea what force could warp momentum space. This seemingly insurmountable problem meant Born was never able to follow through with his intriguing model.

On 31 January 2011, Smolin and a group of fellow researchers including Giovanni Amelino-Camelia published a paper in the electronic journal *arXiv* that proposed an intriguing, and possibly paradigm-changing, new model regarding the curvature of momentum space. This paper suggests that if we do exist within a curved momentum space then any observers within that momentum space can never totally agree on any measurements made within space-time. In simple terms, we all perceive subtly different versions of time. Even the oddness of Einstein's model of space-time has as one of its central pillars that while space and time are relative to each observer, the unified concept of space-time will always be the same for all observers, irrespective of location or velocity. What is stranger is that in this new model the mismatch between one observer's measurement and another's increases with distance over time. As Smolin states: 'The further away you are and the more energy is involved, the larger the event seems to spread out over space-time.'

In her *New Scientist* article, Amanda Gefter commented on the implications of this subjectivity by giving the following example:

> . . .*if you are 10 billion light years from a supernova and the energy of its light is about 10 gigaelectronvolts, then your measurement of its location in space-time would differ from a local observer's by a light second. That may not sound like much, but it amounts to 300,000 kilometres.*[63]

It is important to appreciate that by this we mean both observers would be absolutely correct in their measurements. It is just that locations in space-time are relative. Researchers are now using the term 'relative locality' in relation to this mind-blowing possibility.

If Smolin and his associates are correct then we create time by observing it. We all carry within us our own form of time, one that is unique to us. This puts consciousness at the centre of temporal flow. We will look at this idea again in a later chapter when we explore the work of J.W. Dunne. This new model is only the latest of a series of assaults on the bastion of common-sense belief that the world we perceive through our senses has an independent existence beyond our own perception of it.

Living in Platonia

We have just discovered that time may be a personal construct. Here we find ourselves back in this curious borderland between physics and philosophy. In recent years, physicists have tended to leave the philosophizing to others and have focused simply on the results of their experiments. But one mathematical physicist has not only applied his knowledge to the nature of time but has also written an amazing book that may yet provide an answer that is acceptable to all parties in the debate. His name is Julian Barbour (1937–) and his book, *The End Of Time*, proposes a model that does exactly what the title says.

Barbour is one of the most original minds of his generation. As we have already seen, the idea that time is an illusion has been suggested throughout history by such great thinkers as Aristotle, Leibniz, Schopenhauer, Kant and McTaggart. But in the final analysis all these individuals were philosophers rather than scientists. Barbour is both a scientist and a philosopher and his book *The End of Time* is a tour de force of intellectual rigour.

Barbour, an Oxford-based mathematical physicist, argues that time is an illusion created by the senses. He believes that the true nature of the universe is a timeless state that he calls 'Platonia'. In an interesting variation of the famed Everett's Many-Worlds Interpretation, Barbour proposes that at each quantum event the universe does not split into two versions of itself but simply one physical version and one probability state. He writes:

> But in that scheme (the Many-Worlds Interpretation) time still exists: history is a path that branches whenever some quantum decision has to be made. In my picture there are no paths. Each point of Platonia has a probability, and that is the end of the story.[64]

To quantum physicists, it is impossible to know where a sub-atomic particle (such as an electron) is located at any given moment. It is said to be somewhere within a 'cloud' of possible locations. The densest area of the cloud represents the more probable of its locations. So it is with Barbour's idea of 'outcomes'. Barbour believes that actual events are more likely to take place where the 'probability mist' is at its densest. Some 'nows' have a higher probability of taking place in the same way that the probability of finding a sub-atomic particle in a particular place is higher in some locations than in others. In Platonia, the 'nows' that are experienced are the ones with the higher probabilities. Barbour recognizes that this theory causes profound problems with how time is understood by human beings:

> All this seems like a far cry from the reality of our lives. Where is the history we read about? Where are our memories? Where is the bustling, changing world of our experience? These configurations of the Universe for which the probability mist has a high density, and so are likely to be experienced must have within them an appearance of history – a set of mutually consistent records that suggest we have a past. I call these configurations 'time capsules'.[65]

But these 'time capsules' have no external reality. They are simply models that we create within our minds, models that may seem to be part of the past but, in fact, exist as part of the present moment in the way that everything else that exists does.

So, if time does not exist then how is it that we perceive motion? After all, motion can only exist in time. At one point in time an object is in one position and then it moves to be found in another position at a later point in time. Barbour shows in a reasonably convincing way that motion may not actually exist outside our own perception.

It is important to realize that we 'see' reality as a light-stimulated image on our retina. Within this statement the important term is 'image', that is a singular picture like a photograph. We perceive motion in exactly the same way that cinema film gives the illusion of motion. A series of static images are flashed across the field of vision at such a speed that they 'fuse' into a single moving image. This is because the preceding images are held in the brain and superimposed upon the next image. This single image has a duration in time that gives an illusion of motion. This is known as 'persistence of vision' or the 'Phi phenomenon'. It must be stressed that the sense of motion is exactly that, an illusion.

As Barbour explains:

Suppose we could freeze the atoms of our brain at some instant. We might be watching gymnastics. What would brain specialists find in the frozen pattern of the atoms? They will surely find that the pattern encodes the position of the gymnasts at that instant. But it may also encode the positions of the gymnasts at preceding instants. Indeed it is virtually certain that it will, because the brain cannot process data instantaneously, and it is known that the processing involves transmission of data backwards and forwards in the brain. Information about positions of the gymnasts over a certain span of time is therefore present in the brain at any one instant. I suggest that the brain in any instant always contains,

as it were, several stills of a movie. They correspond to different
positions of objects we think we see moving. The idea is that it is
this collection of 'stills', all present in any one instant, that stands
in psychophysical parallel with the motion we actually see. The
brain 'plays' the movie for us, rather as an orchestra plays notes
on the score.[66]

This observation can be dramatically illustrated by the case of a
Swiss woman who suffered a most peculiar perceptual problem:
motion blindness. The woman, called 'Ingrid' by the famous neuro-
scientist Dr Vilayanur ('V.S.') Ramachandran, suffered bilateral
damage to an area of her brain called the middle temporal (MT)
area. Her eyesight was normal as long as she was looking at a
stationary object. However, if she looked at a person running or
a car driving past then strange things took place. Instead of seeing
motion she saw a succession of static, strobe-like snapshots.
Ramachandran describes her perceptions:

She said that talking to someone in person felt like talking on the
phone because she couldn't see the changing facial expressions
associated with normal conversation. Even pouring a cup of coffee
was an ordeal because the liquid would inevitably overflow and
spill on the floor. She never knew when to slow down, changing
the angle of the coffee-pot, because she couldn't estimate how fast
the liquid was rising in the cup.[67]

For this unfortunate woman reality was being perceived in
'chunks' rather than in a wave-flow. It is almost analogous to the
'quantum' rather than 'wave function' behaviour of sub-atomic
particles. So what is happening to her concept of temporal flow,
indeed, of time itself? If she sees movement in 'snapshots' what
has happened, in relation to her perception, of the time between
the images?

This is where time starts to become a real enigma. So far we have discussed time as a construct of external reality. By this I mean a phenomenon that we all perceive in a similar way. If two of us stood in front of a clock and watched its second hand sweep around its face we would both agree that a minute had 'passed'. But would we both have perceived that minute as having taken the same 'duration'? It is clear that we all carry an 'inner time' that does not relate to external or consensual time. I have known this for many years but it was a strange event that took place just under a year ago that really brought home to me just how subjective time perception really is. I describe it in the next chapter.

CHAPTER 6
THE SUBJECTIVE NATURE OF TIME

The penny drops

On the afternoon of Sunday 21 November 2010, I was sitting in my study, having just finished tying my shoelaces, and was preparing to go outside when I heard a scream. It was my wife, Penny, who was upstairs. I just had time to think: 'Oh, bloody hell, another spider crisis!' (Penny hates spiders and is prone to a spontaneous scream if she sees one.) But this scream sounded different. I got up from my chair and went to the foot of the stairs. I have just measured this distance and it is about four metres. As I arrived, I saw Penny, literally in mid-air, falling down the stairs. I positioned my body to catch her in my arms. I even had time to angle her body so that her head did not smash against the door frame. She had fallen about two metres, at speed, head first. Had I not been in that exact position I have no doubt she would have hit the wall at the bottom of the stairs and broken her neck or cracked her skull. We are both sure she would have been killed.

We were both in a state of shock and Penny was clearly quite traumatized by it all. After we calmed down (I have never experienced such a rush of adrenaline) we looked at each other and realized that what had just happened was impossible. Let's break it down:

Penny trips on the stairs and launches into space. As she does so she screams. I am in the study four metres away when I hear her scream as she starts to fall. My brain processes the sound waves that travelled from Penny to my ears. These are then converted into electrical impulses that are presented to my conscious awareness. I have 'time' to think that this is probably Penny encountering a spider in the upstairs bathroom. The sound of her voice tells me that this is not the case. I get up and go to the foot of the stairs. I recall not being in a great hurry as my intention was to call up the stairs and ask if she was okay. I get to the foot of the stairs to see Penny in mid-air, flying down the staircase. I have time to evaluate the trajectory of her fall and catch her in such a way that her head does not hit the protruding door frame to my right. I also position my body so that Penny's momentum does not knock me over and push me backwards into the wall (thus injuring both of us).

I was so intrigued by this that I took my video camera and I timed how long it would take for me to react to a sound from a sitting position in my study and get to the foot of the stairs. The video runs for four seconds. In my opinion there was no possible way that I could have crossed the distance any quicker. This suggests that either Penny was 'in flight' for nearly four seconds or something very strange took place with regard to time on that potentially fateful afternoon. In some yet-unexplained way I was able to expand time or shrink space, or possibly even both. The distance between my chair in the study and the foot of the stairs cannot be traversed faster than four seconds and yet I was at the foot of the stairs watching Penny in mid-air. In other words, at the point when she had just started to fall, my mind had managed, in some amazing way, to do the impossible. It had affected the flow of time itself.

What took place that afternoon? Clearly, I seemed to enter some form of altered state of consciousness in which I was able to warp time or space, or both. To say that this was a subjective experience is simply incorrect. I managed to cross a distance in a time scale that was simply impossible. Is this evidence that time perception is far from fully understood by modern science?

Slowly does it

Here is an experiment to try: look at your own eyes in a mirror and concentrate your attention on the reflection of your left eye.

Then move your attention to your right eye and then back again to the left. The time it takes for the eyes to change focus from one section of the reflection to the other takes tens of milliseconds. This is much more than a blink of an eye and yet you never see your own eyes move. What happens to the gaps in time when your eyes are moving? Why doesn't your brain care about the small absences of visual input? Indeed, why is it that when we sometimes glance at the second hand of a clock it seems to stop momentarily before continuing? Furthermore, it is regularly reported that time slows down during times of stress such as car crashes and falling accidents. For example, a few years ago a contact of mine described an incident that took place on the M6 motorway in the north of England. He and his wife were driving south for a much needed holiday in Devon. Suddenly, they felt a jolt to the car. My contact looked into the rear-view mirror to see the caravan they were towing begin to disintegrate into shards of fibreglass. As the caravan began to fall apart, the bonnet of a car appeared through the shattering remains. The driver realized that they had been 'rear-ended' by another vehicle. He watched in amazement as the other automobile slowly smashed into the back of his car. For the driver, the flow of time had slowed down dramatically. He described to me how he saw bits of paint detach themselves from the boot of his car and rise slowly into the air. He turned to look at his wife and was intrigued to notice that she was bouncing slowly backwards and forwards, constrained only by her seatbelt. He told me how he felt no fear; indeed he had a curious feeling of elation and humour. The thought crossed his mind that they were both going to die but this generated no sensation of dread, just a feeling of resignation. He thought how ironic it was that they had recently spent thousands of pounds for his wife to have a double hip replacement and that this would all have been wasted. He then took a leisurely look ahead and realized that his car was being pushed towards a line of other cars in the fast lane of the motorway. Taking control of the steering wheel, he slowly negotiated his vehicle around the other cars, back into the middle lane and then squeezed the car into a gap between two large articulated trucks and on to the hard shoulder at the side of the motorway. By now he had detached the rear of his car from the cause of the initial impact and so was able to bring it to a perfect halt at the side of the motorway. His initial thought was of calm exhilaration as if he had just alighted from a fairground ride. And then, in an instant, time recovered its normal flow. He was overcome with fear and began to shake uncontrollably. His body was wracked with pain and he looked with concern towards his wife. They had both suffered minor bruises but otherwise were fine. He was at a loss to explain how he had negotiated a series of amazing driving manoeuvres to get across a crowded motorway with cars travelling in excess of 70 miles per hour (112 kph), but negotiate it he had and in doing so had probably saved his own life, and his wife's.

But this sensation of time dilation can happen in less threatening situations. Someone named 'Semele' recently posted the following on my web forum:

I was standing at the back door trying to pick up the cat's dishes. It's raining and I don't want to step down two steps and out in the rain – pure laziness. So, I am bending outwards with left hand grabbing the door frame and right arm outstretched to reach the dishes. Of course, I lose my balance. I am fully aware that I will have to fall, there is no other way and yet I am calmly searching in my mind for a way to protect myself from a bad fall. Time has definitely slowed down for my perception as I am reaching for the rain water pipe; I grab it with both hands and fall on the patio, as if on a soft mattress, hugging the pipe that has come apart. I got up totally unharmed, not even a bruise.[68]

I have discussed in some detail my own time dilation experience when I caught my wife as she fell down the stairs. I know that what I did was impossible. Something very curious happened with time that Sunday morning and ever since that event I am keen to know exactly what is taking place when these temporal anomalies are experienced.

One academic who is trying to find answers is Dr David M. Eagleman of the Baylor College of Medicine in Texas. When he was a youngster, Eagleman fell off a roof and was amazed that time seemed to dilate as he was falling. Such was the effect of this incident that he has focused his academic career on trying to understand the neural basis of time perception. For Dr Eagleman, the experiences discussed above suggest something of great importance in terms of our understanding of human perception. Does time really slow down or is it simply that our recollection of the event dilates the time as we recollect it?

In 2007, Eagleman, together with a handful of colleagues, set up an elaborate experiment to see whether time really does slow down during life-threatening situations. In this experiment, volunteers fell backwards from a 50-metre tower into a safety net. During the fall they were asked whether it seemed that they were dropping for longer than the three seconds of objective time that the descent involved. All reported that they subjectively felt that the fall took longer. According to neurologists, this sensation is caused by the linking together of time and memory. When the subject recalled the fall they felt that it took longer than three seconds. The team hypothesized that if time really does slow down for them then the subject should be able to perceive things that are usually denied to a mind functioning at a normal level of temporal perception. For example, the subject should be able to see the wings of a hummingbird when it is in flight, or the individual frames of a cine film.

According to Dr Eagleman, a traumatic memory is processed by the amygdala, the part of the brain that responds to fear-inducing situations. When processing these perceptions, he suggests, the amygdala lays down denser, more detailed memory formations than normal. And it is this that may contribute to the sensation that events seemed of longer duration than they were in reality. This makes sense to me. However, I have certain observations to make in this regard.

Firstly, in the summer of 2007, quantum physicist Michio Kaku hosted a BBC television series discussing time. In one episode he featured Dr Eagleman's time-dilation experiment in which subjects fall off a 50-metre tower. The programme recreated the experiment exactly as it was set up originally. The subjects wear, what Dr Eagleman called, a 'perception chronometer' on their wrist. This device is like a huge LED wristwatch that displays random numbers, which flash up at a speed that is slightly too fast for the human mind to register under normal circumstances.

In the programme, one subject, called Jesse, is first asked to confirm that he cannot see the numbers on the wristwatch's LED screen and is then sent to the top of the tower. He leaps off backwards in such a position that he is looking directly at the wristwatch screen for the full three-second descent until he lands in the safety net. Back on solid ground, Jesse is asked to report what he saw on the screen. He immediately states that he saw the number 56. Dr Eagleman reports that the number that was actually presented was 50. As Dr Eagleman states:

> *The zero looks a lot like a six so what this means is that he was mostly able to see a presentation rate that he was not able to see under normal circumstances. It suggests to me that he can take in more information than he was before.*[69]

The experiment is repeated and this time Jesse reported that he saw 96. The actual number was 98. Dr Eagleman then states:

> *These results are very encouraging because this is the first evidence that somebody's brain can speed up and they can see the world more slowly during a high adrenaline situation.*[70]

The presenter Michio Kaku then adds his own comment:

This is the first demonstration that time really can slow down.[71]

However, Dr Eagleman himself is of the opinion that there is absolutely no evidence that there is any form of temporal resolution during stress situations. On his website he states:

By measuring their speed of information intake, we have concluded that participants do not obtain increased temporal resolution during the fall – instead, because memories are laid down more richly during a frightening situation, the event seems to have taken longer in retrospect.[72]

Jesse had a 1 in 100 chance of getting the number right on both occasions. I admit he did not identify the correct number but as Dr Eagleman acknowledged in the programme, 56 and 50 are very similar shapes as are 96 and 98. Remember Jesse had a short glimpse of these numbers while in a highly unusual situation.

Secondly, and much more significantly in my opinion, the circumstances that Jesse and his fellow subjects found themselves in were not in any way like a car crash or a near-death situation. They were well prepared for what was about to take place. They knew in advance that they were going to fall 50 metres. They also knew, and this is of utmost importance, that they were not in any danger of dying. In a real near-death situation, such as a car crash or climbing accident, the situation is totally unexpected and the outcome is far from certain. Surely the two sets of circumstances cannot in any way be considered to be equivalent. Indeed, in relation to my own time-dilation incident, I am intrigued as to how it can be explained that my body moved from one location to another in space far quicker than is physically possible. My situation was not that of perceiving time dilating but of an actual event occurring in three-dimensional, consensual space.

The Zeitraffer-Erlebnis Phenomenon

The closest neurological equivalent to what happened to me that morning is a recognized mental state known as the Zeitraffer-Erlebnis Phenomenon. In German a 'Zeitraffer' is an apparatus that accelerates the apparent motion of a film and is used in a similar way to time-lapse photography.

It seems that for some people this apparatus is not needed. Under certain, little understood, neurological conditions, the world is suddenly perceived to be speeded up. One particularly fascinating case is cited by Ferdinand Binkofski of the Department of Neurology of the Heinrich Heine University and Richard A. Block of the Department of Psychology at Montana State University. The paper, published in the journal *Neurocase*, was entitled 'Accelerated Time Experience After Left Frontal Cortex Lesion'.

Block and Binkofski report that a right-handed, 66-year-old retired clerk with no history of neurological disease was driving his car along a German road. The man (known as BW) was horrified to discover that external objects had suddenly started rushing at him at great speed. He said it was as if somebody had pressed a fast-forward button. He also found that his car was running at extremely high speed. He could not control the car as his reaction time remained 'normal'. He found himself driving through a set of traffic lights on red because he simply could not stop. He slammed his brakes on and stopped the car and watched in horror as the world around continued to run around him at super-speed.

This state continued for two days until, in a state of great stress, BW was admitted to the Heinrich Heine Neurological Hospital. He described what was happening as an 'accelerated motion of events, like a time-lapse film'. He complained that he could no longer tolerate watching television because the progression of events was too quick for him to follow. He also described that life had begun to pass too quickly for him.

At the hospital he was given a series of tests. He showed no difficulty with time orientation; it was just that, for him, time was going faster. However, when asked to decide how long a 60-second period was for him, some strange things were discovered. BW was told to say when he wished to start the counting period and then remain silent until he thought that a minute had gone by. He was then to say 'stop'. They repeated this test many times and BW's subjective average 'minute' was found to be 286 seconds long.

He then underwent a CT scan, which revealed a tumour centred in a region of the pre-frontal cortex of the left hemisphere of his brain known as 'Brodmann's area'. Sadly he died soon after without ever regaining normal time perception.

What is interesting about this paper is that the two scientists suggest some possible explanations, including that we all have an internal 'pacemaker' that controls how we subjectively perceive time duration. They finish off by writing: 'It is unclear how best to explain the phenomenon.'

I am of the opinion that there could be another explanation for this Zeitraffer-Erlebnis Phenomenon. It is known that on long, monotonous journeys drivers can become hypnotized by the regularity of the sensory inputs received by the brain. There are regular sequences of sounds such as the tyres on the road or, even more significantly, visual patterns that repeat over and over again. An example of this is driving along a slatted fence or a line of tall trees when the light filters through in a pattern of light and dark stripes. Could it be that the Zeitraffer-Erlebnis Phenomenon is simply caused by the driver going into a hypnotic trance? After all, people regularly report time loss on very long straight roads such as the one that crosses the Nullarbor Plain in Australia. Many fall into a form of automatic pilot when simply driving a route that is well known to them. Is there a link between hypnotic trance states and subjective time dilation?

One researcher who investigated how hypnotism can affect the way the conscious mind perceives time was Dr Milton Erickson (1901–80). Dr Erickson's interest in the nature of perception was stimulated by his own limitations in this area. He was tone deaf, colour-blind and dyslexic. According to his wife Betty, he had the most common type of colour-blindness, known as 'dichromatopsia', in which red and green are confused. It seems that purple was his favourite colour, which he would have perceived as a darkened blue. Such was his liking for purple that it was to become his own personal trademark.

For many young people, such perceptual problems could have inhibited their intellectual development. Not young Erickson. For him, these sensory limitations were of great fascination and he was keen to understand more about the base-line nature of perception. There is evidence that the young Erickson's mind compensated for these drawbacks by developing other, more extraordinary skills. For example, when he was 6 years old, Erickson was at first unable to distinguish between the number three and the letter M. Clearly, this was related to his dyslexia. However, the difference later became clear to him in what seems to have been a form of visual hallucination. He described this in his biography:

> Can you imagine how bewildering it is? Then one day, it's so amazing, there was a sudden burst of atomic light. I saw the M and I saw the 3. The M was standing on its legs and the 3 was on its side with the legs sticking out. The blinding flash of light! It was so bright! It cast into oblivion every other thing. There was a blinding flash of light and in the center of that terrible outburst of light was the 3 and the M.[73]

Erickson and Cooper

Indeed, this was the first of many spontaneous 'flashes of light' or 'creative moments' that he perceived during his life. These are described in detail in the paper 'Autohypnotic Experiences of Milton H. Erickson'.[74]

Erickson was to embark upon a lifelong study into how and why the human mind can, when distracted, slip outside normal 'clock time'. In 1954, working with his long-term associate, Linn F. Cooper, he realized that this curious subjectivity can be reproduced during hypnotically induced trance states. In one session, they placed a female college student into a light trance. In her mind she perceived that she was sitting at a table and gazing out of a window. She had shown a great interest in dress design as a future career so Erickson and Cooper suggested that she let her mind idly mull over some potential designs. After about an hour of quiet reflection she decided to sketch her ideas on to a drawing pad on the table in front of her. She was pleased that she had completed a full design, particularly as in a normal, fully conscious state it could take her up to ten sessions of two or three hours each to get to this stage. However, the real shock was that in actual clock time that had elapsed the session had only lasted ten seconds.

In another experiment performed that year, Cooper and Dr Erickson persuaded a hypnotized subject to perceive ten seconds as lasting ten minutes. The subject was then asked to sort out a particularly difficult problem. The issue proposed was that there was a young couple who wished to marry. However, the mother of the girl was an invalid. The subject was told that she had ten minutes to prepare her advice. Cooper and Erickson then described how, after ten seconds of real time had elapsed, the following took place:

> The subject reported that she saw and talked to a young man and girl about their problems. She discussed the matter at length with them, asking the girl various questions and receiving answers. She suggested that the girl work after the marriage in order to support her mother, who she felt should not live with the young couple but rather with some friend of her own age. Her account was amazing in the fullness of detail and the amount of reflection it apparently indicated. This was especially surprising in view of the fact that in waking life the subject is not prone to speculation on

such matters. When told she had thought the problem through, not in 10 minutes but in 10 seconds, she was astonished.[75]

The evidence here was quite clear. It is not that time is transcended but that mental processes simply speed up.

Dr Erickson developed his own experimental-clinical-therapeutic hypnotic processes that he applied in various cases. Many of these involved the use of hypnotically-induced subjective time distortion to alleviate symptoms of illnesses. A classic case involved a 50-year-old woman who was referred to Dr Erickson by her family physician for hypnotherapy. This woman had experienced an average of 45 severe and incapacitating migraine headaches over many years. Despite various tests, no organic basis could be found for these attacks. The headaches could last for anything from three hours to three weeks and were clearly destroying her quality of life. Curiously, the subject wished the headaches to continue but to be less frequent.

Fortunately, she proved to be an excellent hypnotic subject and Erickson was able to induce a deep hypnotic trance state within ten minutes. In this state, she was informed that subjective time could be expanded or condensed for her. She was then told that at some point in the following week she would experience a migraine attack that would last no more than three hours. Finally, within the trance state she was told that in the second week after the session she would experience an even more severe attack. This headache would also last three hours. However, this three hours would be experienced by her within her own subjective time perception. The duration of the attack as measured by a stopwatch would be no more than five minutes.

When woken from her trance state, the subject had no recollection of what she had been told while under hypnosis. She was told to return in two weeks' time.

On her return, she described how in the previous two weeks she had experienced two migraines. The first had lasted for two hours and fifty minutes and the second one seemed to her to be much longer than the first. However, she was stunned to realize that, on checking her stopwatch, the actual duration of the second headache had been under five minutes of 'clock time'. Dr Erickson describes this:

> The first headache had developed at 10 am and had terminated at ten minutes to one o'clock. The other had begun sharply at ten o'clock and she had seized her stopwatch for some unknown reason and had proceeded to lie down on her bed. After what had seemed to be many hours, the headache had terminated as suddenly as it had begun. Her stopwatch gave the duration as exactly four minutes and fifty-five seconds. She felt this to be an error since she was certain that the time must be somewhere near mid-afternoon. However, checking with the clocks in the house corrected this misapprehension. With this account completed, the next procedure was to outline the course of her therapy for the next two weeks. To insure her full cooperation instead of her wary acquiescence, she was instructed that she was first to scrutinize them carefully for their legitimacy and then to answer fully a number of questions.[76]

Pleased with the apparent success of the hypnotic suggestion, Dr Erickson again put the woman into a trance state and told her that her next migraine would begin at ten o'clock on the next two Monday mornings and both would last less than five minutes. Again, the hypnotic suggestion was effective and on both occasions the subject said she felt confused because as far as her subjective time perception was concerned both headaches had taken place over a two-hour period.

She was then informed about what she had been told in her hypnotic state. From then on she was able to control the amount of objective time during which her migraines played out. With ritualistic care she was able to evoke the migraines at ten o'clock every Monday morning. These would last around 50 to 80 seconds of 'stopwatch time'. Within her subjective time, however, the headaches took place over a period of hours. This fulfilled her need to continue with the headaches while freeing up a considerable amount of objective time that she was able to fill with social events.

In a fascinating later article added to his seminal 1954 work *Time Distortions in Hypnosis* (co-authored with Linn Cooper) Dr Erickson described a couple of fascinating time-dilation effects reported to him by his subjects, one described by a student of his and another by a hypnotized subject. This female student regularly attended Dr Erickson's hour-long lectures but was only really interested in the demonstrations that took place at the end of each one. The young woman would seemingly go into a trance state at the start of the lecture and only come out of this state in time for the demonstration. Dr Erickson had noticed this and after one lecture decided to ask her exactly what she was doing. Her response was quite surprising. 'Oh,' she replied, 'I just stopped the clock. I didn't want to wait all that time while you lectured.' I am surprised that Dr Erickson doesn't see fit to comment whether he found this rather negative observation about his lecturing disturbing. He did, however, ask for further clarification and received this response:

> You see, you start the lecture, I go into a trance and stop the clock and right away the lecture is over and it is time for the demonstration. That way I don't have to wait.[77]

The second case is even more intriguing. A male subject claimed that, during his trance state, he had been both distracted and fascinated by the sporadic movement of the minute hand of the laboratory clock. To him, the minute hand had ceased to move consistently and systematically but instead moved in short 'jerks' and then stopped. He explained that the minute hand would:

. . . stand still for a while, then jerk ahead for maybe five minutes, pause, and then jerk ahead for another fifteen minutes. Once it just slid around for a full thirty minutes in about three seconds' time.[78]

As Dr Erickson comments: 'In other words he, too, had "stopped the clock"'. So what is actually taking place here? If these cases are taken at face value then it is clear that our perception of time duration can be slowed down and, in some cases, actually stopped. Time is not being manipulated as such, but what is taking place is that the mind is able to control the speed at which time is processed by the brain.

Time for tea

A few years ago, I was told by a business associate that her internal 'pacemaker' once went totally out of control. I will call her 'Margaret', although that is not her real name. Margaret explained to me that she was visiting a female client and the two of them were settling down to a quiet chat in the company restaurant. As her client began to pour a cup of tea, Margaret heard a sharp snap in her right ear and, much to her surprise, her client stayed quite still just as the tea began to appear from the spout of the teapot. At first she thought that the other woman had simply stopped moving for some reason. However, as the seconds became minutes Margaret began to feel very scared. She watched as the tea slowly made its way down from the teapot into the cup below. Something had happened to Margaret's brain to slow down her perception of time. In the background, she could hear a low humming sound. To her horror she realized that this was the sound of people talking. She explained to me that she had no idea how long she was in this weird state. It seemed to her to last for days, if not weeks. She watched as the cup slowly filled up and then she heard another snapping sound. Her client finished pouring tea, sat back and asked Margaret if she was okay. As far as her client was concerned,

Margaret had simply stared at her for a second or so and then 'come to'. Margaret was so concerned that she arranged to see her doctor who arranged for a full neurological examination. It turned out that Margaret had experienced what is known as a 'petit mal absence' brought about by a small epileptic seizure in the right temporal lobe of her brain.

This is a classic example of how the release of certain chemicals in the brain can affect how we perceive the flow of time. It is as if our attention to incoming sensory signals can, in certain neurological states, increase our metabolic rate. This is brought about by a measurable release of certain neurochemicals. Clearly time perception can be influenced by neurochemistry. In many ways, this is the area that modern science is most comfortable with when it comes to time perception. In the next chapter I will be looking at the effects that these chemicals have on subjective perceptions, specifically looking at the outer reaches of psychology and psychiatry – yet another area that is not quite as well charted as modern science would have us believe.

CHAPTER 7
THE NEUROLOGY OF TIME

The doors of perception

While researching material for my first article back in 2001, I discovered an intriguing example of short-time 'future memory'. I was working my way through Princeton psychologist Julian Jaynes' classic book *The Origin of Consciousness in the Breakdown of the Bicameral Mind*. In this book, Jaynes presents his theory that something of profound significance took place within the human brain around 1500 BCE. From this period onwards there is strong evidence that we ceased to perceive our own inner dialogue as the voice of the gods and became aware that these voices were simply our own thoughts. Jaynes argues that the illness known as schizophrenia mirrors the mind-state of our ancestors. Jaynes was keen to give his readers as good an understanding of this mysterious illness as possible. He does this by extensively citing the work of the great Swiss psychiatrist Eugen Bleuler (1857–1939). As well as coining the term 'schizophrenia' in 1911, Bleuler wrote some profoundly influential books on the nature of aberrant states of consciousness. One particular quote from Bleuler really caught my attention. He wrote:

> *A janitor coming down the hall makes a slight noise of which the patient is not conscious. But the patient hears his hallucinated voice cry out, 'Now someone is coming down the hall with a bucket of water'. The door opens and the prophecy is fulfilled.*[79]

Now for me this event was of extreme significance. Here we seem to have evidence of short-term precognition. The schizophrenic patient describes an event that is about to happen *before* it takes place. Yet this seems to be of no significance to Jaynes. He presents a swift and somewhat cursory explanation of what took place that day in Zurich over a century ago:

> *The nervous system of a patient makes simple perceptual judgements that the patient's 'self' is not aware of and these may be transposed into voices that seem prophetic.*[80]

Jaynes seems to dismiss this unusual event by making the voice that the patient hears only 'seem' prophetic. My reading of this quotation suggests to me that the voice did not 'seem' prophetic at all; it *was* prophetic. The schizophrenic patient predicted that somebody would walk down the hall carrying a bucket of water and that seems to be what was witnessed by Bleuler.

If this was an isolated case then one could conclude that it was the result of chance and the particular mindset of that particular patient. However, those who experience episodes of schizophrenia regularly claim precognitive ability. The following example was cited by another influential psychiatrist, Alfred Binet:

> *A chronic schizophrenic woman who had an exacerbation of her illness seemed to have lengthy episodes of déjà vu, which she used in a psychotic way to indicate she knew everything that was going to happen next. For example, she began an interview by stating 'I know all about this. I've been through this same thing many times before. I know what is going to happen'. She continued by describing the situation in minute detail to prove her foreknowledge.*[81]

There is clearly something profoundly mysterious about schizophrenia. Recently, I had the opportunity to speak with a recognized world authority on this 'illness'. As a professor of psychiatry, my contact had spent over 40 years studying, observing and writing about schizophrenia. I asked him what he thought schizophrenia actually was. His answer stunned me. He stated quite matter-of-factly that he had 'no idea' and went on to state that 'neither does anybody else'. He explained to me that he was of the opinion that it was not one disease but a series of symptoms that are conveniently grouped under this all-encompassing term. He ended our conversation with the observation that whatever schizophrenia was it offered us a glimpse into a reality that is denied to most of us by the way our own brains are structured.

This reminded me of the theories of the philosopher Henri Bergson (1859–1941) who regarded the brain as an 'attenuator'. He said the brain acted as a filter to stop consciousness from becoming overloaded with too much information. Indeed, Bergson suggested that our brain allows only a tiny percentage of sensory information to be presented to consciousness.[82] This, in turn, reflects the oft-quoted lines by William Blake:

If the doors of perception were cleansed everything would appear to man as it is, infinite.[83]

I have long admired the power of this quotation, although it continues to intrigue me as to why Blake used the analogy of doors being cleansed rather than windows. I have long suspected that he mixed up his imagery and initially either meant to have the windows cleansed or the doors 'opened' but ended up with the doors being cleansed. Suffice to say it conveys the idea that our senses keep us in the dark and in doing so deny us the wider vision of the world as it really is. Is this what happens with those who experience schizophrenia? Are their 'doors of perception' flung open by neurochemical imbalances in the brain? Are they given glimpses of a reality so pure and real that it literally drives them mad?

Imagine a scenario in which the normally rigid flow of time becomes elastic. Where events are perceived before they happen and the past seems to crash into the present. An associate of mine, Ed, has a son, who we shall call 'M', who is both schizophrenic and autistic. Ed and I have often discussed how this young man's concept of time is completely at odds with the way the rest of us regard it.

Over the years, Ed has collected a whole series of events, in many cases witnessed by others, in which his son had shown powers of perception far and above those of normal human beings. For example, one day Ed and his wife left their son at the clinic of another associate of ours, a professional psychotherapist called Tony, who was working with M to try to bring this young man out of his insular world and into our own. Ed and his wife travelled into the centre of Liverpool, leaving M with Tony three miles away in the suburbs. While sitting in a coffee shop, Ed and his wife were delighted to hear playing on the internal music system a song by Jimmy Ruffin, the 1960s soul singer. Ed and his wife discussed the work of this singer and wondered whatever had become of him. This actual wording was of significance because Ruffin's biggest hit was a song called 'What Becomes of the Broken-Hearted'. An hour or so later they returned to Tony's clinic to collect their son. As they walked into Tony's office, M turned to them and greeted them with the question: 'Whatever became of Jimmy Ruffin?'

Tony also heard this question and was clearly puzzled by it. But not as puzzled as Ed and his wife. It seems that M had tuned into the conversation that his parents were having three miles away. Ed has assured me that there is no way their son would have any idea who Jimmy Ruffin was, having been born many years after Ruffin had had his short flirtation with fame.

Ed has often observed that M exists in his own version of time. His perceptions seem to jump from the future to the past with only occasional visits to the present. His 'predictions' occur on a regular basis and have often come true. Indeed, Ed is sure that the ones that have not come true are not incorrect, but are simply yet to happen.

It seems that schizophrenic patients such as M exhibit a form of hypersensitivity to time that means they perceive a different kind of time from that experienced by non-schizophrenics. In a series of fascinating descriptions of schizophrenic temporal perceptions recorded in the 1920s, we encounter the following intriguing experience, referred to by the Swiss psychiatrist Luc Ciompi in a paper published in 1961:

I stop still, I am being thrown back into the past by words that are being said in the hall. But this all is self-evident, it must be that way! There is no present anymore, there is only this stated being related to the past, which is more than a feeling, it goes through and through. There are all sorts of plans against me in the air of this hall. But I don't listen to them, I let my mind rest so that it doesn't corrode. . . Is there any future at all? Before, the future existed for me but now it is shrinking more and more. The past is so very obtrusive, it throws itself over me; it pulls me back. . . By this I want to say that there is no future and I am thrown back. . . Strange thoughts enter my mind and drive me off into the past. . . It pulls me back, well, where to? To where it comes from, there, where it was before. It enters the past. It is that kind of a feeling as if you had to fall back. This is the disappearing, the vanishing of things. Time slips into the past, the walls are fallen apart. Everything was so solid before. It is as if it were so close to be grabbed, as if you had to pull it back again: Is that time? Shifted way back![84]

This falling out of time is reported regularly in studies of acute schizophrenia. In the same 1961 paper, Ciompi made the following crucial observation:

The patient elevates herself above normal boundaries of time without totally surmounting them. The distinction of the present and the future is not cancelled out as the patient still speaks about both dimensions, yet the line between the actual present and the only maybe-possible and unreal future becomes swaying and possible to cross. Both dimensions encapsulate and overlap each other without a steady transition. The future fuses with the present and vice versa and experiencing acquires a flickering twilight character which is radically distinguished from how a healthy person anticipates the future in day-dreams and the like. . . The edge between the present and the past is swaying as well. At the same time and in a totally different way, the past is included in and fuses with the events of the present as well as usually the present is part of the past. There is a kind of condensation of time; the present is not distinguished amidst the continuous, steady flow of the past any more, but at the same time the present is not filled with something past as it usually is with normal people; in this case it overlaps. . .[85]

The three temporal locations of past, present and future therefore seem to overlap in the psychotic experience of the patient in a peculiar form of simultaneousness without really invalidating the distinction of past, present and future.

The finite interval

Let us now revisit the incident described by Bleuler. Here we have Bleuler's original wording, which is slightly different from that cited by Jaynes. Bleuler writes:

Perceptions can also be transposed into voices without the patient being at all aware of it. In that event the voice becomes prophetic; a patient hears, 'Now someone is coming down the hall with a bucket of water'; then the door opens and the prophecy is fulfilled.[86]

Clearly Bleuler considers the idea of the future being known before it actually comes to pass to be scientifically impossible. From the viewpoint of the present moment the future has no existence. It is simply a potentiality, nothing more. As such it cannot be precognized. However, in 1963 the playwright J.B. Priestley broadcast a TV request for examples of time anomalies and received hundreds of letters in response. (More on this amazing collection later.) One of these letters seems to echo the incident reported by Bleuler. In this letter, a woman from Cheshire describes how her dying son seemed to 'fall out of time' during his final hours. I am in the fortunate position of having read the original letter, which is kept in the historical documents archives at Cambridge University library. In this letter the mother writes:

> On the third day of his illness he said to me, 'A dog is going to bark from a long way off.' A few seconds later I caught the first faint bark coming across the fields. Less than a quarter of a minute afterwards, he said 'Something is going to be dropped in the kitchen, and the middle door is going to slam.' Within seconds, my aunt, who was working in the kitchen, dropped a pair of scissors on the tiles, and the middle door slammed. My doctor arrived a little later and while it was fresh in my memory I related this to him. He said he had not known of this happening before, but plainly my son's brain was working just ahead of time.[87]

What is taking place here? If time is an external reality that exists outside the mind then how can such anomalies be perceived? Is it simply that certain neurologically-based illnesses manipulate subjective time perception, or is it that time is a psychological construct and as such is always capable of being changed?

A change of perception is not a perception of change. Our conception of what is happening 'now' is known by philosophers as the 'specious present', while psychologists call it 'the perceptual moment'. According to the *Oxford Companion to Philosophy*, the 'specious present' is defined as:

> . . .the finite interval of time embracing experiences of which the mind is conscious as happening 'now', and constitutes the boundary between the remembered past and the anticipated future. That it exceeds a mere instant is demonstrated by our capacity to perceive continuous movement.

In other words, that perception we call the 'now' is not a specific point in time in which the future becomes the past but it is a small, but nevertheless extended, interval of time.

The specious present

Although the term 'specious present' is usually associated with the great American psychologist William James (1842–1910), it was, in fact, an idea first suggested by E. Robert Kelly in his book (published anonymously) called *The Alternative: a Study in Psychology*. Kelly was an Irish immigrant to the USA who ran a cigar company, which he built into a highly successful concern. As a result of this financial success, Kelly was able to take early retirement and spend his time as an enthusiastic amateur philosopher. James quotes Kelly directly in his classic text *The Principles of Psychology*, although chose to name his source 'E.R. Clay'. Whatever the reasons for this use of a pseudonym, Clay/ Kelly's words ring as true to experience now as they did back in the late 19th century:

The relation of experience to time has not been profoundly studied. Its objects are given as being of the present, but the part of time referred to by the datum is a very different thing from the conterminous of the past and future which philosophy denotes by the name Present. The present to which the datum refers is really a part of the past – a recent past – delusively given as being a time that intervenes between the past and the future. Let it be named the specious present, and let the past, that is given as being the past, be known as the obvious past. All the notes of a bar of a song seem to the listener to be contained in the present. All the changes of place of a meteor seem to the beholder to be contained in the present. At the instant of the termination of such series, no part of the time measured by them seems to be a past. Time, then, considered relatively to human apprehension, consists of four parts, viz., the obvious past, the specious present, the real present, and

the future. Omitting the specious present, it consists of three. . .
nonentities – the past, which does not exist, the future, which does
not exist, and their conterminous, the present; the faculty from
which it proceeds lies to us in the fiction of the specious present.[88]

He called it 'specious' because he regarded it as a 'false' present that describes an experience that may seem to be in the present but is actually part of the very recent past. However swift our cognitive processes may be, it takes time for light to reach our eyes from the objects in our visual field and our brain then requires even more time to process that information. In other words, whatever we perceive has to be, in a very real sense, part of the past. We can never comprehend the present moment.

The German mathematician Edmund Husserl (1859–1938) had long been intrigued by exactly what we are perceiving when we experience the 'now' and started writing about the subject around 1904. His extensive personal and lecture notes, which were finally published in 1928, contain some fascinating ideas regarding the nature of this perception.

For Husserl, our experience of temporal objects is processed by three separate perceptions. He called these 'protention', 'retention' and 'primal impression'. These perceptions overlap to give us an extended perception of the 'now'. Retention is when a part or phase of a perceptual stimuli is held within our consciousness after the stimuli has, in effect, ceased to be in the present moment and has disappeared into the past. Protention, on the other hand, is our advanced perception of the next moment, in actual fact our internal modelling of a moment that is still within the future and is yet to become actualized in the present. It is unclear as to whether Husserl considered this to be a simple anticipation or whether it is indeed some form of precognition by which consciousness can comprehend the contents of its immediate future. As we shall discover later with the work of Dick Bierman and Dean Radin, this is not such a strange suggestion as it seems. Husserl suggested that perception has three temporal aspects in which protention moves through to the present moment and becomes the retention for the next moment. In their paper 'A Brief History of Time-Consciousness: Historical Precursors to James and Husserl', Anderson and Grush present a musical example of the way this process works:

> When listening to a melody, for instance, at any given moment a specific note will be playing. This currently-given-as-new note is the primal impression. But this note is not heard as an isolated note, but as part of a temporally extended whole. The notes that have just been heard remain in consciousness not as auditory images or echoes but in what Husserl calls 'retention'. Retention is a process by which contents are held in consciousness and experienced-as-just-past, after having been given in primal impression when they were experienced-as-present. Part of the explanation for why the third note of the main theme of the final movement of Beethoven's Ninth Symphony sounds the way it does is the context which is perceptually available in consciousness, a context provided by retention of the notes that immediately preceded it. Without retention of the preceding notes, the third note would in some sense be the same note in primal impression, but would nevertheless not sound the same. And as time passes, the third note will in turn sink into retention and provide part of the temporal context for the experience of the fourth note.[89]

This suggests that there is something hard-wired into our perceptual process in which we can smear out the 'specious present' to take in information that actually has yet to come into existence. We seem to monitor the contents of our immediate future to create an accurate model of the present moment. This is an interesting idea but what hard scientific evidence do we have to suggest that such a perceptual ability exists in reality?

I have long been fascinated by why it is that I sometimes seem to react a split second before I hear a loud, unexpected noise, such as a door slamming shut. I have recently executed a very unscientific straw poll of people attending my lectures and somewhere in the region of 80 per cent of people recognized that this happened to them as well. What can we make of this? Is there some form of monitoring system within our sensory apparatus that is aware of the noise before our conscious mind becomes aware of it? Can we sense the subtle change in air pressure that occurs when a loud noise is created? Clearly, it would be a very useful survival trick for any organism to be able to react to danger before it has consciously processed the threat. You may be surprised to know that a series of ever more elaborate experiments has taken place in which it has been shown that human awareness may indeed extend into the future. If this is the case then our idea of exactly what time is may need to be revised. It all started with the work of the American neurologist Benjamin Libet (1916–2007). Be prepared to be surprised.

In 1958, Libet was a psychologist at the University of California School of Medicine, in San Francisco. He was particularly interested in the process of nerve transmission within the body. In that year his friend Bertram Feinstein set up a neurosurgery unit at a nearby hospital. Feinstein was experimenting with a new operation to control the tremors and tics caused by brain conditions such as Parkinson's disease. In order to isolate the source of the tics within the brain, Feinstein applied a technique discovered by pioneer neurosurgeon Wilder Penfield (1891–1976) in the 1930s. Penfield was aware that the brain itself does not feel pain. By giving a conscious patient a local anaesthetic only (to dull the pain of the incision through the scalp and skull), Penfield was able to remove a section of the skull and stimulate the exposed surface of the brain with an electrode pen. This device applied a small electrical stimulus to the brain that, in turn, stimulated a sensory response that the conscious patient was able to describe. Penfield focused his attention on an area known as the somatosensory cortex. This section of the brain conveniently runs in a strip along the surface of the brain and so is easily accessed. Each section of this strip is linked to a specific part of the body. For example, stimulation of a point on the left of the somatosensory cortex can produce a sensation of tingling in the subject's right arm. In this way, Penfield was able to map the locations of specific areas within the somatosensory cortex that relate to different parts of the body.

Libet was very interested in the potential of this technique. He felt that the stimulation could be used to understand more about his own personal interest, nerve transmissions. Fortunately, his friend, Feinstein, was happy to involve him in his own operations.

Over a period of five years, Libet took part in more than 100 operations. He found that a pulsed current was more effective than a blast of electricity. Using this technique, he was delighted to find that he could stimulate some powerful sensations including the sensation of water trickling down the back of the neck and a feeling that a ball of cotton wool was nestling in the palm of the hand. But it was something else that caught his attention. Libet noticed that he needed to apply the current for about half a second before the patient reported any sensation. This surprised him. He could not understand why the sensation did not start immediately. He experimented and found that if the train of pulses was stopped at 470 milliseconds the patient sensed nothing but once the current passed the 500 millisecond mark they became aware of the sensation. Between the two time periods the response was more varied.

Libet decided to insert the electrode even deeper into the brain, first into the thalamus and then into the brain stem. The effect was the same. Clearly this result had something to do with the way the brain conducted information to our consciousness. He was so intrigued by these seemingly consistent results that he decided to apply a newly fashionable technique known as evoked response potentials (ERP). ERP was a huge advance on the previous system known as electroencephalograph (EEG) recordings. Whereas EEG picked up every crackle of electrical activity that occurred within the brain, ERP could be fine-tuned to focus on specific areas of activity. Another advantage was that normal EEG signals were detected only after passing through the skull whereas using ERP he could pick up the signals directly from the surface of the brain and even from within the cortex itself. In this way Libet would now be able to find out exactly why there was this consistent delay between the stimulus and its conscious perception.

After setting up the ERP equipment, Libet gave a quick electric shock to the back of his subject's hand. He then recorded the response from the somatosensory cortex over the course of 500 trials. The traces showed that the brain responded within 10 to 20 milliseconds of the electric shock being administered to the hand. This was exactly the length of time that a nerve impulse would take to travel the distance from hand to brain. Libet therefore knew that whatever caused the perceived 500 millisecond delay was not due to the conductance of the nerves. The brain was aware of the pain exactly when it should have been. Yet, again, the patients did not react for around 500 milliseconds. Initially Libet considered that this delay may be in some way due to the patient evaluating the pain and processing it. However, repeated experiments showed that this was not the case.

In 1964, Libet published his findings in the *Journal of Neurophysiology*. The response was immediate. At that time science was going through a period of extreme materialism. To establishment scientists, only the physical world, that which could be measured and quantified, had any existence. The suggestion that anything other than chemical and electrical processes were occurring within the brain was regarded as totally unscientific. According to the followers of a still influential theory of mind known as 'eliminative materialism' both 'consciousness' and 'mind' are simply elements of 'folk psychology' that belong to a pre-scientific age. The materialist philosopher Gilbert Ryle (1900–76) had dismissively termed the idea that we have an inner life that is not part of the physical world the 'ghost in the machine'. Yet Libet's findings controversially suggested that this may, indeed, be the case. The Nobel Prize-winning Australian neurologist John Eccles (1903–97) was one scientist who was determined not to be a part of the eliminative materialist establishment. Eccles was a controversial figure in that he was a keen supporter of another theory of mind, known as 'substance dualism', that was in total opposition to eliminative materialism. This model suggests that there are two fundamental kinds of entirely separate substances: mind and body. For Eccles and his associates, the fact that we all experience an inner life of private thoughts, motivations and sensations, was self-evident. We perceive this inner world at all times, both in waking life and in dreams. To deny this inner life as some kind of self-deluding illusion is, in the opinion of the substance dualists, denying the evidence of everyday experience.

For Eccles, the brain was merely an inanimate vehicle for the conscious soul and the results of the Libet experiments seemed to confirm this. Indeed, in a fascinating example of how modern science is a belief system rather than an objective way of trying to understand the nature of reality, Libet found that his association with Eccles destroyed his credibility with mainstream scientists.

Persistence of vision

Concerned about this turn of events, Libet returned to his laboratory and tried to find an alternative explanation that would be acceptable to the eliminative materialists. He was aware of another mysterious sensory phenomenon known as 'backward masking'. This is an illusion whereby a strong stimulus can block awareness of an earlier perceived, weaker, sensation. For example, if somebody is shown a weak flash of light and then a tenth of a second later a brighter light is shone at them from the same direction, the first light does not register in the mind. This works for all visual sensations, including pictures and the written word. What is even odder is that if a third stimulus is introduced, the first flash is perceived and it is the second flash that is lost.

In his new experiment, Libet followed the same procedure as before, with the patient's somatosensory cortex exposed and an electrode poised to administer a small charge to its surface. He would then administer an electric shock to the hand of the subject and then, a split second later, apply the electrode to the surface of the brain. In effect, he was bringing about a backward masking effect in that the second charge would mask the first one. And this is exactly what happened.

This presented strong evidence that we do not perceive 'now' but exist in a permanent sensory world of about half a second before. As the classic English folk-rock band Jethro Tull stated, we are 'Living in the Past'.

However, Libet had major concerns about these results. If consciousness lags behind 'real time' by up to half a second then what does that suggest with regard to 'free will'?

Although we perceive external reality after things have happened our bodies still exist in the actual time that is concurrent with reality. If this was not the case then we would fail to protect ourselves from incoming danger. To be aware of a threat 500 milliseconds after that threat becomes manifest is, in many cases, a death sentence.

To help resolve this issue, John Eccles put Libet in touch with two German researchers, Hans Kornhuber and Luder Deecke.

In 1964, Kornhuber and Deecke had discovered a phenomenon that offered a physiological explanation for the events observed by Libet. In a series of experiments to investigate the temporal relationship between neural activity and conscious awareness during voluntary action, the Germans had discovered that the brain activated the action to move a part of the body around 500 milliseconds before the motor neuron stimulates the muscle into action. Kornhuber called this effect the 'Bereitschaftspotential', in English the 'pre-motor potential or 'readiness potential'. In experiments involving complex actions such as a pianist getting ready to play a scale of notes, it was noticed that the delay between mental preparation and muscular movement could be a second or more.

However, and this is again of great significance, the pianist believes the decision to act to be instantaneous. For the subject there is no delay between thought and action.[90]

Libet saw that this experiment offered another way to test his discovery. He asked a volunteer to sit in a chair. He then attached a set of small electrodes to the volunteer's scalp that, in turn, produced changes in voltage that were detected by an EEG. He also attached another set of electrodes to the subject's forearm that sent information about muscle movement to a device similar to an EEG called an electromyograph (EMG).

The subject was then asked to note the position of a rapidly flashing dot of light on an oscilloscope in front of them that moved in a circle around the screen like the second hand of a clock. The device was set up so that there was a 43 millisecond interval between flashes.

The subject was asked to carry out a simple motor activity, such as flexing a finger by pressing a button. The choice of when to flex was left entirely to the discretion of the subject.

All the subject had to do was note the position of the dot on the oscilloscope screen the moment they first became aware of the 'urge to act'. It was discovered that the EEG-measured brain activity that set in motion the flexing occurred, on average, 500 milliseconds before the button was pressed. This showed conclusively that the 'readiness potential' preceded the conscious intention to flex.

This was a stunning result. It showed yet again that consciousness not only lags behind 'reality' but also that we never make free decisions because the brain has already decided what to do before consciousness makes the decision. This has massive implications with regard to our concept of free will. We are fooled into believing that we are in control of our bodily movements yet the experimental evidence suggests otherwise.

Future perception – Radin and Bierman

In the late 1990s, another series of experiments was to add to the ever-increasing suspicion that the human mind functions from a place in which future and past seem to meld into one permanent 'now'. Together with his associate Dr Dean Radin, parapsychologist Dr Dick Bierman placed a group of subjects in front of a computer screen. Each subject's left-hand index and middle finger was connected to a device that measured small changes in the electrical conductivity of the skin. It has long been known that because the sweat glands are controlled by the sympathetic nervous system any arousal of a psychological or physiological nature will be reflected in changes in the electrical resistance of the skin. This provides an objective measure of arousal without the conscious input of the subject. Once the subject had settled down and the computer screen was turned on, he or she was then asked to start the test by pressing a key on the keyboard. After 7.5 seconds a randomly selected picture was displayed on the screen for a specific length of time. The pictures had been carefully selected to either bring out a strong emotional response or to relax the subject. The relaxing pictures involved landscapes, household objects or fruit. The arousing images were either of a sexual nature or involved pictures of fatal accidents, murder victims or threatening animals. The skin conductivity was measured before, during and after each image was shown at a rate of five samples per second.

As expected, the results clearly demonstrated a significant difference in skin conductivity between the response to emotionally calming and emotionally arousing stimuli. However, and this is hugely significant, what was more surprising was that the skin conductivity response to the emotionally arousing stimuli occurred before the picture was shown on the screen. In other words, the subject was aware that the next picture was going to be disturbing even though at that time they had no conscious idea what the next picture would show. This result suggested to Bierman and Radin that human consciousness had the ability to monitor the contents of its own immediate future.

A major objection to the interpretation made by Bierman and Radin is that, as more pictures are shown that are calming, the subject's anticipation that the next one will be emotionally arousing is raised. The subject knows that sooner or later another powerful image will be presented. As each calming picture is projected the fear that the next one will be shocking increases. This effect is popularly known as the 'gambling fallacy'. This is the belief, held by most people, and not just gamblers, that the longer the wait for an anticipated exciting or stimulating image the greater their level of expectation. In simple terms, if the ball on a roulette wheel keeps falling into a black slot in a sequence it increases the chance that the next time the ball will fall into a red slot. So somebody gambling on the ball falling into the red slot will show an increase in heart rate every time the ball lands in the black slot in anticipation that the next roll of the wheel will bring about a winning result. This may be the wrong conclusion but nevertheless it is a natural reaction. It has been argued by some that this is what is taking place during the Bierman and Radin experiment.

Indeed, this would be a convincing explanation if such anticipatory reactions were confined to a frightening or arousing response. However, there is another fascinating experiment in which the subjects are in a totally relaxed state and have absolutely no expectations. Indeed, in this experiment the subjects seem to have access to information that they could not possibly know about. It is all to do with a peculiar effect of vision first noted a century ago.

The Phi phenomenon

In 1910, the Czech psychologist Max Wertheimer (1880–1943) noticed a strange visual illusion. If two light sources are flashed through a small aperture in a darkened room they can, when set to a specific timed sequence, appear to an observer to be a single light moving backwards and forwards between the positions of the two light sources. The two sources are actually stationary but the mind creates the illusion of movement. Sixty-seven years later, this odd discovery was revisited by two perception psychologists, Paul Kolers and Michael Von Grunau. An associate of theirs, philosopher Nelson Goodman, had asked them a very simple question: what would be observed if the two light sources were different colours and the observer is not told this in advance? For example, the first light that is illuminated is red and the second one, illuminating shortly after, is green. If the observer has no idea what the second colour will be then logic (and temporal causality) suggests that the observer will initially see a red light changing to green the instant the second light is switched on. In other words, for the whole sequence the light will be red with a flash of green appearing as the illusionary moving light source starts to move back upon itself.

The experiment was set up. A subject was asked to look in the direction of the two light sources. On the left side a red light was switched on for 150 milliseconds and then switched off for 50 milliseconds. After the 50 milliseconds was over, the right-hand green light was immediately switched on. The subject was then asked what they saw. Much to the utter astonishment of all involved the subject stated that they saw the red spot move to the centre of their field of vision and then abruptly turn green, staying green to the end of the movement. Goodman was later to write:

How are we able to fill in the spot at the intervening place-times along a path running from the first and second flash before the second flash occurs?[91]

I first came across this stunning, and totally counter-intuitive experiment, in Daniel Dennett's fascinating book *Consciousness Explained*. This was 12 years ago and I have still to find any explanation for what is taking place. Indeed, even Dennett was mystified. He wrote:

> Suppose the first spot is red and the second, displaced, spot is green. Unless there is 'precognition' in the brain (an extravagant hypothesis we will postpone indefinitely), the illusory content, red switching to green in midcourse cannot be created until after some identification of the second, green spot occurs in the brain. But if the second spot is already 'in conscious experience' would it not be too late to interpose the illusory content between the conscious experience of the red spot and the conscious experience of the green spot? How does the brain accommodate this sleight of hand?[92]

For me, there are only two conclusions that can be drawn from this. Either the brain buffers information before it presents it to consciousness (in which case how does the brain know when it has all the information it needs to give a coherent model?) or we are able to monitor the contents of the immediate future before it happens and react to it. This information can be received visually, aurally and by impact on the surface of the skin. Indeed, this may explain an incident that has long fascinated me, the case of 'Maury's Dream'. Alfred Maury (1817–92) was a French physician who specialized in the study of dreams. His interest had been stimulated by a series of curious events that took place when he was a young man, inspired by the mass executions known as 'The Terror' that followed the French Revolution. He describes this in some detail:

> I was slightly indisposed and was lying in my room; my mother was near my bed. I am dreaming of The Terror. I am present at scenes of massacre; I appear before the Revolutionary Tribunal; I see Robespierre, Marat, Forquier-Tinville, all the most villainous figures of this terrible epoch; I argue with them; at last, after many events which I remember only vaguely, I am judged, condemned

to death, taken in a cart, amidst an enormous crowd, to the Square
Of Revolution; I ascend the scaffold; the executioner binds me to
the fatal board, he pushes it, the blade falls; I feel my head being
severed from my body; I awake seized by the most violent terror,
and I feel on my neck the rod of my bed which had become
detached and had fallen on my neck as would the blade of the
guillotine. This happened in one instant, as my mother confirmed
to me, and yet it was the external sensation that was taken by me
for the starting point of the dream with a whole series of
successive incidents. At the moment that I was struck the memory
of this terrible machine, the effect of which was so well produced
by the rod of the bed's canopy, had awakened in me all the images
of that epoch of which the guillotine was the symbol.[93]

It seems that the young Maury's unconscious had created a whole dream to account for the impact of the canopy on to the back of his head. Indeed, either the dream was fabricated in the split second between the sensation of the impact and his conscious mind registering the blow, or else the dream itself was perceived 'back to front'. That is, the dream started with the blow and worked backwards to the trial. Either option means that time was warped in one way or another. Maury concluded from this that dreams arose from external stimuli, instantaneously accompanying such impressions as are acted upon the sleeping person. In other words, the subconscious mind has the ability to process outside sounds or events immediately and then completely and subjectively incorporate them into a dream. This is all done in a microsecond. You may recall that in the opening section of this book I discussed how author Rian Hughes had a dream back-created in time to accommodate the sound of an alarm bell. Clearly, this phenomenon is not unusual and may be a natural element of perception. Indeed, I wonder if it is of significance that Maury was, as he terms it, 'slightly indisposed' which sounds to me like a quaint 19th-century way of stating that he was ill, possibly with a fever or something similar that increases the metabolic rate of the body. If this was the case then it is also reasonable to suggest that here we have confirmation of Hoagland's findings that body temperature has an effect on the way we perceive time.

The end of free will

Of possible significance in this regard is that in 2003 James Spottiswoode and Ed May completed a study that suggested that the body can respond to loud noise two or three seconds before that noise is heard. In their experiment, a noise of one second duration was sent to a pair of headphones worn by the subject. These noises, sent at random, were loud enough to bring about a 'startle response'. The subject's finger was attached to a machine that measured skin conductivity much like the procedure followed by Bierman and Radin. Could it be that Maury's subconscious was already aware of the impact of the headboard and it sent the information back in time so that the 'dream choreographer' could create a dream based upon the guillotine-like impact of the head-board on the back of the young man's neck? Similarly, for Rian Hughes, did the sound of an alarm bell create a dream based around the bell used to announce the end of a boxing round?

Of course 'future' perception, be it of events a thousandth of a second or a minute ahead, is still, as far as our present scientific model is concerned, impossible. However, many will argue that half a second delay suggests that something is being misinterpreted or misunderstood. A recent series of experiments, which took place at the Bernstein Centre for Computational Neuroscience in Berlin, has shown that Libet's delay of 500 milliseconds is far too conservative. A small team led by neurologist John-Dylan Haynes at the Charité-Universitätsmedizin in Berlin asked 14 subjects to lie inside a functional magnetic resonance imaging (fMRI) scanner. Each subject was supplied with a hand-held console with two buttons, one on the left and one on the right. While the scanner analyzed their brain activity, the subject was asked to spontaneously decide to press either the right or left button. The decisions could be made at any time but as the decision was made they were asked to report the exact moment they made the choice by looking at a clock-like device within the scanner.

The researchers kept a close look on the subjects' brain activity, both before and after the decision was made, using a sophisticated computer program that scanned micro-activity in the frontopolar cortex, an area right behind the forehead. The patterns of micro-activity indicated whether the subjects had chosen the right or left buttons. Haynes and his team were surprised to notice that the earliest brain patterns fired about ten seconds *before* the conscious choice. The researchers recorded that the micro-activity correctly predicted the choice of right or left button 60 per cent of the time. In an article published online in *Nature Neuroscience* Haynes wrote:

> The outcome of a decision is shaped very strongly by brain activity much earlier than the point in time when you feel to be making the decision.[94]

So, yet again it seems that the decision had already been made before the conscious mind became involved. In other words, the mind had no choice in the matter, the decision had already been made and it had no option but to follow it. Such was the interest in this experiment that the BBC sent a crew over to Germany to film Oxford mathematician Marcus du Sautoy taking part in the experiment for himself. Du Sautoy was placed inside the fMRI scanner and given the hand-held console with the two buttons and was asked to press either the left- or right-hand button at random. On finishing the exercise, Haynes revealed the results of the test. The experiment showed that the micro-activity in du Sautoy's frontopolar cortex lit up to indicate which decision he was about to make (whether to press the left or right button) a full six seconds before he was consciously aware of making the decision and then pressing the left or right button.

After leaving the laboratory, du Sautoy sat down in the Berlin sunshine to assimilate what had just taken place. The film was part of a series of programmes that du Sautoy had made for the BBC called *The Secret You*. This had involved some fascinating examples of how mysterious the human mind is. But this particular incident had obviously left him feeling disturbed. In a fascinating piece of television, du Sautoy states, almost as a personal comment, 'That must be the most shocking experiment I have experienced on this journey.' He is clearly stunned by the implication that this has for the concept of 'free will'. Du Sautoy added: 'The fact is that when I become conscious of making a choice John (Haynes) can, six seconds earlier, predict what I was going to do before I even realized what I was going to do.' Put another way, John's own consciousness, by observing the computer screen, knows what decision was to be made six seconds before the consciousness that is actually making the decision.

Libet discovered a delay of only half a second. This experiment showed that the delay could be as much as six seconds. Only two conclusions can be drawn from these results: either our concept of free will is an illusion or the consciousness can, in some way, bring about a backwards causation in time. Perhaps this is a self-preservation mechanism and consciousness can make a decision and then send a message back in time to ensure that we can react immediately to any threat before it takes place. Is this why we jump before we hear a loud noise?

It is reasonable to conclude that consciousness can somehow affect the state of the brain in the recent past. Indeed, in this regard I am reminded of the John Wheeler experiment that we discussed in an earlier chapter. It will be recalled that Wheeler showed that the 'act of observation' now can affect the state of sub-atomic particles millions of years in the past. Can we not apply this to the Haynes experiment? By making a decision to press one or other of the buttons the subject's consciousness is, in effect, observing that action in the same way that a consciousness 'observes' which slit the quasar photon passes through. In doing so the consciousness back-creates a physical reaction that took place within the brain six seconds before.

More importantly, in my opinion, is the suggestion that the subconscious mind can, facilitated by certain neurological states, access this future information and use it to create dreams that contain information directly related to events yet to happen. Indeed, there is strong statistical evidence that people use this intuition to avoid accidents. In the mid-1950s, American parapsychologist William E. Cox (1861–1942) carried out a survey of passenger statistics on the US railway network covering a number of years. The survey showed that significantly fewer people travelled on trains at the time of accidents, compared with the number who travelled on the network during the 7, 14, 21 and 28 days before the accidents occurred. Possibly of even greater significance was that Cox's results showed that in every case there were fewer passengers in the carriages directly damaged in the accidents. From this it can be suggested that the future-monitoring for danger is mostly subliminal. It seems that the subconscious processes the future data and ensures that everyday consciousness does not place the physical body in harm's way.

The global consciousness project

In September 2001, a series of events took place that shook the world. The terrorist attacks on the World Trade Center's 'Twin Towers' in New York, and the Pentagon in Washington, were to have a profound effect on the collective psyche of humankind. If such events can resonate through time then it should be the case that certain sensitive individuals may pick up on these 'backwards-in-time' communications. You will recall that physicist John G. Cramer has suggested that the mystery of wave-particle duality can be explained if we accept that there are two forms of electro-magnetic waves. He calls these 'retarded' and 'advanced'. Retarded waves travel in the perceived forward-direction of time, whereas advanced waves are time-reversed. In effect, they travel backwards in time. He calls this the 'Transactional Interpretation' of quantum physics and presents it as a more effective solution than either the Copenhagen Interpretation or the Many-Worlds Interpretation. In a paper published in 2000, Cramer was quite precise in how he saw his model working:

The transactional interpretation asserts that at the quantum level time is a two-way street, in which at some level the future determines the past as well as the past determining the future.[95]

Could it be that the human mind can pick up on information contained in these advanced waves? After all, a form of electromagnetic energy is used to send information across the globe and into the vacuum of space. We know this form of energy as radio waves. In this way, the subconscious can pick up messages from the future and modulate it into dreams. Indeed, could this explain why something quite unusual was recorded by the Princeton Engineering Anomalous Research (PEAR) laboratory, based at Princeton University in New Jersey, USA in 2001?

The Global Consciousness Project (GCP) is an ambitious study set up in 1998 by Dr Roger D. Nelson of the PEAR laboratory. His basic idea was that any form of collective fear or anxiety generated by a large number of minds may physically affect the workings of the sensitive devices his team used called Random Number Generators (RNGs), and known to the researchers as 'EGGS'.

Nelson and his team meticulously recorded any changes or fluctuations in the usually random sequence of data generated by the machines. The team kept a particularly close watch during times of worldwide emotional interest such as television broadcasts of the FIFA World Cup or the Oscar awards. After the researchers noticed an intriguing response following the death of Diana, Princess of Wales in 1997, it was agreed that this project should be expanded to create a permanent network of RNGs running continuously. The GCP currently maintains a network of RNGs linked to computers at 65 locations around the world. All the data are then sent to a server at Princeton's PEAR laboratory.

On 11 September 2001 these devices did indeed record a significant level of activity. But what is intriguing is that the increase was recorded some hours before the events occurred. In referring to a sequence of readouts posted on his website, Nelson observed that:

> *The main figure traces the variability among the 37 RNG devices reporting on September 10, 11, and 12. Early in the morning of the 11th, the EGGS (RNGs) began showing consistently large variance, and that tendency continued until about 11:00 or a bit later. Then the variance became compressed, and remained smaller than usual on average until early evening. This is a remarkable figure in many ways. The peak departure on September 11 has odds of less than one in a thousand, and is essentially unique; no other day in four years shows such a large deviation. Moreover, if we read the graph directly, there is a perhaps more startling note: the EGG network began to react well before the first plane hit the World Trade Center towers.[96]*

Is this evidence that not only can we collectively sense a disaster is going to take place, but also that this awareness is somehow subliminal, only reaching day-to-day awareness for some of us? In my book *The Daemon – A Guide To Your Extraordinary Secret Self* I suggest that we may all have within our memory banks some stored memories of our previous lives. These are the recurring lives lived in a model similar to that suggested by Nietzsche and Ouspensky. I also suggest that there is a part of us that knows the future, a being I call the 'Daemon'. This entity uses this knowledge to protect its partner in life, the everyday, non-clairvoyant being I call the 'Eidolon'. It is not my intention here to explain why I come to this conclusion because the case is expounded, in great detail, in both *The Daemon* and my first book, *Is There Life after Death? The Extraordinary Science of What Happens When We Die.* However, my model could explain why many of us felt the impending disaster of 9/11 without being aware of it. This is because, although our lower, everyday self, our Eidolon does not have access to these 'memories' our higher self, or Daemon, does. I would like to suggest that it was the collective fears of the world's Daemons that brought about the variance recorded by the Random Number Generators.

Warning signal

I recently received an email from a young man called Bill Doyle who was keen to tell me about an incident that took place in 1996. On that day Bill, his mother and sister were being driven by his father Colin along a narrow country lane in Cheshire, north-west England. The journey had been uneventful. But as they approached a local landmark called the Backford Dip, suddenly, and for no apparent reason, Colin pulled over on to the grass verge and stopped the car. The family were quite confused by this action. The lane ahead seemed clear, although visibility was obscured by a large bend in the road ahead. Bill's mother asked Colin why he had stopped so suddenly. His response was that he had simply felt a great urge to pull over. As he continued to explain, his voice was drowned by the sound of a huge tanker lorry approaching at speed from round the bend. This lorry was so big that it filled the lane from side to side. There was no way it would have been able to stop had it encountered the family's car in the centre of the lane. In his email to me, Bill explained that in his opinion a head-on collision would have been unavoidable and would have resulted in all of them being killed.

So here we have an example of precognition actually saving lives. Colin did not see a future event. There was no 'vision' of a potential catastrophe, just an urge to do something different, in this case to pull over on to a verge. Could it be that this 'higher self' is continually monitoring the future and changing our life's course in order to avoid future dangerous consequences? If so, then we will never know what dangers have been avoided because they never came to pass. Indeed, is this why every single person reading this book has survived a life full of dangers in order to be taking in these words? Could it be that each consciousness will, by necessity, survive all life-threatening circumstances because each personal universe needs an observer to bring it into being? Is death something that only happens to other people? Could there be alternative futures that contain all outcomes of all events?

If a part of us has lived this life before then sometimes a sudden recognition of a set of circumstances may 'leak' over from our 'Daemonic memory banks'. Many of us experience watching a movie and vaguely recognizing the plot. As the story develops we realize that the reason for this vague sense of precognition or familiarity is because we have, in fact, seen the movie before but had forgotten. If the Eternal Return is more than a simple philosophical exercise and is a genuine possibility then we should all have this sense of recognition as we watch the movie of our life over again. According to recent research, at least 70 per cent of people will experience this sensation of recognition, more popularly known as *déjà vu*. For me, this phenomenon is the greatest evidence for the reality of the Eternal Return there is.

CHAPTER 8
THE DÉJÀ PHENOMENON

The Windrush incident

One day in the summer of 2011, I decided I needed a break from writing this book. My wife and I had recently moved back to West Sussex. As the summer had been particularly good we invested in a guide book of country walks, our intention being to follow the back roads, footpaths and bridleways and in doing so learn more about this beautiful county. The weather looked particularly promising so I decided to abandon the laptop and get some good country air.

Quite at random, we picked a short walk around the small village of Loxwood on the West Sussex–Surrey border. This was particularly interesting as much of it followed the route of a famous old canal, now being renovated, called the Way-Arun. About an hour into our journey we found ourselves walking along a wonderfully named road called Pigbush Lane. As we approached a junction with the B2133 Guildford Road, a really odd occurrence took place. For no apparent reason, my mind was taken back nearly a third of a century to a specific time and place. I recalled a long-forgotten incident whereby my then girlfriend, Jane, announced that we had been 'summoned' to her parents' house in West Wittering, a particularly attractive village on the southern coast of England. I recalled this strange choice of words – 'summoned to. . .' She then gave the name of her parents' house. I had never been there before, nor had I ever associated with a section of society that gave their houses names, like pets or children.

However hard I tried, I could not recall the name of the house. This was unusual for me as I usually have a really good memory for these things. I also know that if I make my mind go blank, or think about something else, information simply pops into my mind. I mentioned to Penny about the incident all those years ago and, rather curiously, I found myself explaining how strange it was that I could not recall the house name. We continued chatting about West Wittering as we crossed the main road. As we did so the name of the house suddenly appeared, as expected, unbidden from the recesses of my memory banks. 'Windrush', I announced to Penny triumphantly. 'That is what the house was called, "Windrush".'

Penny looked at me with her usual pained 'why did I marry this guy?' kind of look, nodded and started to read the next instruction in the guide book. She read out: 'Walk along the right-hand verge of the B2133. Walk along to Oakhurst Lane and follow the Sussex Border Path to Oakhurst Farm'. This was Penny's subtle message that she was less than interested in the name of a house from my past and more interested in negotiating the instructions. The entrance to Oakhurst Lane was no more than 30 metres away and took less than a minute to walk to. Immediately on the left-hand side of the lane was a large country house. At the back was a pebbled drive leading to a garage. Unusually for homes in this part of the country, the garage could be seen clearly from the road. Parked outside the garage was a Volkswagen Golf, which was about 10 years old. Why I looked at this car I have no idea. It was on the opposite side of the road from where Penny and I were walking and there was absolutely nothing unusual about it. We had passed many parked cars on the walk and I had barely noticed them. But this car was different. My attention was immediately drawn to it and, much to Penny's surprise, I crossed the road and encroached slightly on the private gravel path. I was as confused as Penny as to why I had done this. But my answer came swiftly. I found myself looking at the rear windscreen of the Golf. This had a sticker announcing the name of the garage that had supplied the car to the original purchaser 11 years before. My heart leapt to my throat as I quickly realized the significance of this. In clear letters the supplier's name announced itself as 'Windrush' – the very name of the house that had resurrected itself unbidden from the miasma of over 30 years of memories less than three minutes before.

Penny was puzzled as to why I looked so shocked. She walked across the road to join me. Without saying anything I pointed at the sign in the rear window. Penny looked stunned. Even she found this hard to take in. Much to my surprise she immediately offered an explanation. 'You have walked down this road before in your last life and your subconscious recognized the road. Last time you talked about Jane's parents' home after you had seen the car. Last time the car stimulated the memory. This time the circumstances triggered the association.' I couldn't help but agree. Yet, another option was available. Could it be that I had simply experienced a form of *déjà vécu* sensation in which I subliminally precognized my encounter with the Golf and that in turn generated the association with the house in West Wittering?

Was this an example of a past-life memory or simply a stunning example of the most common of all psychic phenomena, *déjà vu*?

That strange sensation

The term *déjà vu* first appeared in a paper written by M. Bonac, a professor of philosophy, in 1876. Professor Bonac was intrigued by a particular form of memory that he had experienced throughout his life. He described these memories by using the term *le sentiment du déjà vu*. Unfortunately there seems to have been little reaction to this paper and we have to wait 20 years before the term reappears. In that year a M. Arnoud suggested at a meeting of the French Société Médico-Psychologique (SMP) that this term should be used to describe the strange sensation that one is living again a moment that one has lived before. Indeed, in this meeting it was suggested that the term used should be *déjà vécu* (already lived) rather than *déjà vu* (already seen).

As was typical of the jingoistic world of the late 19th century, British psychologists and psychiatrists had their own terms for this feeling, calling it 'promnesia' or 'paramnesia'. However, in 1895 the renowned researcher Frederick Myers (1843–1901) put jingoistic attitudes aside and used the French term in his major work *The Subliminal Self*. In doing so he gave us the first modern definition of the phenomenon:

> . . .*a suddenly evoked reminiscence of a past dream may give rise to the feeling of 'déjà vu', of having witnessed the actual scene at some indefinite time before. . . The really important question. . . is whether the connection may be other than casual, whether the dreamer may in some super-normal way have visited the scene, or anticipated the experience, which he was destined afterwards to behold or undergo.*[97]

In many ways this accurately reflects the various reports of the sensation that have come down to us in the diaries and novels of earlier writers. Indeed, it is of possible significance that prior to 1800 the experience can only be implied from reports involving reincarnation and the belief in the transmigration of souls. To find a specific reference to the sensation of having relived an incident we have to turn to the world of literature. The earliest examples found so far are in the writings of Sir Walter Scott (1771–1832). On 17 February 1828, Scott entered the following in his diary:

> *I cannot, I am sure, tell if it is worth marking down, that yesterday, at dinner time, I was strangely haunted by what I would call the sense of pre-existence, viz.; a confused idea that nothing that passed was said for the first time; that the same topics had been discussed and the same persons had stated the same opinions on them. . . the sensation was so strong as to resemble what is called a mirage in the desert and a calenture on board ship. . . it was very distressing yesterday and brought to my mind the fancies of Bishop Berkeley about an ideal world. There was a vile sense of unreality in all I said and did.*[98]

It seems fairly reasonable to conclude that this sensation occurred to him more than once because he wrote of a similar experience in his novel *Guy Mannering*, which was published in 1815. However, the most famous passage relating to the subject was by Charles Dickens (1812–70) in his book *David Copperfield*. Published in 1850, the work includes a specific comment on the sensation:

> *We have all some experience of a feeling that comes over us occasionally. Of what we are saying or doing have been said and done before, in a remote time – of our having been surrounded, dim ages ago, by the same faces, objects and circumstances – of our knowing perfectly what will be said next, as if we suddenly remembered it.*[99]

Dickens was not using this simply as a literary device. In his autobiographical travel book *Pictures from Italy* he wrote the following:

> *At sunset, when I was walking on alone, while the horses rested, I arrived upon a little scene which, by one of those singular mental operations of which we are all conscious, seemed perfectly familiar to me, and which I see distinctly now. There was not much in it. In the blood red light, there was a mournful sheet of water, just stirred by the evening wind; upon its margin a few trees. In the foreground (of a view of Ferrara) was a group of silent peasant girls leaning over the parapet of a little bridge, looking now up at the sky, now down into the water. In the distance a deep dell; the shadow of approaching night on everything. If I had been murdered there in some former life I could not have seemed to remember the place more thoroughly or with more emphatic chilling of the blood; and the real remembrance of it acquired in that minute is so strengthened by the imaginary recollection, that I hardly think I could forget it.*[100]

By the time Dickens was writing, interest in all forms of psychic phenomena was very much in vogue. It is possible that he may have come across the work of the English doctor A.L. Wigan. In his highly influential book *The Duality of Mind*, Wigan describes a curious *déjà vu* sensation that overtook him in 1817 while attending the funeral of Princess Charlotte at Windsor. As all the local eating houses were closed as a mark of respect, he had had little to eat and had spent a sleepless night in uncomfortable lodgings. As such, he was in a fairly weakened state. After standing for nearly four hours in St George's Chapel he states that he was very nearly fainting. Suddenly, as the princess's coffin was being lowered into its place of rest, he:

> . . . *felt not merely an impression, but a conviction, that I had seen the whole scene before on some former occasion, and had heard even the very words addressed to myself by Sir George Naylor.*[101]

This experience mystified Wigan to such an extent that he wished to try to understand what was taking place. In doing so he proposed the first neurologically-based theory of the *déjà* phenomenon. Wigan suggested that *déjà vu* is caused by faulty communication between the two hemispheres of the brain. He argued that one hemisphere is simply not following what it is receiving from the senses. The attentive hemisphere thus processes the information a short time before the tardy side. As a result, consciousness receives two identical messages but with a slight delay between them. Wigan believed that the mind will only be fully aware of the delayed input and so the earlier message is not fully realized. As the later message is received, the person experiences a vague feeling of familiarity.

Robert Efron and the optical pathway hypothesis

From now on, *déjà vu* would be regarded as a neurological, not a psychological, issue. Anybody who proposed that a *déjà* experience was an example of anything other than faulty wiring in the brain would be swiftly accused of dabbling in pseudo-science and ignored by the main body of scientific enquiry. Indeed, Wigan's theory of double consciousness, although crude by modern standards, has become the generally accepted explanation for *déjà vu*. Many years later it was to be updated and given a more solid scientific base by the work of Robert Efron.

Efron's 1963 paper, entitled 'Temporal Perception, Aphasia and *Déjà Vu*' was seen by many as a proposal that at long last freed the *déjà* phenomenon from the clutches of pseudo-science and brought it back into the mainstream. Efron's suggestion was both simple and convincing. He explained that in order to identify an event in temporal order a person has to place that event along with other events. In other words, there has to be both 'information' and 'sequence'. Under normal circumstances, both hemispheres of the brain receive sensory stimuli from the external world at the same time. However, Efron suggested that should one hemisphere receive information before the other (even if the delay is only a few milliseconds) then there will be an echo of stimulus in which consciousness will perceive the information twice. As subjects believe they have already come across this information (albeit only milliseconds before) they have a sensation of *déjà vu*. Efron believed this principally applied to the brain's visual pathways, and so the theory is sometimes known as 'optical pathway delay'.

On first encountering the Efron proposal, when researching material for my first book, I found it a particularly unsatisfactory explanation. For example, how much information can be processed in a fraction of a second? It takes longer than that to realize that *déjà vu* is taking place. Indeed, it is the totality of the experience, not a tiny split second of perception, that causes the feeling of strangeness. In addition, neurologically speaking, the right and left hemispheres process information from the outside world in totally different ways so it is therefore unlikely that confusion would occur.

Recent findings have now raised serious doubts about the Efron model. In order to be effective, a dual-processing theory such as that of Efron has to involve the visual pathways of the brain. It is literally an explanation of *déjà vu* (already *seen*) rather than *déjà vécu* (already lived). It is important to make the distinction between the two clear. If I feel that I have *seen* this event before then I am experiencing *déjà vu* and the Efron thesis proposes to explain it. The Efron explanation depends upon one hemisphere receiving sensory information before the other and in doing so there is a feeling of an event that has already been perceived being perceived once again. This works fine for the way in which the visual pathways in the brain work. It is possible that we might process a visual image in one hemisphere, not be consciously aware of having done so but still see it subliminally, only to receive the same image from the dominant hemisphere.

However, the neural pathways for *hearing* take a very different route and as such there cannot be a similar 'echo' effect. Therefore Efron's theory cannot explain the phenomenon known as *déjà senti* (already felt).

It can be argued that a *déjà* sensation is more than just vision-stimulated. When I have the feeling that I have experienced an event before it involves *all* my senses, not just what I am seeing. If vision alone were involved the experience would, I am sure, feel far less strange. I would have a sensation of vague double vision, as if I was seeing the same few frames of a film one after another. This is quite specifically what I do not perceive and, on questioning individuals who have regular *déjà* sensations they, similarly, do not have this sensation; specifically sight and hearing.

In 2006, after my first book had been published, a paper appeared in an academic periodical that proved that Efron's thesis could not explain all *deja* experiences. One can reasonably conclude that the 'visual pathways theory' is, as they say, dead in the water. The paper was written by Dr Akira O'Connor and Professor Chris Moulin of the psychology department at Leeds University, in the north of England. The two researchers describe how their subject experienced powerful *déjà* sensations while undoing a zip, hearing a piece of music, holding a plate in the school dining hall and hearing a snatch of conversation. All these experiences triggered profound feelings of having experienced those moments before, of living them time and time again. Although powerful, these are still very typical *déjà vu* sensations. What is of significance is that the subject was blind. His *déjà* sensations were sensed through hearing, touch and smell and not vision, and so none of them could be explained using the Efron thesis. O'Connor wrote:

> It is the first time this has been reported in scientific literature. It is useful because it provides a concrete case study which contradicts the theory of optical pathway delay. Eventually we would like to talk to more blind people, though there's no reason to believe this man's experiences are abnormal or different to those of others. Optical pathway delay is a quite antiquated theory, but still widely believed – and was the basis for the déjà vu *sequences in Joseph Heller's novel* Catch-22. *But this provides strong evidence that optical pathway delay is not the explanation for* déjà vu. *The findings are so obvious, so intuitive, that it's remarkable this research has never been done before.*[102]

For me, this confirms what I have always believed, and experienced, and that is that my *déjà vécu* sensations involve all my senses, not just sight. It is literally a recreation of a total experience. But added to that is also this strange feeling of disassociation, as if my mind is experiencing a recording rather than an actual event.

The dream theory

I regularly lecture across the UK and I usually ask the audience members to describe their own *déjà* experiences. All of the experiencers I have spoken to describe this odd feeling. Could this be that a *déjà* sensation is exactly what it feels like; a sudden realization that this world we experience is a form of illusion that we have been through before, possibly many, many times?

What does surprise me is that the Efron thesis is still trotted out as the definitive explanation by those who should know better. It is as if the O'Connor paper were never published and that those who believe it are in some form of denial. In my opinion, this is because the alternative explanations are simply too disturbing for many commentators on the subject. They cannot take the suggestion that the *déjà* phenomenon may indicate the reality of short-term precognition. However, one commentator who is not in any way disturbed by such conclusions is consultant psychiatrist Professor Vernon Neppe, of the Pacific Neuropsychiatric Institute in Seattle.

In 1983, while still living in South Africa, Professor Neppe published a groundbreaking book on the subject entitled *The Psychology of Déjà Vu*. For many, this is the definitive review of this enigmatic subject. Neppe's definition of the phenomenon, from an earlier paper, is still the one that is used by most researchers in the field. This is:

> *Any subjectively inappropriate impression of familiarity of the present with an undefined past.*[103]

Neppe says it is important to understand precisely what we mean when we use the term *déjà vu*. He argues that it is not a feeling but an impression; a cognition rather than an effect. He also thinks that it is equally important to differentiate *déjà vu* from other similar phenomena such as flashbacks, 'cryptomnesia' and actualized precognition. He explains:

> *Initially, let us consider the phrase in the* déjà vu *definition 'present experience with. . . past'. For familiarity to occur there must be a comparison. Déjà vu experience is firmly rooted in the PRESENT; and the comparison is made with the PAST. By stressing*

the present, one is able to differentiate the interpretative component of déjà vu *with the purely experiential flashback.*[104] *In the flashback experience, one may see facets of one's past life passing before one's eyes. One may for that brief period conceive of oneself as not in the present but actually back in the past. Flashbacks (also called 'playbacks') are different from conventional vivid memory: in a vivid memory, the imagery and percepts of the past come into focus but the subject is firmly rooted in the present. Both differ from* déjà vu: *for* déjà vu *to occur there needs to be an experience which is happening at that moment and it is that experience which seems familiar.* Déjà vu *also differs from cryptomnesia*[105] *(literally: hidden memories): for in the latter the person will have a memory of something which did not happen to him but there is no comparison with the present, just a sense of past ideas which are familiar yet should not be because they apparently do not exist.*[106]

This is a very precise definition. For Neppe it is of utmost importance that the sensation involves an *undefined* period in the past. If the subject could define where the original event had taken place then the mystery would be of a totally different nature. In this case the past would be, as Neppe says, 'actualizing itself' in the present. The technical term for this sensation is 'pseudo-presentiment'. This is the sensation that the present situation has been foretold. This is different from precognition, which is the foretelling of some future event, an event by its very nature that has yet to take place. To experience pseudo-presentiment one must be at that point in time when the precognized event actually comes to pass. However, in the case of *déjà vu* the subject cannot recall the prediction; only a sensation that it has now come to pass. Neppe considers this to be a particular form of the *déjà* phenomena and terms it *déjà pressenti.*[107]

The Switzerland-based US psychoanalyst Dr Arthur Funkhouser is an important associate of Neppe. Funkhouser is of the opinion that all *déjà vu* experiences can be attributed to dreams. Funkhouser says that it is from dreams that all precognitive phenomena arise. The issue is that dreams are nearly always forgotten on waking. Therefore when the foreseen circumstances come to pass they are a surprise to the observer.[108] This sensation is reflected in the following description found in Neppe's book on *déjà vu*. The narrator was a 56-year-old pensions clerk who attributed all his *déjà vu* experiences to dreams. However, it was only after the events took place that he acknowledged them as being from a dream. He claimed that he never remembered his dreams for more than a short time after waking:

> *It happened in connection with my work recently. It signified something I had done. It proved what you had mentioned about* déjà vu *and* déjà entendu. *I had a sense of familiarity about the whole thing because I had dreamt it. But I couldn't remember the actual dream or when I dreamt it. Each thing that came up was familiar. I felt like a prophet because I knew what was coming up. I could have proved I was a prophet if I had mentioned it to someone before it happened, but I hadn't done so. It started off when the name of one of my clients was mentioned. I had to go through the file (as part of my work) and felt I knew what was coming next. I've had several instances like this – all dreams coming true but I can only remember this one well.*[109]

This experience seems to vindicate Funkhouser's 'dream theory'. However, Funkhouser is still puzzled by one aspect of the phenomenon:

> *. . .why are* déjà vu *experiences so banal? Why am I given a preview of just this everyday situation, and not something more striking, or at least more meaningful? Is this just some random event, like radioactive decay, or is there some hidden, meta-purpose involved?*

I had the opportunity to discuss this with Dr Funkhouser and we both agreed that if these sensations are simply a form of memory then banality will be part of the overall sensation in the same way that our past memories seem to regularly involve very ordinary circumstances. A much quoted example of the sheer ordinariness of spontaneous memories was given by the French writer Marcel Proust (1871–1922) in his classic meditation on memory and time, À la Recherché du Temps Perdu (In Search of Lost Time), when he describes how a long-lost memory of his childhood appeared in his mind totally unbidden when tasting a piece of madeleine cake dipped in tea. However, what is less known is that the writer regularly experienced déjà vu sensations, as he described in À la Recherché:

> . . .and at the same time in the context of a distant moment, so that the past was made to encroach upon the present and I was made to doubt whether I was in one or the other. The truth surely was that the being within me which had enjoyed these impressions had enjoyed them because they had in them something that was common to a day long passed and to the present, because in some way they were extra-temporal, and this being made its appearance only when, through one of these identifications of the present with the past, it was likely to find itself in the one and only medium in which it could exist and enjoy the essence of things. That is to say; outside time.[110]

Indeed, it may be of significance that Proust's cousin, Louise Neuberger, married the great French philosopher Henri Bergson. We have already encountered Bergson in relation to his theories that the human mind acts as an attenuator and filters out much of the information received by the senses. In 1908 Bergson wrote an intriguing paper in which he reviews a psychological phenomenon that he calls 'false recognition'. I am sure Proust would have known about this paper when be began writing À la

Recherché in 1913. In 1952, a paper was published in the *International Journal of Psychoanalysis*, suggesting an intriguing explanation that has echoes of Proust's overall philosophy on the nature of memory and time. Psychoanalyst Eli Marcowitz argued that *déjà vu* was simply a wish for a second chance to correct unresolved guilt. He believed that *déjà vu* involved transient psychotic episodes, and was motivated by an extreme wish to turn back time.[111] As such, *déjà vu* is really *encore vu* because the unsatisfactory had been repeated as the satisfactory. In many ways this model has echoes of the Eternal Return as suggested by Peter Ouspensky.

The research into *déjà vu*

Clearly the *déjà* phenomenon has much to tell us about the nature of time, dreams and precognition. Indeed, in my opinion, it may offer us a crucial source of empirical information in our attempt to understand the relationship between conscious awareness and the underlying nature of reality. But just how common is this phenomenon?

Surprisingly enough, the earliest report on the incidence of *déjà vu* appeared as early as 1884. The researcher in question, an American by the name of Osborne, used the term 'illusions of memory' to describe the sensation as the term *déjà vu* had not become part of common terminology. Osborne reported that half of his subjects claimed to have experienced reliving a particular moment. However, the first attempt to use recognized statistical methodology to chart the incidence of *déjà vu* was made by Morton Leeds in 1944. Leeds interviewed 100 'normal' subjects; that is, none of them suffered from any form of psychological or physiological abnormality. Of these, 85 stated that they had 'experiences that had happened the same way once before'. Later in this exercise, three more subjects reported similar experiences giving him an 88 per cent 'yes' response in total. Leeds came to the reasonable conclusion that under the right circumstances all people experience *déjà vu*.

In Britain, the first fully reported study involved 110 students at Aberdeen University in 1954. Again it was found that a significant majority of the subjects, 71 per cent, reported *déjà vu* experiences.

As regards psychiatric patients, the results have been even more interesting. In 1970, researchers at Yale University asked 84 acute psychiatric hospital admissions if they had experienced a feeling of having been somewhere before when first encountering a place. An amazing 92 per cent answered yes, with 15 per cent stating that they had this experience on a regular basis. This high incidence of *déjà vu* in those with psychiatric conditions was reinforced in 1977 when Greyson asked a similar question to schizophrenic patients in Virginia. Of these, 65 per cent of the 20 questioned responded in the affirmative.

Professor Neppe carried out the first of his studies of the phenomenon in 1979. He took the opportunity to question 84 women who were attending one of his lectures in South Africa. In a not altogether surprising group of results, Neppe found that 96 per cent claimed to have had *déjà vu* at some time in their lives, 30 per cent in the previous six months and 19 per cent in the previous month. However, one cannot escape the fact that an individual who chooses to attend a lecture by a known expert on *déjà vu* may well be motivated by personal experience of the subject. Therefore the amazingly high incidence is not altogether surprising as the subjects had, in effect, self-selected. However, the results did seem to confirm one of the few 'known facts' about the incidence of *déjà vu*, which is that it occurs in inverse relation to age: the younger the subject the more likely it is that they will experience it. Over 90 per cent of respondents aged over 40 had experienced *déjà vu* at some point in their lives but recent experience of *déjà vu* was more common among the younger respondents.

Neppe was also involved in a later study carried out in the early 1980s. This was an extremely structured and objective exercise and involved both an interview and the use of a questionnaire devised by Neppe himself.

Neppe was keen to understand if the *déjà* experience was related in any way to abnormal psychiatric conditions. As a comparison, he questioned a group of selected individuals who had been diagnosed with psychiatric conditions. He compared the results with the same set of questions asked to a random group of 'normal' (that is, non-psychiatric) subjects. He was surprised to discover that the incidence of *déjà* experiences in the 'normal' group was surprisingly high. Of the 76 subjects in this group, 71 per cent reported experiencing *déjà vu* at some point in their lives, with 47 per cent experiencing the phenomenon in the previous six months. With regard to the psychiatric group, the responses that particularly fascinated Neppe were those from the one specific category, subjects diagnosed with a neurological condition known as temporal lobe epilepsy (TLE). If you have read my previous books you will know that I am particularly fascinated by this enigmatic 'illness'. Those who experience TLE regularly report perceptions that suggest that they can, in some way, override the Bergsonian 'attenuator'. It is as if the neurochemicals responsible for this form of epilepsy open up consciousness to a far wider awareness of 'reality' than is normally available. This belief is very much supported by the results of Neppe's survey.

Neppe wanted to discover at what age *déjà vu* began to be experienced. As already mentioned, it has long been known that the young experience *déjà vu* with the greatest frequency and this drops off as they get older. This does not seem to be the case with the TLE group as 12 of the 14 said that they had experienced *déjà vu* consistently throughout their lives. Of those 12, ten had had an experience in the past month and all 12 within the past year. Eight of the 14 subjects had experienced at least 50 *déjà vu* experiences in their lives. Two claimed to have experienced *déjà vu* 'thousands' of times and seven said they had these experiences at least once a week.

In response to the question of how long the *déjà vu* experience lasted, 11 of the 12 said that the sensation lasted longer than a minute. If this is correct then the subject has had time to take in fully what they can see and feel. For those with TLE, *déjà vu* is not a fleeting sensation that has passed before they realize what is taking place. They relive the memory for longer than a minute. They find themselves back again at a point in their own memories. If Neppe's respondents can be believed, and their perception of *déjà vu* really does last 'more than a minute', then this is again clear evidence that the Efron explanation simply does not work.

Efron's theory is further invalidated by the TLE subjects' perception of the overall experience. For over 50 per cent of them, the sensory perception of *déjà vu* was described as 'vivid' or 'very vivid'. This does not square with the fleeting nature of the sensation implied by Efron's explanation.

Neppe was concerned that the term *déjà vu* was an inadequate and misleading term for certain forms of the experience as the words literally mean 'already seen'. As Neppe argues, quite rightly, in many cases the subject is experiencing a much wider sensation. In order to reflect this Neppe suggested the term *déjà vécu* (already lived) as being far more accurate. It then comes as no surprise that the TLE group show a much higher incidence of this experience than ordinary *déjà vu*. Three out of the 12 felt that they were 'reliving the whole'. Indeed, that *déjà vécu* is in some meaningful way an essential part of the whole TLE illness is echoed by the American psychiatrist Dr Strauss. For Dr Strauss, *déjà vécu* is a special kind of *déjà vu* with a deep qualitative component, going far beyond familiarity with an intensity sometimes so great that the impression of reliving the same situation resulted. Dr Strauss considers that this special type of *déjà vu* occurs significantly more often in those with TLE than with the general population.

For those with TLE, the *déjà* experience has one other simply fascinating side effect. Nine out of the 12 (75 per cent) reported that during the sensation they have a higher awareness of their environment and their senses are far more acute. Some 50 per cent stated that this awareness was greatly enhanced. This implies that they had more time available to process incoming sensory signals. This changed awareness of time will be visited again in a later chapter. Suffice to say at this stage that time becomes elastic during a *déjà vécu* experience.

Neppe's questionnaire itself showed that TLE subjects' experiences of *déjà vu* are qualitatively and quantitatively different from that of 'normal' subjects. The questionnaire consisted of 11 questions to which the subjects answered 'yes' or 'no'. The number of 'yes' responses was indicative of the degree of *déjà vu* experienced. The average positive response to the questions was 32 per cent. But for those subjects with TLE the average positive response was 48 per cent. When this is factored together with the actual numbers of lifetime experiences recorded, it is clear that TLE and *déjà vu* have a strong correlation. As Neppe says:

> *When frequency in individuals is considered, temporal lobe epileptics generally have* déjà vu *far more frequently than other groups.*[112]

However, there is a period in everyone's life when time seems to have a very liquid form, and this is in early childhood. For a few short years we all inhabit a wonderful world where magic and mystery exist everywhere and our imagination is as real as the world that our parents take for granted.

Infant precognitions

In his autobiography, British writer Colin Middleton Murry (1926–2002) relates how, as a child, he unwittingly disconcerted grown-up company by foretelling what was about to be said. He would do this a few seconds before the adult spoke. The curious thing is that he saw nothing odd in this ability and it was only because of the embarrassment of others that he stopped using it. As he grew older this ability stopped. It will be recalled that those approaching death sometimes also show this ability. It could be that in some way certain individuals can 'attune' to another part of the brain's memory store. The word 'memory' is not an error here, it is the memory store that is being accessed, not a vision of events that are yet to occur. Suffice to say that these individuals for some reason perceive things that ordinary adults do not. Here is an example given to me by a personal contact:

A few years ago when my son Alex was around 18 months old a very strange thing happened. At this age he was able to walk and was very dextrous but was not yet talking. We were concerned at the time that his speech skills were a little slow developing. It was some time in the afternoon, when completely out of character at that time, he became VERY agitated and time after time pointed to the window and indicated that he wanted my wife to go to the window with him. The window ledge at that time was a few inches above his eye line and therefore the other side of the window was clearly beyond his field of vision. My wife went over to the window a number of times and could see nothing. Eventually, after a few more minutes he (still agitated) started to sort through a pile of books in search of something particular. He then flicked through the pages until he came to a page with a picture of an American (bright yellow) school bus, at which point he pointed to the picture of the bus and then immediately pointed out of the window again. Again my wife went over to the window, still there was nothing to be seen. By now he was becoming extremely upset and was lying on the floor kicking and screaming because my wife did not understand what he was trying to say. He continued to gesticulate towards the window. To my wife's great surprise, a few minutes had elapsed when she heard the sound of a lorry coming along the road. (We lived in a quiet cul-de-sac and were rarely ever visited by lorries.) She watched the lorry approach and stop outside our house. It was a big bright yellow council lorry of the type used for drain clearing. As she picked him up to look at the lorry he smiled and immediately calmed down. My wife is convinced that he somehow sensed that the event was about to take place. When

I returned from work, my wife relayed the story and I thought that I should eliminate the possibility that it was a coincidence. Based on what she had told me, I opened the book to the picture of the bright yellow bus and said to Alex, 'Did you see one of these today?' at which point my son immediately started gesticulating towards the window and clearly indicated a positive response. I too firmly believe that Alex knew in advance that the lorry was coming. During his first couple of years of life similar things did happen, for instance Alex always knew about 20 minutes before I arrived home from work that I was due home, this could not be accounted for by daily routine as even when I left work early he still seemed to know.

Certain children continue this ability for a few years after infancy. However, as with adults, it seems to become part of a previous dream rather than a concurrent perception. Writer Rosalind Heywood describes an event that is all the more believable because of its ordinary, low-key nature. She describes how her young son casually informed her of his precognitive abilities:

He and his brother came out from school in England to spend their summer holidays with us at Rehoboth, a seaside town in Maryland. On arrival he said casually, 'I know this place, I have dreamt it. I know what's there and there (pointing east and south) but not what is there and there (pointing west and north).' I replied equally casually, for I never discussed ESP with the children, 'Well, if you do, lead us down to the sea.' The way to the sea was obvious enough, one walked downhill, but what was less obvious was our flowered sun umbrella, which was one of hundreds on an enormous beach. Without hesitation he threaded his way between them until he reached it. I followed. 'How did you know that one was ours?' I asked. 'I dreamt the pattern on it.' The pattern was very distinctive and like no other on the beach. 'Do you often dream ahead?' 'Oh yes, it is very useful at school.' He again said

this as indifferently as he would have said that it was useful to
be able to swim if you fell out of a boat.

So it seems that some young children have an ability to tune into the thoughts of another part of their 'memories'. They are at the start of their lives and as such can tune into 'memories' of the future. There is evidence that the same thing takes place at the end of a life. This ability seems to be carried into adulthood by certain individuals such as those who experience TLE. One particularly intriguing example of just how strange these perceptions can be was described by one of Neppe's patients:

It occurred one year ago. He was in the Johannesburg waiting room of a certain doctor for the first time. He felt a little anxious and agitated. Suddenly, lasting a flash of a second, the whole place became familiar; the walls, the curtains, the receptionist, the counter, the ceiling. This experience was identical in quality to previous experiences he had had, and he therefore knew he would have a blackout. With the feeling started an experience of intense, unexplained unprecipitated fear which lasted about thirty seconds. During this phase everything was unfamiliar again, and he developed the intense uncontrollable desire to go away. He then blacked out. [113]

This is a particularly fascinating example of a form of time anomaly in that it is more than simply a precognition. It seems that he knew what was about to happen next (his blackout) and this is what happened. It seems to be that time itself loses its ability to flow in the way we normally expect. As we have already seen, there is strong evidence that time flow is an illusion created by the mind. If this is the case then 'real' time consists of a permanent 'now'. This perceived flow can be disrupted by certain neurological conditions, both natural and pharmacologically induced. Sometimes this consists of an immediate future cognition, but sometimes it involves time itself running backwards or forwards. There is one case that continues to intrigue me since first encountering it many years ago.

In the film *The Matrix* there is an incident in which Neo, the central character, has what is termed a *déjà vu*. He sees a cat walk past a door and then sees what he takes to be a second cat do exactly the same thing a second later. His companions tell him that it was indeed a replay of the first incident and that all *déjà vu* experiences are caused by 'reality' being reprogrammed. This is, of course fiction. This kind of thing does not happen in the real world because if it did it would lead us to doubt what external reality really is. Bear this prejudice in mind as you read the following account reported by a maid and taken from J.B. Priestley's masterwork, *Man and Time*:

> *The only time that time became misplaced for me happened when I was working as a maid in a place called Dunraven Castle in South West Wales. There were three of us in the servery just after Saturday luncheon – Hans, the odd-job boy, Renate, the senior maid and me. The floor of the room was a terra cotta orange colour. I saw Renate pick up a jug, a white jug, of chocolate sauce. As she turned to hand it to Hans she dropped it. It smashed and the pastel-brown sauce formed a very definite pattern on the floor, something like an amoeba as shown in a school biology textbook. As I looked the whole scene melted and, like a loop of film, started again. It was terrifying! I remember shouting to Renate, as she picked up the jug, not to touch it, and screaming in horror as I watched the sauce make its pre-destined shape on the orange floor. I tried to explain to them how I had watched the scene take place a couple of seconds before it had – and, of course, they said that if I had not shouted the whole thing wouldn't have happened.*[114]

What had happened here? It was as if time had somehow rewound itself, running backwards into the past. This suggests that what we perceive as reality may be a form of recording, something encoded in the brain as digital signals are burned on to a DVD disc by a laser beam. This could mean that the record of our whole life may be found somewhere deep within the neuronal pathways of the brain. Indeed, some have suggested that all these records are downloaded into one huge record that has within it the information describing every event that has ever occurred since the first nanoseconds of the Big Bang. If this is the case then this may help explain one of the greatest mysteries of human experience, circumstances whereby people seem to find themselves in the past or, in some cases, the future. It is to the enigma of time slips that I would like to turn our attention.

CHAPTER 9

TIME IN DISARRAY

Incident at Miletus

In 1984 I was travelling round Turkey with a small group of 15 or so people. We had seen some amazing sites in Eastern Anatolia and along the Lycian Coast and we were making our way back to Istanbul along the Aegean coastline. As you may be aware, that part of Turkey has an amazing number of ancient Greek and Roman sites.

On one particularly hot afternoon, we arrived at the remains of the Greco-Roman city of Miletus. I knew nothing of this place but I was looking forward to a leisurely wander around the ruins.

Miletus was like every other site we had visited up until that time. We had the whole site to ourselves. Well, that was not quite true. There were also lots of goats and sheep, the occasional tortoise and the incessant buzz of the cicadas, but that was about it.

On arrival, I really had the urge to be alone. As my then girlfriend, Jenny, and the rest of the group headed down to the Roman theatre, I walked off in the other direction. I noticed a pink dome rising out of the trees a short distance away and I went to investigate.

On getting closer, I realized that it was a somewhat derelict mosque. Islamic art and architecture have always fascinated me so I decided to check it out. Inside it was very overgrown and I decided, for some odd reason, to climb up on to the roof area around the dome. After a difficult and somewhat dangerous scramble, I found myself on the roof.

The view was splendid. I could see across the site and in the distance I could see Jenny and the others sitting in some shade next to the ancient theatre. There was nobody else around. Even the goats seemed to have left me to my solitude.

Then something really strange happened. The only way I can

describe it is that the air around me became electric. I felt a tingling all over me. The view I was looking at seemed to shiver like a TV screen losing its signal. Time seemed to stop. As the air calmed down again I suddenly found I was looking out over an entirely different scene. Moments before I had been viewing the swaying cotton fields of the Menderes River's flood plain but now it was different. The flood plain had turned into a wide estuary filled with water. What had been hills in the distance were now offshore islands. The water lapped in as far as the ruined theatre that I could see further down the valley. I really could not take in fully what I was seeing but it was totally vivid. I can still see it now in my mind's eye. But what happened next snapped me back to 1984. As I looked over at one of the islands I saw the prow of a ship appear from behind the island, not of a modern craft but of a type of ancient Greek galley known as a trireme. It had a distinctive curved shape to the front. This was the image that was to shake me out of the 'dream' and back into 'reality'. The ancient trireme and the strange vista vanished. The electric sensation ceased, to be replaced by the buzz of the cicadas that greeted me as I returned to the 'present'.

It took me a few seconds to recover. My girlfriend, Jenny, then turned up and took a photograph of her weird boyfriend sitting on the roof of a mosque (a photograph I still possess and have now posted on my Blogsite). When I came down from the heights (both actually and metaphorically) I was still in a strange state of dislocation. A state that would take me many days to fully recover from.

When I returned to the UK, I was keen to know more about the original geography of the area. I was amazed (but not really surprised) to discover that what I had seen was exactly how the coastline looked in ancient times. The Menderes River was a large fjord-like inlet from the sea and the hills present today were then, as I had 'seen', offshore islands. Boats, mostly triremes like the one I had seen, would unload right next to the theatre.

But this event had a strange coda. A few weeks later, *The Sunday Times* ran an article about that part of Turkey. The reporter, a person whose name escapes me, described how when he was near 'the mosque' at Miletus he experienced a 'curious timeless state'. He said nothing more about this but I wonder what he actually meant. Had he experienced some weird time slip, as I had? Somewhere in our loft is the original article from 1984. It so stunned me that I kept it.

Hypnagogia

I have never experienced anything like this since and the event will always puzzle me because I know that it was not a daydream, because of its vivid, ultra-real properties. So what did I experience?

Throughout written history, people have claimed that, under certain circumstances, time seems to lose its structure and the past overlaps with the present. In some cases, the future even seems to impinge upon the present. It is as if the real nature of time is a permanent 'now' and it is simply our brain that presents time to us in a linear fashion. The question is, what is the mechanism by which consciousness can transcend the temporal prison and gain access to the 'timeless now' in which all events occur concurrently?

In my opinion, there was something very odd about atmospheric conditions that day. An oppressive feeling of heaviness was in the air. It is the feeling one experiences just before an electric storm. I also recall that there was a strong smell of ozone in the air. Added to this was a strange vibration all around me that made my skin tingle in anticipation of something portentous. Looking back, I am of the opinion that the atmospheric conditions facilitated the generation of certain neurotransmitters in my brain that, in turn, caused the tingling sensation. Indeed, I am reminded of the effect that glutamate has on certain individuals when they experience a condition called 'Chinese Restaurant Syndrome' (a severe reaction to the seasoning monosodium glutamate, or MSG). If this is correct then my consciousness was placed into a semi-conscious dream state known as 'hypnagogia'. This is the border state between wakefulness and dreams. Most people experience this as they go to sleep at night or, occasionally, as they wake up (in which case it is technically known as 'hypnapompia'). However, recent research has suggested that we sometimes lapse into this state while we are fully awake. When this happens wakefulness and dreaming overlap and we seem to enter a state of altered consciousness. Is the world we encounter in these 'waking dreams' simply an illusion or is it something more?

Many, many reported cases of time slips and time anomalies are accompanied by descriptions of peculiar atmospheric conditions, thunderstorms and an odd feeling of dislocation from ordinary reality that British writer Jenny Randles calls the 'Oz factor' after Dorothy's comment in the famous movie *The Wizard of Oz* that 'we are no longer in Kansas, Toto'. A classic example of this was experienced by a woman named Lynn in 1997. She was driving through a small Australian town when something strange happened:

> I was driving toward the main intersection, when suddenly I felt a change in the air. It wasn't the classic colder feeling, but a change, like a shift in atmosphere. The air felt denser somehow. As I slowed at the intersection, I seemed to be suddenly transported back in time to approximately 1950. The road was dirt, the trees were gone and coming toward me to cross the intersection was an old black car, something like a Vanguard or old FJ Holden. As the car passed through the driver was looking back at me in total astonishment before he accelerated. From what I could see he was dressed in similar 1950s fashion, complete with hat.[115]

She describes the 'shift of atmosphere' that I sensed that day in Turkey. She suddenly found herself directly involved in an incident from the past. However, it was clearly more than a snapshot of something that had happened years before, a 'recording' of events that somehow have been recreated by odd meteorological conditions. The man in the car reacted to her presence. He was clearly as astonished to see her as she was to see him. Is it possible that in the early 1950s a man driving an FJ Holden car suddenly glimpsed a woman from the future in a strange-looking vehicle? If so, did he ever mention it to anybody? If this story is to be taken at face value then what we have here is not a time slip in the classical understanding of the concept but an 'overlap' of incidents; two situations located in different places within space-time that suddenly share the same temporal location.

The Versailles mystery

Of all the famous cases of time slips, the one that is cited more than any other is the strange incident that befell two English women during the hot summer of 1901. Miss Annie Moberly, principal of St Hugh's College Oxford, and her friend Miss Eleanor Jourdain, the vice-principal, were sightseeing in Paris when they decided that the Palace of Versailles was close enough to be worth a visit.

They spent a leisurely few hours looking round the palace itself and then set out in the warm but muggy afternoon to look for the Petit Trianon, a small château located in the grounds. As they wandered around, the atmosphere became heavy and oppressive. It was clear that a thunderstorm was brewing. This atmosphere began to affect the two women and they started to feel strange. Suddenly, two men dressed in 'long greyish coats with small three-cornered hats' appeared. It is unclear whether Miss Jourdain and Miss Moberly asked the men for directions or whether the men spoke to the women first, but the two oddly dressed figures directed the two women to the Petit Trianon. As they approached the main building, the women noticed a small cottage standing in isolation within the grounds. In the doorway stood a woman and a young girl. Both were wearing white kerchiefs fastened under their bodices. Then something quite strange happened. The woman was holding a jug and, as she leant forward and the girl stretched out her hands to take it from her, the two figures seemed to freeze in time. Many years later Miss Jourdain described the incident:

> *She might have been just going to take the jug or have just given it up I remember that both seemed to pause for an instant, as in a motion picture.*[116]

I find this very curious. The description suggests that Miss Jourdain had seen a 'motion picture'. However, remember that she is describing the event many years afterwards. The world's earliest motion picture had been produced 13 years earlier, in 1888, so it is possible that she may have seen a 'movie' but somewhat unlikely.

At this stage, the women were more concerned about the strange atmosphere around them than the people they had encountered. Indeed, the atmosphere was becoming even more oppressive and unpleasant when they encountered a pavilion standing in the middle of an enclosure. A man was sitting outside the pavilion. He, too, was oddly dressed – his clothing was completely different from the fashions of the very early 20th century. However, what disturbed both women was how awfully disfigured the man was, possibly due to a very severe case of smallpox. Just like the woman and girl in the cottage, the man showed no interest in them whatsoever.

Clearly, what they were seeing was very odd. However, they did not speak about it to each other but continued walking through this peculiar tableau. Soon, they came across a small country house with shuttered windows and a terrace on either side. In front of the house was a manicured lawn where a very elegant lady stood holding a large sheet of paper. The two women could not tell if the lady was looking at the paper or drawing something on it. They were both later to recall in some detail that her clothing was unusual, like the others. She was wearing a summer dress with a long bodice and a very full, but also very short, skirt. Round her shoulders was a pale green kerchief and on her head was a large white hat.

The two women then spotted a second house. As they approached it a door was flung open and a young man came out. He walked off at a fair pace towards the Petit Trianon and they decided to follow him. Something very strange then happened. As if a switch had been thrown, they found themselves in the middle of a wedding party. This consisted of a crowd of people all dressed in the fashions of 1901. They were suddenly back from what they called *An Adventure*, the title of the book they co-wrote describing the events of that odd August day.[117]

To protect their reputations Miss Jourdain and Miss Moberly published the work under the pseudonyms Elizabeth Morison and Frances Lamont. Since then, the incident has become one of the most popular, and much debated, cases in the history of psychic research. Much has been made of the fact that Annie Moberly had claimed a number of psychic experiences before the events of 1901. Indeed, these events continued afterwards. According to a 1957 review of the case by Lucille Iremonger, Miss Moberly reported that she had a similar experience during a visit to the Louvre in Paris in 1914. There she saw an odd-looking man who had 'a small golden coronal [wreath] on his head and wore a loose toga-like dress of some light colour'. After some research, she came to the conclusion that she had seen the ghost of the Roman Emperor Constantine.[118] Unfortunately, this claim was somewhat undermined when a newspaper pointed out that a very eccentric artist regularly frequented the Louvre dressed as a Roman citizen. Clearly, Miss Moberly was rather too keen to believe in a romantic interpretation of facts in the face of more prosaic answers.[119]

One could also argue that after the events of 1901 Miss Moberly's concept of time had been severely compromised and she was desperately trying to re-experience her 'adventure'. However, in 1976 Dr Joan Evans wrote an article in which she referenced a 1966 biography of an eccentric French nobleman called Robert de Montesquiou-Ferenzac. It seems that this individual, who lived at the turn of the 20th century, was fascinated by the fashions and etiquette of the 18th century and regularly hosted fancy-dress parties in the grounds of Versailles. Could this have been what the two ladies stumbled across that hot summer's day in 1901?[120]

Could it be that what I had experienced in Turkey was a similar illusion in which I had interpreted what was a perfectly normal scene as something more mysterious? Now, it is reasonable to conclude that two Edwardian ladies who were walking round the grounds of an imposing 17th-century building such as the Palace of Versailles would be thinking of the past. Therefore, when they encountered an event staged by Montesquiou-Ferenzac it would seem in keeping with the history of the location. However, when I sat on the roof of the derelict mosque in 1984, ancient Greek history was not on my mind in any way. I accept that we had visited many ancient Greek and Roman sites over the course of the previous week or so, but this particular location was not of that time. So why did my imagination create a seascape over a river valley? Why did my mind's eye imagine offshore islands?

The Oz factor

In my previous books, I have suggested that altered states of consciousness may be facilitated by changes in metabolic processes in the brain. These can be the result of migraine or temporal lobe epilepsy (TLE), or may simply be brought about by a lowering of blood sugar levels. There are many cases where time slips seem to occur when people are overtired or hungry. In her fascinating book *Time Storms*, researcher Jenny Randles cites a particular case that took place in 1974. A Swedish resident of California called Bo Orsjo was hiking in the area of Mount Lowe just outside Pasadena. Halfway along his walk he came across an extremely attractive hotel. He was particularly taken by the fact that it was painted green and was therefore in keeping with its surroundings. The location was so idyllic that he decided that this would make a nice place to stop for his lunch. He was clearly hungry and much in need of the break. He sat down and watched a maid who had come out to do some chores around the outside of the building. He had noted that the scene was bathed in a shimmering, misty light that seemed to add to the overall ambience. He then made his way back to his friends and told them about the beautiful hotel he had seen.

Much to his frustration, nobody believed him. His friends often walked in the area and they insisted that no such hotel existed. Determined to prove them wrong, he returned with a friend a few weeks later. He was both dismayed and surprised to discover that the view from his picnic spot consisted of nothing but rubble. Intrigued, he decided to research the history of the location. He was amazed to discover that a millionaire by the name of Lowe had decided to build a railway going all the way up to the top of the mountain. The plan proved too expensive and the railway line was terminated just halfway up. But Lowe liked that spot so much that he decided to build a magnificent hotel on the site. The records clearly stated that the green hotel had burned down in 1937. So it was not at all surprising that Orsjo could find no evidence of the hotel in 1974. All that was left was the rubble that he discovered on his subsequent journey up the mountain.

In her book *Time Storms*, Jenny Randles has collected many fascinating time anomalies like this that have been described across the years. One in particular caught my eye. Randles describes how a sailor called Bill told her that in 1928 he was crossing the Atlantic on board a large tanker. At about 8.00 pm one evening the ship was suddenly becalmed. The sailor described the sensation as 'like being inside a bottle'. There were none of the sounds he would expect to hear aboard ship, such as the regular beating of the water against the hull. What was even stranger was that the rest of the crew seemed to have disappeared. Bill thought that they may have abandoned ship without telling him. He stated that:

Things were not normal. There was a grey misty sheen around us. Everywhere I looked, the sea and the sky blended into one wall

of seamless grey. The monotony went on for ever. I could see no
horizon. Nothing was moving. It was exactly as if time stood still
and I was no longer part of the world.

This continued for a few more minutes. Then he heard his fellow crew members running towards him. They had noticed him missing and they were concerned that he had fallen overboard. At this point he realized that everything had returned to normal.

Some cases seem to suggest that these time storms involve people travelling to our time from elsewhere. A woman named Edith Sage experienced a very strange encounter on 4 August 1980 in the Medway area of Kent. She was on the way to the shops in the late afternoon when something caught her attention.

Out of the corner of my eye something in the sky made me jump.
It was like a smoke ring going round and round with sort of sparks
coming out of the edge of it.[121]

From behind the mist, Edith could see what looked like a futuristic helicopter. It was a large transparent bubble with military camouflage markings. Inside the object were two very normal-looking human beings wearing what Edith was later to describe as 'jump suits'. Edith found herself in the curious timeless and muted state that Randles calls the 'Oz factor'. Edith then felt dizzy and disorientated. She claims that she heard the two men talking. However, their voices seemed to be inside her head rather than coming from outside. They seemed to be very concerned that something had gone wrong, that they had allowed themselves to be seen. One said: 'You said it would be all right' with the other replying 'I know, I know', and 'it's all right. She thinks we are in the army.' Yet somewhat oddly, Edith acted perfectly normally. With the helicopter still in sight she entered the shop, bought her groceries and even had a conversation with the shopkeeper about a wedding that was about to take place, and then continued about her normal business for the rest of the day. Randles doesn't describe when the 'helicopter' disappeared from Edith's sight. Randles states: 'As the hours passed [Edith] simply forgot about it.'

I find this strange. Why did Edith act so normally after such an extraordinary event? Indeed, why did the episode simply vanish from her mind? Did she undergo some form of hypnotic state in which her memory of the event was wiped clean, or at least manipulated to be perceived as somehow mundane? Randles finds this odd, too, but fails to explain that if it was expunged from her memory why did Edith subsequently feel the need to report the event and describe it in such graphic detail. What re-stimulated the memory?

Strangely enough, as her memories were recovered, Edith felt that the alleyway in which she had had the encounter had now changed in minor ways. The steps were narrower, for example, and a house now had a path when there had not been one there before. Intriguingly, she also describes that there is now a tree in the location that did not exist when the earlier encounter took place. Edith makes the point that, had the tree been there on the day: 'I could not have seen what I did. It would have blocked my view of the smoke.'

Out of time or out of body?

This sensation of unreality has been reported many times during time slips. Could it be that the person involved is, in fact, experiencing a form of altered state of consciousness in which they are able to access an alternative location in space-time rather than just being involved in a time slip? In my last book, *The Out of Body Experience – The History and Science of Astral Travel* I suggest that out-of-body experiences involve trans-dimensional travel to another 'version' of earth. In doing so, I explain why it is that famous 'astral travellers' and 'distance viewers' such as Ingo Swann and Robert Monroe never succeeded in accurately describing what they saw during the out-of-body (OOB) state. Some of the information they obtained proved to be correct but some was not. Just like Edith, both Monroe and Swann described people and objects that did not exist in consensual (shared) reality but were clearly perceived in the out-of-body state. In many ways, this state is similar to another phenomenon known as 'lucid dreaming'. In this state the subject suddenly becomes 'self-aware' during a dream. They experience the dream as if it were real. Could it be that during time slips the person falls into a waking-sleep state?

One of the cases Randles includes in her book features an incident involving a young man she calls 'David' that occurred when, on a warm summer's evening in 1966, he was walking his girlfriend home. The route took them through a small area of woodland and over a bridge that crossed a stream. Coming towards them was a group of lads clearly in a state of some agitation. It seems that they were being chased by something. Then, as David described it:

> Suddenly everything appeared abnormally quiet – even for night time. My ears felt as if they had been closed – like when you fit your fingers in them. Then it was a numb feeling. Then a strange depression set in. It was a feeling of heaviness and I had a sense of moving my head in slow motion. I turned to look at my girl-friend, who also seemed concerned. . . she felt giddy. . . the voices (of the running teenagers) sounded as if they were coming from a valley that caused them to echo.[122]

He noticed a white mist about six feet (around two metres) above the ground. As the mist swirled around them, David felt time start to slow down. He noticed that the smoke from his cigarette spiralled upwards more slowly and that his own movements were slow and laboured. Sounds seemed odd and 'hollow':

> It was like a record being played at a slower speed and we could not understand what we were trying to say to one another. I would

have got up and run, but I felt so heavy and my girlfriend was now clinging to me in hysterics.[123]

Fascinatingly, in this case there was an external form of time measurement that confirmed that this had been a subjective (but somehow shared) time dilation – David's cigarette had not burned down. Time really had slowed down for both of them. Of course, the idea that a dream can be shared by two or more people is not scientifically possible, according to our current understanding of brain processes. Yet there are many reported cases in which individuals who have a particularly strong emotional bond can indeed share dreams. An example was given to me by a young woman who attends my author meetings in Liverpool. She told me that she had been dreaming of eating a particular form of fast food involving chicken with a coating from the southern states of the USA. When she awoke, her husband told her that he had been dreaming of them both being in a fast-food restaurant eating this particular form of chicken. On discussing the circumstances of the dream, it was clear to both of them that they had been sharing the same dream. Could it be that 'David' and his girlfriend had entered a mutual lucid dream that evening? As we have already discovered, time expands during dreaming so this would explain the mutually experienced time-dilation effect. The question then must be what triggered the session of microsleep experienced by two fully awake individuals? Could it be caused by unusual atmospheric conditions?

On 28 July 1974, Peter Williamson and his family were having a barbecue in their garden when there was a violent electrical storm. The family dog was spooked and ran under a tree. As Williamson rushed towards the dog to rescue it, there was a huge flash and the man vanished. The police were called and Williamson's wife Mary, who was severely distressed, was put under sedation. At 8.00 am three days later, Peter was found unconscious in nearby shrubbery. He was lying with one foot in a pond. It was as if he had appeared out of nowhere. He was taken to hospital and asked about his experiences but had no recollection of what had happened to him. Of great significance for me is that after the event he started to experience powerful dreams that became more and more lucid. These dreams involved him finding himself standing in an unfamiliar garden; he is soaking wet. He leaves the garden in a very confused state and begins to wander along various roads. Eventually he is spotted by somebody and taken to a hospital where he spends some time and is given a series of tests.

This is the basic outline of his dreams but they became more and more vivid. In one dream, he describes how the hospital walls 'shimmered'. (This is exactly the same effect described by lucid dreamers such as Robert Waggoner and my associate Marc Crowshaw.) As Williamson's condition improved, the medical staff allowed him to take a walk in the hospital gardens. As he walked down the lane he felt as if he knew it from somewhere. According to his dream, this was the point when he woke up by the pond.

Alternative universe

This case reminds me of the experiences of out-of-body traveller Robert Monroe. In his groundbreaking book *Journeys Out of the Body*, Monroe describes how he found himself in a world that was very similar to earth – but not quite the same. He calls this place 'Locale 3'. Monroe occupied the body of a person he came to call 'I There'. Monroe's 'possession' of this doppelganger sometimes brought about all kinds of problems. On one occasion, 'I There' was presenting his new invention to a group of potential investors. Monroe, who was in 'possession' of 'I There' at the time, knew nothing about the invention and so had to 'wing it' while Mrs 'I There' looked at her husband in total confusion. As Randles observes in her book, could this be what happened to Peter Williamson on that summer day back in 1974? He had swapped lives with another version of himself in an alternative universe. Interestingly enough, Monroe did these swaps during supposed out-of-body states that could be interpreted as a form of lucid dreaming – something that Williamson began experiencing on his return to our 'reality'.

Later, Randles describes a fascinating case that seems to be a mixture of a time slip and a near-death experience (NDE) that was reported in a letter to the October 1986 edition of a magazine called *Exploring The Supernatural*. It took place in Cleveland, Ohio, in 1986 and concerned a person by the name of Mr West. This man was in hospital recovering from heart surgery. As he tried to get out of bed to go to the toilet he suddenly realized that there was no sound. Everything around him had become silent and still. He noticed that a man in a neighbouring bed seemed somewhat distressed but this seemed of no concern to him. He had the overwhelming sensation that he had to travel to the past. Suddenly the scene changed and he was looking at a new location. He was to describe this later as seeming as if he was inside a TV drama. He could see a woman giving birth and a doctor dressed in very old-fashioned clothing, including a stovepipe hat. Mr West then felt a strong tugging sensation as if he was being pulled down by an anchor and saw himself lying in bed surrounded by medical staff who were giving him emergency treatment. He was clearly in a bad way. In fact, his heart had stopped. Mr West then blacked out and the next thing he knew he was regaining consciousness in the hospital bed.

What had taken place here? In many ways this is a classic near-death experience (NDE) except that it involved no 'going towards a bright light' or encounters with dead relatives. This was more of a time slip or a movement into an alternative universe. What does this tell us about the nature of the NDE? Is it really a passing over or is it simply that consciousness locates itself in another reality?

The Bold Street triangle

My home city of Liverpool seems to be a focus for strange time slips in which the past overlaps with the future. Are these cases to do with a form of short-term lucid dreaming in which the subject glimpses an alternative reality, as in Monroe's 'Locale 3', or are they really glimpses into the past? They seem to centre around a specific area of Liverpool, in the vicinity of a popular shopping thoroughfare called Bold Street.

The most famous case took place in July 1996 when Tom, an off-duty police officer, was shopping in Liverpool city centre with his wife Carol. At Central Station the two decided to split up. Carol wished to visit Dillon's bookshop to purchase a copy of Irving Welsh's *Trainspotting* and Frank was keen to purchase a particular CD. After a visit to a music store where he made his purchase, Tom made his way to the pre-arranged meeting point at the bottom of Bold Street. As he entered this normally lively area he felt as if he was in a 'bubble of quiet'. Sounds seemed muffled and distant. The change of atmosphere disturbed him and he absent-mindedly stepped into the traffic. As he did so he was startled by a small van that sped across his path, the driver honking a warning. Tom looked up to see a curiously old-fashioned vehicle with the name 'Cardin's' written on the side. He then walked across the road and towards Dillon's bookshop, where his wife was to meet him. As he approached the bookshop he became quite confused. It was not a bookshop at all. Its window was no longer full of books but of women's handbags and shoes. He looked up to see that the store was now called 'Cripps'. It was then that he took account of the people around him. It was a typically busy Liverpool afternoon but these people were wearing clothes from the 1940s. Shaking his head in disbelief, Tom then spotted a young girl in her early 20s dressed in the style of the mid-1990s. This reassured him and he smiled as they both entered the shop. As they did so the scene changed from a 1940s shoe shop back to that of a 1990s bookshop. He grabbed the girl's arm and asked her if she had seen anything odd. She replied that she was confused. She said she had entered what she thought was a shoe shop to discover it to be a bookshop.

Subsequent research has discovered that both Cripps and Cardin's were going concerns in Liverpool during the 1940s but are no longer in business. Cripps was a famous women's outfitters that did occupy the site in Bold Street where Dillon's bookshop was located (and where Waterstones now stands). Cardin's was a Liverpool firm that owned a fleet of vans at the time.[124]

What is fascinating about the Bold Street mystery is that people who have no idea about the area's reputation continue to report strange happenings in the vicinity. An example of this was posted on the 'yoliverpool' forum on 25 February 2010. A person called Bernadette asked the question: 'Has anyone ever had a strange experience in Bold Street, Liverpool?' She then goes on to describe her experience:

> *Several years ago I was coming out of the exit from Central Station that leads directly into Bold Street and I thought I'd walked into a film set! There were cobblestones and horses and carriages and people dressed in bonnets and long dresses. I'm not sure what period it was but they looked like the people on the Quality Street tin. I was totally disorientated for a few seconds because in my mind I was just going to cross Bold Street and into Waterstones but suddenly all these horses and carriages and people were in the way. First thing I thought was 'They're shooting a film and I've walked on to the set, silly me.' But as soon as I'd told myself that, everything was back to normal, present day and I was left scratching my head as to what had happened. I definitely needed a cuppa before I did anything else and I think I sat in Cafe 53 for about an hour trying to work out what on earth I'd just experienced.*[125]

According to local researcher Steve Parsons, the centre of this activity seems to be the pedestrian ramp that runs from Liverpool Central Station into Bold Street and the area around Waterstones and what used to be the Lyceum Post Office. It has been suggested that these events may be related to the fact that directly below this location is the electrified railway line of the Liverpool metro system. Could it be that some form of powerful electromagnetic field may be generated by a combination of the rail lines and the local geology? As we have seen, one sensation associated with these time slips that is consistently reported is a feeling that the air is 'electrified'. This was exactly the feeling I had in Turkey in 1984.

Bold Street is also known for other curious events. A builder was working on the old Lyceum Building when he put his helmet down for a second. When he went to pick it up again it had disappeared, even though there was nobody nearby. When he looked down at his watch he discovered that it had gone back two hours.

The literature is full of cases where individuals have experienced similar events when time has been lost or gained. These cases are nearly always experienced by just one person. As we know, time is a subjective construct so there is no way of proving that such experiences represent real events. However, if two people share such an event then we have corroborative evidence. We have already encountered the shared time dilation effect experienced by 'David' and his girlfriend, as reported by Jenny Randles and cited earlier. However, the couple did not actually lose time, rather time just seemed to slow down. But a case of shared 'lost time' was reported to me by an associate of mine, Richard Fleming.

In 1995, Richard was apple-picking in the Kent countryside with a friend of his called Gary Harmer. At the end of their first day's labour, Richard and Gary decided that they would pick up their earnings at Broadfield Farm, in Plaxtol, and drive the short distance to a nearby pub, The Chequers, in Ightham. They collected their day's pay at the farm at 4.30 pm and headed off to Ightham. Much to their disappointment, they found that The Chequers was closed so they decided to drive to another popular Kent country pub, The Plough, in the intriguingly named village of Basted, near Borough Green. Richard has informed me that this journey was no longer than two miles (three kilometres) to The Chequer's and possibly another two miles to Basted. Within a few minutes, they were driving into the pub car park and looking forward to a pint after a hard day's work. They ordered their drinks and sat down. Before they had a chance to take the first sip of beer they heard one of the pub regulars ask the landlord the time. He replied that it was 'ten past six'.

Richard and Gary looked at each other in amazement. They checked their respective watches and, to their surprise, discovered that the landlord was quite correct. It was, indeed, ten minutes past six o'clock. It had taken them one hour and forty minutes to drive four miles along empty country lanes. Both of them were stunned by this and, even to this day, Richard is at a loss to explain what took place that summer evening.

What is unusual about this case is that the time slip was shared by two people, both of whom felt that no more than 15 minutes had elapsed when in external 'clock' time a total of 100 minutes had gone by. The subjective speeding up and slowing down of time is not uncommon, as Einstein pointed out in his example of time spent sitting with a pretty girl and sitting on a hot stove. This form of time perception is intensely personal and cannot be measured against the time perception of another person. However, in the case of Richard and Gary, the two men shared the experience of having lost time.

The question is, where did they go during that lost time? Clearly they must have been somewhere. Did they both share some form of communal blackout? One of them (Gary) was driving a car. To black out anywhere is dangerous but at the wheel of a car on a country lane is particularly so. Could it be that they stopped the car for some reason? If so, why did they not recall stopping?

Perhaps they were abducted by extraterrestrial aliens? Such events have been reported time and time again across the world, such as the famous Betty and Barney Hill case. On 19 September 1961, the Hills were driving back from Canada to their home town of Portsmouth on the coast of New Hampshire, USA. Just south of Lancaster, New Hampshire, Betty spotted something moving in the sky that she at first took to be a shooting star. It soon became clear that this was an alien craft and that it was approaching them. The craft hovered over them, forcing them to stop the car. They then had a direct encounter with up to 11 humanoid beings that came from the craft. During their encounter, events became very vague for both of them. They found they had travelled 35 miles (56 kilometres) south of where the encounter had first taken place. Like Richard and Gary, they had both experienced lost time. However, and this is the important point, their 'close encounter' had started before the Hills lost consciousness. Something odd had already begun to happen. For Richard and Gary, there was no such event. It had been an apparently seamless journey.

Phone call from another world

Similar reports have regularly been recorded on the Nullarbor Plain in southern Australia. However, all the reports begin with an encounter with something odd or unusual. Could it be that these two young men, as the Hills had claimed, were snatched by aliens on the road between Plaxtol and Basted? But if this was the case then they would both have recalled coming to in the car. Indeed, it is highly likely that one would have become conscious before the other and in doing so would have noted that the car had stopped and that the other person was unconscious. None of these events took place. It was simply a case of lost time; 100 minutes had been erased from the lives of Richard and Gary, never to be recovered. Of course, there is another, rather disturbing possible answer to this question; could it be that in all the reported cases the alien abduction had not gone to plan and the abductees had been able to recall some of the events that occurred to them. In other words, this kind of thing happens regularly but because the victims' memory of events are seamlessly extracted they have absolutely no recollection of anything strange taking place and are only aware of the time that is mysteriously lost?

One of the most amazing reports I have ever read on my

discussion forum was posted by medium Susan Leybourne.[126] She described an event that suggests that time slips may be even more complex than a simple loss of time or a return to the past.

In the early summer of 2011, Susan was at home in Northamptonshire when her mobile phone rang. On answering it, Susan heard a rather flustered female voice. 'Is that Susan?' said the voice. 'Yes,' Susan replied. Sounding relieved, the woman responded: 'Oh good, I wanted to let you know I'm going to be a bit late meeting you for lunch.' Susan was somewhat disconcerted at this as she had made no such plan. As far as Susan was concerned this was simply a wrong number. Much to Susan's surprise, the caller asked: 'Are you not Susan Leybourne, the medium?' Feeling a gathering sense of confusion, Susan replied that she was indeed that person but added quickly that she had no lunchtime meeting arranged for that day. Things then became markedly more strange. The caller was adamant that she had a lunch meeting with a medium called Susan Leybourne at 1.00 pm in Leeds. As Susan had recently moved from Leeds to Northamptonshire, she began to suspect that this lady did actually know her but had simply become confused. Susan explained that she had moved from Leeds a few months previously and that she was taking this call at her new home. The woman sounded even more confused. 'But I'm in your class in Leeds!' the caller insisted.

It was at this point that Susan started to suspect that somebody else had set up a training course in Leeds and was using her name to attract students. She was keen to know more about this course and asked the caller what was the subject matter. 'It's a Psychic Development class, it's Farida speaking!'

In a flash, Susan recalled that at least 15 years ago she had indeed run a Psychic Development class at a night school in Leeds and that one of her students was called Farida. 'Ah, Farida! I remember you. Are you the same lady who bought me the Georgio perfume and body lotion one Christmas?' Susan replied.

'Yes, but I'm in your class now, in Leeds!' insisted Farida. Susan was now starting to feel rather unsettled. It then dawned on Susan just how odd this situation was. In 1996 Susan did not own a mobile phone. The question that immediately arose in her mind was how could Farida possibly know her 2011 mobile phone number and call her? How could one of her old students ring her 15 years later on a mobile number that hadn't existed at that time?

She concluded that this ruled out one possibility that had occurred to her, that her old student had bumped her head and was confused. However confused she may have been, she could not have randomly chosen a mobile number that just happened to be the correct one. Desperately trying to rationalize what was happening, Susan recalled that one of her male cousins had married a woman called Susan, so there was another Susan Leybourne in Leeds. However, this other Susan was not a medium, and certainly not someone who ran a Psychic Development course that Farida could have attended.

Nevertheless, Susan suggested that this may be the reason for the confusion. But Farida stated that this was certainly not the case. Indeed, she recognized Susan's voice as that of the woman she knew.

As Susan later described it to me, things started to turn into something that Lewis Carroll would have written. Farida stated that she had better stop chatting as she was in danger of being 'even later meeting you than I already am!' Farida was still adamant that she was meeting Susan Leybourne, her teacher, the medium, in Leeds at one o'clock. As the call came to its natural end, Susan received an overpowering feeling that perhaps there existed another, alternative reality where she was still living in Leeds and that class was still meeting. As these thoughts crossed her mind, the caller abruptly hung up.

For a few minutes or so, Susan sat and pondered the implications of what had just taken place. If indeed she had just had a conversation with somebody from a parallel universe, then other incidents that happened in the reality she now occupied may not have taken place in the other one. In her communication with me Susan wrote:

> *But she was gone and that was the end of that. I wanted to ask in that World is Nicola still alive? I hadn't thought of Nicola in many years, but she had died unexpectedly in the first month of the first term. I got a feeling in that World Nicola was still alive.*[127]

But this was not the first time that these curious alternative-universe scenarios have been experienced by Susan. In the posting she goes on to describe another, even more curious event:

> *I have had other experiences like this too, and it reminded me of the time I was speaking at a large conference in Blackpool. After my lecture I sat down in the audience ready to listen to the next speaker, as there was a little break while the next person set up her projector and got her slides ready. Two ladies in front of me turned around and both told me they had read my book and it was brilliant, and how it had inspired them. 'I'm sorry, I don't have a book out,' I said. 'Are you sure you mean me, there are other well-known writers here?' 'It's you,' the more vocal woman insisted. 'Susan Leybourne, definitely.' Then again getting curious asked, 'What is [the book] about?' and they both said, interrupting each other to fill out the full picture, 'It's about you and your Spiritual life and your adventures in Africa and Borneo and places like that, it's very funny too.'*

Susan went on:

> *Now that book does exist, but on my old laptop. It took 11 years to write and 5 years to edit, and eventually got shelved. I never even printed out a hard copy for myself or close friends, and only my ex-partner had ever heard snippets of it. But in some weird reality these women had not only read my book but said it had*

inspired them. They couldn't have been mistaken as they described things in the book which could not have been guessed at and are very specific to my life. So is there another dimension where I not only have 1 but possibly 2 or 3 books in print? Perhaps this other me is fabulously successful and I go on book tours to California . . . who knows!

Could this be evidence of Everett's Many-Worlds Interpretation that we encountered before when discussing the physics of time? Susan's final comment certainly suggests that she believes there may exist another version of her that does inhabit an alternative reality in which another time-line has been followed. Could this be in a future that actually shares the timeless 'now' with us? If this is so then do we have any evidence of time slips into the future? All the cases so far have involved time slips from the present into the past. A sceptic could rightly argue that this is because it is much easier to fabricate a story based upon known information than use information that can only be confirmed by those events coming to pass later on. We have already discussed another possibility, precognitive dreams, but those are subtly different. The protagonist dreams of an event and then, following the usual course of time's arrow, they progress to the future to experience the events revealed in their dream. A time slip into the future involves an encounter with the future in waking-life, one that involves all the senses that we use to perceive the phenomenal world. This experience ends and the observer finds that they are back in the present with knowledge of events that have yet to take place.

The time tunnel

The idea that we can travel into the future is in many ways much harder to accept than a journey into the past. In a very real sense, the past has already happened and as such has already been 'recorded'. In our everyday lives we encounter images from the past all the time. We watch old movies, recorded television programmes, we look through old photographs. These provide clear evidence that the past may no longer be with us in the present but it did exist as an absolute reality. The future is different. We cannot photograph the future and nor can we film it. This is because it is yet to happen. The future exists as a series of potentialities dependent upon actions taking place now. Every small decision made in the present helps create the future. In a very literal sense, the future cannot exist until it becomes the present moment.

But sometimes time slips are literally that; a split second in which a future event is perceived before it happens. I came across an intriguing example of this when, in February 2010, I was given access to a large number of letters sent to the playwright J.B. Priestley. In March 1963, Priestley was invited to appear on a Sunday evening BBC TV programme called *Monitor to* discuss his forthcoming book *Man and Time*. At the end of the programme, Wheldon made a request that if any viewers had experienced similar time anomalies they could write to Mr Priestley care of the BBC. Priestley had expected to receive a few hundred responses at most. Over a period of a year or so he received in the region of 3,000. Of these, he included about 20 in the final manuscript of the book that appeared in 1964. The rest were collected together in a series of boxes and languished in Priestley's library until his death in 1984. His son, Tom, collected these together and donated them to the historical documents archives at Cambridge University library. I met Tom in 2009 and he suggested that I might like to look through these letters with the objective of writing a book about them. I became the second person after Priestley to sift through this amazing collection. As well as being a wonderful snapshot of Britain in the early 1960s, the letters also contain some amazing personal accounts of anomalous occurrences. I was particularly interested in the letters that described visions of the future. A handful stunned me. I will be discussing the implications of these letters as we make our way through this book.

One was sent by the actor Charles Scott-Patton. In this letter, written by hand, Scott-Patton describes how, in 1933, he was sitting at home with his mother in Hampstead waiting for lunch to be served. He heard what he thought was a terrible accident outside. He went to the window to look. His mother joined him there and asked him why he had run to the window.

> I told her that I had heard very clearly a car in collision with what I thought was the brick wall in front of our house and that I heard glass falling (and) presumed that the lamp post outside had been hit. At the same time I heard a girl's cry. My mother heard nothing at all and had only run to the window because I had.

As he started to explain what he had heard, the noise of the collision and the sound of the glass smashing was repeated. He discovered later that a doctor was driving along Belsize Park Gardens when he hit the side of a bicycle ridden by a schoolgirl. He lost control, knocked over a lamp post and crashed into the wall. The cry Charles had heard was that of the schoolgirl. If we apply the results of the Bierman and Radin experiments, the work of Libet, and the fascinating implications of the Global Consciousness Project, it is reasonable to conclude that we can, contrary to the generally accepted model of reality, monitor the contents of our immediate future. The incident described by Charles Scott-Patton presents supportive, albeit subjective, evidence for this. The neurological evidence suggests that future cognition can cover no more than a few seconds at maximum. Yet I have come across many cases that suggest that future cognition can in fact cross many, many years, perhaps far into the future. We can then apply the model of particle physics suggested by John G. Cramer, that sub-atomic particles can travel from the past into the future and from the future into the past and in doing so can carry information. Indeed, as Richard Feynman suggested, the anti-matter particle called the positron is simply an electron travelling back in time. In that case Scott-Patton had simply heard the contents of his own immediate future.

This involved just one of his senses, however, hearing. It could be argued that sound takes time to travel from its source to another location in space. Occam's razor is a principle often applied by sceptics. Its premise is simple; when faced with competing hypotheses that are equal in other respects, select the one that makes fewest assumptions. One could therefore apply Occam's razor to this case and suggest that there may be a simpler answer, perhaps unusual atmospheric conditions had caused the sounds to echo in some way. Charles alone had heard the initial impact and scream and then both he and his mother had heard the echo. Such a model cannot explain another of the Priestley letters, however, sent by a woman living in South Wales. She describes an incident that took place in 1939 or 1940, when she was 12 years old.

She explains that at that time she would often visit her aunt who had a 'modern' flat on the third floor of a building in Westgate Street in the centre of Cardiff. These flats backed on to the cricket ground. While her mother and aunt had tea, she would amuse herself by running to the lift, going down to the ground floor, leaving the lift, running through an archway that led to the back of the building, going up the fire escape to the back to the third floor, entering the building and then repeating the exercise. She had done this four times and was about to run down the front steps and go through the arch again when she stopped abruptly with a mounting feeling of dread:

I not only was afraid to step forward but that it was dangerous to step forward because instead of the courtyard there was a harbour with dark, glistening water, old-fashioned sailing ships and, in general, a completely different scene. It was uncanny.

She looked at this scene for about 30 seconds and then ran back up the front steps to the safety of the lift. She never saw the scene again. However, 'five years ago' she opened the evening paper to see an article discussing the area around the Westgate Street flats and the cricket ground. She read that the site had been built over the old harbour where sailing ships were once moored. This was the very scene that she had 'seenwitnessed' that afternoon as a 12-year-old child many years before.

The Liverpool area seems to have more than its fair share of future time slips, as well as glimpses of the past. Local historian of the 'unexplained', Tom Slemen, recently described a curious incident in his column in the *Liverpool Echo*.[128] He wrote how a 44-year-old businessman called Geoff Kingsley was driving through a Mersey tunnel late one night in 1957. At that time there was just the one route under the River Mersey, the Queensway Tunnel, that runs from Liverpool to Birkenhead. In the late 1950s there was a good deal less traffic than there is today and at 11.45 pm the tunnel was almost deserted. As Kingsley was approaching the Birkenhead entrance to the tunnel he noticed something moving at speed in his rear-view mirror. Approaching his Morris Minor was a gold-coloured triangular vehicle with rounded edges. It flashed past Kingsley's car at amazing speed and turned into the wall of the tunnel, disappearing into it as if through a hidden entrance. Had this unusual automobile been witnessed by Mr Kingsley alone then it might simply have been dismissed as a hallucination. However, Slemen claimed in his column that at least a dozen people also reported seeing this car. Had these witnesses been given a glimpse of a future form of transport?

One day at Drem

As with many such cases, there is little corroboration. These events are either experienced by lone individuals such as Priestley's correspondent or else they take place in fairly obscure circumstances with no strong supporting evidence. However, there is one well-documented report that does seem to suggest that something very odd occurred. This is an incident at Drem Airfield involving

Air Marshall Sir Victor Goddard (1897–1987). This also involved a vision of a futuristic form of transport, as in the incident in the Queensway Tunnel in 1957. However, in this case the vehicle witnessed, an aircraft, actually was manufactured a few years after the event.

In 1935, Goddard was a wing commander flying a Hawker Hart biplane from Andover, in Hampshire, England, to Edinburgh, in Scotland, spending a weekend in the area. While there he visited an old First World War airfield at Drem on the outskirts of the city to evaluate whether it could be brought back into use in the future. He found the airfield in a terrible state of neglect. The tarmac and four hangars were in disrepair and the whole area had been given over to cattle grazing, with barbed wire used to cordon the airfield into manageable sections of pasture. It was clear that the local farmer intended to convert the airfield into farmland. On the Monday, Goddard started his flight back to Andover. The weather was poor with low cloud and heavy rain. His plane had no radio navigation aids or instruments for flying in cloud. Sitting in an open cockpit, he was also at the mercy of the elements. The rain beat down on his goggles, which meant he was literally flying blind. He climbed to 8,000 feet (2,400 metres) but there was still no break in the vast cloud bank. Suddenly, he lost control of the plane and found himself in a downward tailspin. His altimeter told him that he was losing altitude rapidly. The clouds parted to give him a view of open water less than 200 feet (60 metres) below him. Although still falling at over 150 miles per hour (240 kilometres per hour), he managed to right the plane. By now he was no more than 20 feet (around 6 metres) above the ground and narrowly missed hitting a young woman who was pushing a pram. He just managed to clear a sea wall and level off, finding himself flying low over a sandy beach. Goddard then spotted the Edinburgh road ahead. He recalled that this road skirted the Drem Airfield and as his eyes adjusted to the gloom he could see in the distance the dark silhouettes of the derelict hangars. Suddenly, he found that he had flown into a different world. In an instant, the rain and clouds had disappeared and he was bathed in bright, warm, sunshine. As he flew over the airfield he couldn't believe what he was seeing. Replacing the tattered hangars were brand new buildings. The broken and shattered runway had been replaced by pristine tarmac. At the far end of the runway, he saw four bright-yellow aircraft. He recognized three of them as standard Avro 504N trainer biplanes but the fourth one puzzled him. It was a monoplane of a design he could not recognize. Indeed, in 1935 the Royal Air Force had no monoplanes and none of their aircraft were painted yellow. Goddard noticed a handful of mechanics working on these planes. The men wore bright blue overalls. Again, Goddard was puzzled. In 1935 all RAF mechanics wore brown overalls.

He flew closer until he was no more than a few feet above the heads of the mechanics. However, it was evident that they could not see him as there was no reaction from the men on the ground. As he headed away from the airfield, the storm returned with a vengeance. He managed to get back safely to his base at Andover. On arrival, he was so relieved that he excitedly told his fellow officers of his adventure. His story was not received well and so he decided that it would be best for his future career prospects if he did not mention the incident again. However, four years later the events on that stormy day were to return to him in a fascinating and totally intriguing way. In that year, new overalls were issued to RAF mechanics. These were the exact shade of blue he had seen during his close encounter at Drem. Not only that, all RAF trainers were now to be painted yellow. The oddest thing of all was the introduction of a new training monoplane called the Magister – the very plane he had seen four years before.

By 1939, the airfield at Drem was reborn with new hangars and a new airstrip. The barbed wire was cleared and the cows sent to pastures new. In that fateful year it was to become home to No.13 Flying Training School before taking its first delivery of Spitfires as part of 609 squadron, preparing for the outbreak of the Second World War.

Had Victor Goddard flown into the future that day in 1935? Goddard went on to have an illustrious career, both within the RAF and then with the US military in the Far East. In 1947, he was honoured by being made Knight Commander of the Order of the Bath. After his retirement in 1951, he became principal of the College of Aeronautics. But it was only in 1966 he felt that he was able to retell his adventure. Why would such a man make up a story like that and jeopardize his reputation by publishing it? It is reasonable to conclude that something very odd happened that day in the skies over Scotland. Of course, it could have been a hallucination brought about by stress – Goddard had experienced a harrowing few minutes before entering the 'future' – but if this was the case, how was it that his hallucination proved to be so factually accurate?

Another letter from the amazing Priestley archive was from a lady who, 13 years before, had experienced a particularly vivid waking-dream state.

She had recently recovered from a second unsuccessful pregnancy and it was thought impossible that she would be able to carry a child to term. One night she was half asleep when she heard a door slam. This woke her up. She turned to her husband and said: 'It was the five boys come in from the pictures.' Her astounded husband replied, 'Whose boys?' She replied, 'They are ours.' Her husband was clearly astounded by this and thought that his wife was going crazy. Although the letter writer does not implicitly state this, I think it is reasonable to conclude that these words were uttered not by her waking self but her 'liminal' personality (that is, on the threshold of sleep) not yet fully awake. In the letter, she goes on to state that she subsequently gave birth to five healthy boys. Clearly, this is an amazing turnaround and something that could not have been predicted by anybody at the time of her 'hypnopompic' interlude. However, it gets stranger. She explained that, a few weeks before the date of the letter, all the boys were out of the house together. They had been to what she calls a 'Brooke Bond Tea Film Show'. On this particular evening they were late. As they came through the door and slammed it behind them she heard herself say to her husband: 'It's only the boys come in from the pictures.' Clearly, this must have shocked both her and her husband as it was a re-run of the event that had occurred years before. Could this be evidence that, in her liminal state, the two time periods had become muddled and that she had experienced some form of time slip?

Another letter caught my attention. The correspondent described how, in 1951, she was recovering from an illness in hospital. She found herself lying in bed in a similar borderline sleep state to that described by the lady above. In this state, she could hear voices speaking in dialect. As the images solidified she found that she was looking down at her hands using a knife to spread butter on to bread. This was all being viewed, as she described it, 'under a diffuse evening light'. A few days later, she suddenly found herself reliving the experience in waking life. The voices in dialect were from a radio play being broadcast in the background. Interestingly, she 'recognized' what was said for 'about a minute whilst I buttered bread exactly as in my dream'. She adds that she was delighted to have pinpointed the precognitive state and that it exists 'somewhere between waking and sleeping'. She adds that it must be intensified by 'one's own emotional state'.

What is it about dreaming and semi-dreaming that seems to access information from the future? This is the most natural of mental states and every human being that has ever existed has experienced the dream state. Is this where we can access the time-less state discussed by physicists? It is to this fascinating possibility that we now turn our attention.

CHAPTER 10
DREAMS & PRECOGNITION

An Experiment with Time

In the introduction to a previous book of mine, *The Daemon – A Guide To Your Extraordinary Secret Self*, I describe a very strange event that took place on 27 October 2000.

On that night, I had a particularly vivid dream. In this dream, I was in a place where I had never been before. It was a low-lying headland with a town visible in the distance to my right. I knew that I was looking out at the English Channel. As I looked, I could see a storm approaching from out at sea. I watched with mounting horror as the storm turned into a twisting tornado. I saw the tornado hit landfall and rip into a town a few miles down the coast to my left. I then realized that it was heading towards us on this exposed piece of land and I looked on in horror as it tore into caravans along the coastline, smashing them into pieces. I awoke with a start with this image still in my mind. The images were so vivid that I can recall them even now, seven years later.

Two days after I experienced this dream I heard on the radio that Bognor Regis had been hit by a freak tornado and that a good deal of damage had been done. I thought to myself that this was interesting in that Bognor was also on the south coast of England. I thought it was odd and possibly a close-hit precognitive dream.

A few weeks later, I visited the town of Selsey with my mother and my wife, Penny. As we got out of the car I had this alarming sensation that I had been to this place before. Everything seemed familiar. It was like a super *déjà vu* sensation. I had experienced these many times in my life but this one was different. I knew what I was about to see next. As we walked towards the seafront I was amazed to find that the view from the headland, known as Selsey Bill, was exactly what I had dreamed. I looked across the bay to my left to see the town that I had seen in my dream had been hit by the tornado. To my surprise and horror, I realized that the town in my dream was, in fact, Bognor Regis. On top of that I could see that between Selsey Bill and Bognor were lines of caravans in exactly the spot I had seen them in my dream. My knowledge of the geography of that part of the south coast was not good so I had no idea before arriving at Selsey that it was that close to Bognor.

On my return to Horsham, I decided to get some further details about the 30 October tornado. On looking it up on the BBC news website I was stunned to discover that my dream had been far more accurate than I had first believed. The reports on the morning of the 30th had only mentioned Bognor but the website gave many more details. Apparently the twister had travelled along the coast towards Selsey and on the way had badly damaged over 150 caravans. This is exactly what I had seen in my dream.

This event stunned me. For the first, and to date, only time in my life I had experienced a classic 'Dunne Dream', named after the Anglo-Irish researcher John William Dunne (1875–1949).

Dunne served as a trooper and an infantry officer in the Boer War but his great interest was aviation. In 1904 he invented a stable, tailless type of aerofoil that was subsequently named after him. However, it was a curious event that took place in 1902 that was to focus his mind on the area of research for which he is now best known, the nature of time and an attempt to give a scientific explanation for that strangest of human perceptions, precognition.

On the night of 8 May 1902, Dunne, while living in South Africa, was fast asleep one warm evening when he had a vivid dream. He was living on an island populated by French-speakers. In the dream, he was approached by many of the locals who told him that a town on the other side of the island had been destroyed by a huge volcanic eruption. They informed him that 4,000 people had been killed.

He awoke the next morning with the dream, and its figure of

4,000 dead, echoing in his mind. A few days later, a copy of the *Daily Telegraph* arrived on his desk. This contained the news of a few days before. As he read through the newspaper he was amazed to spot a headline stating that there had been a volcanic disaster in the French West Indies on the night of the 8th, at exactly the same time he had experienced his dream. The paper announced that 4,000 people had been killed.

Dunne was stunned. Here was absolute proof that precognition was real. He knew that he had experienced the dream and also knew that in some bizarre way he had been given information about an event that was yet to take place. His scientist's mind found this really hard to accept. He was determined to find a rational explanation for this seemingly impossible event.

What was to assist him in devising his fascinating theory that he was to call 'serial time' was the discovery, sometime later, of a curious error in his story. He was talking about the dream to a small group of people when one informed him that his figures were wrong, and as such his dream was not as accurate as first seemed. Dunne was told that the actual death toll was 40,000, not 4,000. Dunne had kept a copy of the *Telegraph* and went back to check. The person was right; the death toll was much higher – 40,000.

Dunne thought about this and realized that in his excitement he had misread the headline. His mind had read 4,000 and he had seen that as proof of his dream. He then reflected upon this and concluded something far more profound. He decided that his precognition was not of the events that took place that fateful night, but a dream interpretation of his reading of the event in the paper, including his misreading of the death toll figure. This was a profound observation. Precognitive dreams, in Dunne's opinion, were personal and prosaic. When somebody experiences a precognitive dream they do not witness the event itself but the moment they became aware of the event.

In 1927, Dunne published his first, and best-known, work, *An*

Experiment with Time. In this he gave numerous examples of the way many of his dreams, when analyzed in the correct manner, were shown to be precognitive. However, what was different about this book was that Dunne spent the second half attempting to explain how it could be that the future could be perceived before it had taken place.

In part four of the book, he leaves his dream experiences and turns to a theoretical exposition. He proposes that there is a whole series of times – or 'serial time', as he termed it. His logic was that time is perceived to have a physical presence. It seems to exist as a block 'out there', as another dimension such as height, length and breadth. This is very much what Einstein's teacher Hermann Minkowski suggested in his concept of 'Block Time'. However, Dunne proposed that, in order for time to be perceived as 'passing', its movement had to be measured by something else. And the only thing that time can be measured against is time. How long does a minute take to pass? Obviously a minute, but the first minute must be measured against the second minute, how else can we perceive the movement unless it is perceived to move against a static background? Of course, this goes to the very root of Einstein's theory of relativity, that the motion of any object is relative to other objects, which, in turn, are in motion. And so it is with time. 'Time One' needs 'Time Two' in order for it to be perceived to flow. 'Time Two', in turn, needs 'Time Three' and so on. Clearly this quickly turns into an infinite regression.

The 'Ultimate Observer'

According to the Roman philosopher and emperor Marcus Aurelius, time can be likened to a river, always flowing in one direction towards the sea. However, this analogy has certain drawbacks. For example, if time is like a flowing river then in order to gauge the speed and, more interestingly direction, of flow, a stationary riverbank is needed. Indeed, there is an even deeper question that can be asked: what would happen if time suddenly slowed down across the whole universe? Could we tell? The simple answer is: no. Absolutely nothing would change. A minute would still take a minute to pass. Indeed, this gets to the heart of the question: a minute passes, passes what exactly? Yet again we have the issue that time can only 'pass' if there is another time that is moving at a different speed. But, in turn, that time needs another time. Dunne was quite right to ask this question because it is of fundamental importance. Indeed, going back to my example of all time speeding up in the universe, the only way this could be measured is against another universe in which time flows differently.

Dunne suggested that each of these separate times needs an observer in order for a perception of time flow to be perceived. These observers in turn end up in an 'infinite regress'. Indeed, although he never stated it as such, it is fairly reasonable to conclude that Dunne's 'infinite regress' ended with the 'Ultimate Observer'. This bears many similarities with the philosophy of the Anglo-Irish cleric Bishop George Berkeley (1685–1753) who suggested that it is only the act of observation that brings 'reality' into existence, or *esse est percipi* ('to be is to be perceived'), as he termed it. Of course, the initial problem with this extreme solipsism is what about the world that continues to exist when nobody is observing it? This is similar to the old conundrum: 'If a tree falls in the forest and there is no one around to hear it, does it make a sound?' Berkeley's argument was simple. There is an 'Ultimate Observer' that observes everything at all times. This 'Ultimate Observer' is God, as is, by implication, Dunne's 'Observer'.

In *An Experiment with Time*, Dunne asks how we rationally define a 'self-conscious' observer in order to distinguish him from a 'non-self-conscious' recorder such as a camera? I find this of great significance. You will recall that in our discussions about quantum physics we encountered something called the Copenhagen Interpretation. First proposed by Neils Bohr and his associate Max Born, it suggests that in order for the 'wave function' to become a point particle in space it needs to be influenced by an 'act of observation'. This act of observation can involve taking a measurement by an inanimate device but ultimately this device will be manipulated by a consciousness, usually that of a scientist. This debate has carried on to the present day with one group of physicists arguing that the wave function can be collapsed simply by interaction with other inanimate particles whereas another group, including luminaries such as the Hungarian-born physicist Eugene Wigner (1902–95), felt, like Dunne, that it needs a 'self-conscious observer' to collapse the wave function and, by implication, bring physical matter into existence.

The three great wheels

In his book *Man and Time* (more of which later), the playwright and essayist J.B. Priestley argued that the 'infinite regress' of observers was unnecessary. Priestly suggested that only three 'observers' would be needed. These would be 'Self One' who is, in effect, simply an object. This observer need not be self-aware in any way. Indeed, I would suggest that this being is the unthinking, responsive being that can be found in the reptilian brain that sits below the higher brain of the cerebellum. 'Self Two' is the everyday personality. This consciousness is 'self-conscious' in that it perceives 'Self One' as a subject of its observations. It is this being that is aware, by observation of 'Self One', that it is not only conscious but also 'self' conscious. The third consciousness 'Self Three' sits above the other two and is utterly detached from events. It simply observes. As Priestley accurately described this triune being:

> . . . that we know (3), that we know (2) that we are conscious (1).[129]

So how did Dunne take this theory and go on to use it to explain precognition?

He suggested that within 'Time One' exists 'Observer One',

'Time Two' has an 'Observer Two' and 'Time Three' has an 'Observer Three'.

In this particular case Dunne was not being entirely original, although that is not to say that he was aware of this. However, the 15th-century poet Juan de Mena had suggested something similar in his poem 'El Laberinto de Fortuna' ('The Labyrinth of Fortune'). In this, de Mena visualizes 'three great wheels: the first, motionless, is the past; the second, in motion, is the present; the third, motionless, is the future'. De Mena uses this to suggest that the future already exists. As such it can be perceived by a consciousness that can just 'see' a little bit further, exactly as Dunne suggested.

For Dunne, each 'observer', and there are an infinite number of them, exists in their own version of time. This time exists, if that is the right word, in a different position from the others. Therefore some can see further into the future than others. A popular analogy that I have also used before is that 'Observer One' is like a passenger on a train as it approaches a station platform. She can only see straight out of the window. So, for her, 'now' consists solely of the contents of the window. As the train progresses, things she has already seen disappear out of view as they are obscured by the windowless parts of the train. These views become her past. As the train continues, the views lost into the past are replaced by new views that appear, as if by magic, from the future. Eventually, the train platform appears in the passenger's 'present' viewpoint. It enters the 'now' position. Imagine another passenger on the roof of the train. For him, the present moment, the 'now', is much more expansive. Not restricted by the viewpoint from within the carriage, he can see far into the past and far into the future. Within his perception, the views experienced two minutes ago within the carriage still exist in his 'now', as does the station platform. He can see the future, but to him it is simply part of the view. One can imagine observers at various 'heights' above the train. In effect, they are existing at a right angle to the normal flow of time, as signified by the train on the ground. The higher the observer is located from the ground, the more of the past and future is encompassed by their version of 'now'.

The viewpoints from these higher positions in 'serial time' can be perceived as being part of a more ordered whole than they seem to be close up. For example, if you place your nose close to a newspaper photograph you see that a photograph is made up of printed dots. It is only as you move away that these dots coalesce into an image. In 1936, Dunne gave a wonderful demonstration as to how 'serial time' worked. Next to him sat a pianist in front of a grand piano. Dunne requested that the pianist play each note, in sequence, from the top to the bottom. 'That,' he said, 'is what everyday life is, just one damn thing after another.' He then requested that the pianist play Mendelssohn's 'Spring Song' and Beethoven's 'Funeral March'. For Dunne, that was the way his 'Observer Two' sees time. This being can choose which notes to play and in so doing create a thing of great beauty. For Dunne, accidental access to the perceptions of the higher entity, either through dreams or precognitions, are equivalent to pushing down the notes in a totally random way. Perceptions through dreams are thus a cacophony made up of perfectly good notes.

Dunne suggested that each of us consists of an infinite number of observers, each one taking in a wider temporal viewpoint. Ordinarily, we are the equivalent of the person in the train carriage but, during certain altered states of consciousness, we can access the information normally only available to a higher observer. One particular altered state of consciousness is sleep. It is here that future events are accessed and presented to the dreaming mind. In turn, that mind weaves the future events into the usual surreal and semi-surreal dreamscapes that fill the mind at these times. This is how our dreams can be precognitive. For Dunne, his Martinique dream was created when his 'Observer Two' perceived the newspaper headline and back-created a dream-story to accommodate the disaster and its French-speaking location.

Dunne may have applied a new theory to the mystery of

precognitive dreaming but such events have been reported for centuries. Clearly, there is something very peculiar taking place in the brain when we dream. Many years ago, I came across a particularly stunning example of a dream-related precognition when reading the classic book *Death and Its Mystery* by the French astronomer Camille Flammarion (1842–1925). Flammarion describes a dream that was reported to him by a priest friend, Canon Garnier. Garnier experienced a particularly vivid dream in 1846 in which he found himself travelling along a road by the side of a large mountain. He arrived at an intersection and stopped to take in the view. My apologies for quoting this at length but the power of any dream, because of the extreme subjectivity of their content, can only really be conveyed by using the actual words of the dreamer. As such, this chapter will have many quotations but, in my opinion, this is the only way to report such perceptions. To paraphrase simply waters down the impact and the symbolism. Canon Garnier describes the dream in this way:

> About thirty feet from the spot where I was standing, opposite me, in a well-levelled court, there rose, close to the road, a charming little house, white as chalk and bathed in sunshine. The only window, which faced the road, was open; behind the window sat a woman well but simply dressed. Red predominated among the bright colours of her clothes. On her head was a white cap of some very light material with openwork embroidery, of a form that was unknown to me. This woman was about thirty years of age. Standing before her was a young girl of ten or twelve years, whom I took to be her own. She was attentively watching her mother, who was knitting and showing her how it was done; she was barefoot, her hair down her back, and was dressed somewhat like the mother. By the side of the young girl were three children, rolling on the ground: a small boy who might have been four or five years old was on his knees, showing something to his two little brothers, smaller than he, to amuse them; these were flat on their

backs before the eldest, and all three were absorbed in their admiration. The two women had given me a rapid glance when they saw me standing there and looking at them, but they had not stirred. Evidently they often saw travellers passing.[130]

He went on to describe how he saw a dog lying beside them. In a doorway could be seen three men playing cards and drinking. They were wearing unusual pointed hats. In a further piece of detail, his dream showed him the card table being approached by a young, inquisitive horse that was given a sharp slap for its intrusion on the game.

Three years later, the canon was visiting Italy for the first time when his group stopped at an isolated inn to change horses. As he took in the scene, he suddenly felt an overpowering sensation of familiarity:

I looked out of the carriage door and sweat comes on me; my heart beats like a tambourine, and I mechanically put my hand to my face, as if to remove a veil which troubles me and prevents me from seeing: I rub my nose, my eyes, like a sleeper who awakens suddenly after a dream. I really think I am dreaming, and yet my eyes are wide open: I assure myself that I am not mad nor yet the victim of a most singular illusion. Before my eyes is the little country scene which I saw long ago in my dream. Nothing had changed! The first thought that comes to me, after I get back my wits, is this: I have already seen this. I do not know where but I am quite sure of it – that is certain. For all that, I have never been here, as this is the first time I have been in Italy. How does it happen? Sure enough, there are two roads that cross, the little wall which holds the earth up at the sides of the court, the trees, the white house, the open window; the mother knitting and her daughter watching her, the three little fellows amusing themselves with the dog, the three workmen, drinking and playing, the colt who goes to take a lesson and receives a cuff, the two horses, the sheep. Nothing is changed: the people are exactly those I saw, as I saw them, doing the same thing in the same attitudes, with the same gestures, etc. How is that possible? But the fact is certain and for fifty years I have wondered. Mystery! First I saw it in a dream; secondly I saw it in actual reality, three years later.[131]

The amazement of the priest speaks to us across the years. Here is a person who has experienced the impossible and knows, with absolute certainty, that what he experienced was real. It was not an hallucination nor was it a misinterpretation of natural phenomena. Of course, there is another possibility; that he was simply lying in order to impress his old friend, the esteemed astronomer Flammarion. But why would he feel the need to do this, particularly as he was a senior priest with a reputation to think about? Indeed, as the Catholic Church takes a very dim view of such things, he was, if anything, taking a considerable risk in allowing this account to be published.

The law of large numbers

Psychologists, particularly those who are unwilling to accept the truth of any experiences that do not fit into the present scientific paradigm, will argue that such events can be explained by a phenomenon known as 'confirmation bias'. In simple terms, this is a tendency to give more attention to data that supports our beliefs than data that conflicts with these beliefs. Another explanation that is growing in popularity is something known as the 'law of large numbers'. Indeed, in a recent book psychologist Professor Richard Wiseman dismissed all precognitive dreams as falling into this explanatory category.

So let us apply these two 'explanations' to Canon Garnier's experience. Confirmation bias suggests that the canon was really keen for his dream to come true. For three years he had been searching high and low for a set of circumstances that would coincide to reproduce his dream. It will be recalled that in order for the dream to come true he would have had to have found a set of circumstances that included two roads that crossed, a little wall, a mother knitting, three children playing with a dog, three workmen drinking, a colt who gets hit, two horses and a sheep. On top of that all these circumstances had to coincide in one location and to follow a specific sequence within time. Finally, the events had to take place in similar weather conditions in a precise location.

All these things had to happen in order to reproduce the dream. Is this really possible? Indeed, in my opinion 'confirmation bias' suggests that the human mind can, in some way, manipulate reality in order to ensure that a precognitive dream comes true. I can accept 'confirmation bias' as an explanation of a single event or incident, but not a series of events. For example, I may dream of meeting a young woman in a red dress. A few days later, with the dream in my mind, I encounter a woman in a red dress. Now this would be confirmation bias and I would accept this as a perfectly reasonable explanation. But in the case of the canon's dream, there are just too many accurate details coinciding for this explanation to hold true.

Let us now turn to the 'law of large numbers'. This states that coincidences are much more likely when dealing with a very large sample. When such large numbers are stretched out over a very long period of time, the chances become even greater that a coincidence will take place.

The most popular example of this is that, in a random selection of 23 people, there is a 50 per cent chance that at least two of them will share the same birthday. But let's turn to really large numbers, an example used by Professor Wiseman to dismiss a belief in precognitive dreams as the solace of the mathematically ignorant.

In his book he focuses on the Aberfan disaster. In 1966 over 140 children and adults lost their lives when a gigantic waterlogged slag heap became unstable and flowed down into a small Welsh mining village, destroying a terrace of houses and the local primary school. Many people reported experiencing dreams depicting a disaster involving the mining debris. Wiseman points out that the debris had been a cause of local concern for some time. He then adds to this the 'law of large numbers':

> *Let's take a closer look at the numbers associated with these seemingly supernatural experiences. First, let's select a random person from Britain and call him Brian. Next, let's make a few assumptions about Brian. Let's assume that Brian dreams each night of his life from age 15 to 75. There are 365 days in each year, so those 60 years of dreaming will ensure that Brian experiences 21,900 nights of dreams. Let's also assume that an event like the Aberfan disaster will only happen once in each generation, and randomly assign it to any one day. Now, let's assume that Brian will only remember dreaming about the type of terrible events associated with such tragedy once in his entire life. The chances of Brian having his 'disaster' dream the night before the actual tragedy is about a massive 22,000 to 1. Little wonder that Brian would be surprised if it happened to him.*

Wiseman then informs us that this is not at all strange. He points out that in the 1960s there were around 45 million people in the UK. By logic there will be one person in every 22,000 who will have a once-in-a-lifetime disaster dream that will coincide with an actual disaster the next day. By extrapolation, Wiseman states with absolute confidence that 2,000 British people will experience such a set of circumstances. He glibly dismisses all precognitive dreaming with the comment:

> *To say that this group's dreams are accurate is like shooting an arrow into a field, drawing a target around it after it has landed and responding, 'Wow, what are the chances of that?'*

But hold on a minute. This suggests that every single night a minimum of 2,000 people in the UK experience a stunning precognitive dream. That is 14,000 a week and 728,000 a year. My question is a simple one. If that is the case, why are our papers not full of reports of people having precognitive dreams? Indeed, let us extrapolate these figures to a worldwide scale.

For example, let us assume that there is a million-to-one chance that when a person has a dream about a plane crash a plane crash happens the very next day. There are seven billion people on this planet. Now, according to a researcher called Hines, each human being has around 250 dream 'themes' in any one night. This is different from a dream. Each dream can have many themes as it unfolds and each one may be recalled on waking. So, by extrapolation, that is 1,750,000,000,000 dream themes every night. Assuming our one-in-a-million chance that somewhere in the world a plane will crash after a person dreams of a plane crash, then up to 1.75 million people may experience such a clairvoyant dream. This is 1,75 million for every disaster that takes place. This is a huge number of people. Assume that on any one day a disaster of some description takes place, then a minimum of 547 million people every year will experience an absolutely stunning precognitive dream that will come true the very next day. Strange how quiet they all are! We can all play with this law of large numbers, you know. Indeed, if this was the explanation, then surely the naïve among us, that is, us ignorant fools who do not understand statistics, will have so much evidence for human precognitive abilities that the case will seem to be proven. But it is not. The numbers of people who report such precognitions are not in the hundreds of millions, far from it. Such amazing precognitions are rare, and that is why they are usually dismissed by sceptics. It seems that Wiseman wishes to have his cake and eat it.

Is it really that simple, though? Let us now apply Wiseman's model to the case of David Mandell. How can the 'law of large numbers' account for this?

The man who paints the future

David Mandell is an artist who lives in Sudbury Hill in north London. His paintings are enigmatic and disturbing. One of his most famous pencil drawings shows two tall buildings in the process of toppling. All who have seen this picture are immediately reminded of the events of 11 September 2001 when the twin towers of the World Trade Center were destroyed by terrorist attack. Of course, it is not at all surprising that such an event would be the subject of many paintings executed after 2001. Indeed, David Mandell did paint this picture on 11 September, but not that fateful day in 2001. His painting was created on 11 September 1996!

On the night of 10 September 1996, Mandell experienced an exceptionally vivid dream in which 'two enormous towers' are shaken by a huge cataclysm. On waking, he rushed off a black and white painting and then made his way down to Barclays Bank in Sudbury Hill. With the painting in his hands, he had a photograph taken of him standing underneath the large time and date monitor in the main area of the bank. He was keen to have irrefutable photographic evidence should any event similar to his dream came to pass.

This may seem like a curious thing to do, but David Mandell is a curious man. For most of his life he has experienced dreams that contained images or circumstances that subsequently came to pass. He had experienced, on average, ten of these dreams a year. He was determined that he would have proof that his dream contained images that he could not have known about at that time.

It therefore came as no surprise to him that in March 1997 'the dream' was to return. This time he was even more convinced that the cause of the disaster was to be a huge earthquake. On awaking he immediately began painting what he had seen. This time the work was larger and it was in colour. Again, the two buildings can clearly be seen but this time he placed a specific clue as to their location. In the background can be seen the Statue of Liberty. He was sure that this disaster would take place in Manhattan. He also brought back from his sleep state a recollection that the tragedy is accompanied by an indescribable noise.

Nine months later, a third dream was to add more detail. In this he 'saw' two twin-engine aircraft flying in different directions and, as he described it, 'hitting buildings'. He again rushed off a quick drawing of the planes he saw.

His dreams became more and more vivid. In one, he was in a car park near what he assumed was an airport runway. He could see three cars, one with a particularly unusual radiator grille at the front. He then saw something fired out of the central car towards the runway. He again executed a line drawing depicting what he saw in his dream. Nine months later the IRA, an Irish terrorist group, parked a car next to the runway at Heathrow and fired a mortar shell into the airport perimeter. As a consequence, several cars were badly damaged. A photograph of the damaged cars appeared a few days later in the British press. The similarities between this photograph and Mandell's drawing are uncanny, specifically the unusual radiator grille that can be clearly seen in both the drawing and the photograph.

However, it was a dream in June 1997 that was to convince many people that David Mandell really is the 'man who paints the future' as he has now become known after a British TV programme of the same name. In this dream, Mandell saw a Concorde aircraft flying past with flames gushing out of its tailend. When he awoke next morning he produced a colour painting of what he saw and wrote underneath the words 'Concorde crash'. He was sure that the incident would either take place in France or would involve a French Concorde. To make this clear in the painting, he placed within it a small French flag.

On 4 April 1999, the dream returned with more details. He was sure that he heard a voice announcing that the captain was attempting to get the stricken aircraft to another airport. He again recorded this. Fifteen months later, a French Concorde crashed at Charles De Gaulle Airport in Paris killing all on board. The last recorded words of the captain were, 'We are trying Le Bourget,' another airport nearby.

These dreams fit securely within the model suggested by J.W. Dunne, in that Mandell has long insisted that his dreams are not 'future memories' of the events being experienced first-hand but memories of reading about the events or seeing them on television. Indeed, in the television programme *The Man Who Paints the Future*, Mandell states:

> *Somebody is saying to me in the dream that this is what you will see in the newspapers when this event happens.*[132]

Here we have a series of dreams that are highly detailed and highly specific. David Mandell's dream of Concorde did not consist of a general image of a generic plane crashing in a non-specific location. He saw the plane as a Concorde, a plane that, until that fateful day, probably had the best safety record of all aircraft. At that time there were only a handful of Concorde aircraft flying and these were used by only two airlines: Air France and British Airways. He was quite specific that the crash would take place in France. He was also quite specific that the tail end of the plane was on fire. His painting shows the aircraft close to the ground with trees clearly visible close by in the background. This matches very well with photographs of the incident.

For me, this suggests far more than a general dream that 'confirmation bias' has shoe-horned into a known event. Mandell's description is very specific. We also have absolute proof that the painting was executed before the tragic events so any suggestion that Mandell is a liar or that he has exaggerated his claims after the event is not tenable.

Now let us apply Occam's razor to the David Mandell case. Either we apply a series of statistics based on a set of assumptions (and, let's be reasonable about this, the claims that we all have 250 dream 'themes' per night and that we are capable of remembering them all are exactly that, assumptions, nothing more) and then add confirmation bias and, hey presto, it is all explained away.

Precognition is nonsense and believed only by the weak-minded. Or we take the incident at face value. Mandell clearly dreamed an event that seemed to come to pass in the future. That this does not fit in with the present paradigm is immaterial and to take this approach is, in my opinion, bad science.

I am happy to accept that airline disasters do seem to feature strongly in the literature. However, it seems that dreams associated with such events act as a form of warning. For example, on 10 April 1973 a chartered Vanguard aircraft crashed into a mountainside outside Basle in Switzerland. Most of the 107 passengers who died were housewives from four villages in Somerset who were on a day trip to Switzerland. One woman, Mrs Marian Warren from the village of Churchill Green, returned her ticket for the trip and, in so doing, possibly saved her life. At some point before the trip, she experienced a vivid dream in which she saw an aeroplane fly over trees and crash into deep snow. She then saw the bodies of her friends being laid out in the snow.

For me this sits very easily within Professor Wiseman's model. Many people are anxious before flying, particularly if it is a comparatively infrequent occurrence. It is possible that Mrs Warren's fears had created a dream scenario involving a crash. It is not clear from the documentation as to how long before the crash the dream was experienced but the fact that Mrs Warren was able to return her ticket and get a 50 per cent refund suggests that it had taken place some time before. Her description of the crash is also of interest. She describes how she saw the bodies of her friends being laid out. This suggests a viewpoint at either distance or elevation. She was an observer to the events rather than a person directly involved.

The Farnborough incident

However, my next case fails to fit into Wiseman's model on so many different levels. It is another letter sent to J.B. Priestley following his request for anomalous time occurrences, now housed in the historical documents archive at Cambridge University. I have now read about 40 per cent of these letters and I consider them to be not only a wonderful collection of extraordinary events recorded by ordinary people but also a priceless snapshot of social history.

One of these letters was written by a gentleman I will call DP. In the letter he describes how, in early September 1952, he and his wife were coming to the end of a camping holiday in Dorset. They decided to drive back early because they wanted to attend the first public day of the Farnborough Airshow in Hampshire. As they left the campsite, DP's wife suddenly announced that she really did not wish to spend any time at Farnborough after all. Puzzled, DP asked what had brought about such a change of heart.

She explained that, the night before, she had experienced a vivid dream in which one of the aircraft had exploded during its display flight and crashed into the crowd. She described the plane as silver with swept-back wings. Not wishing to miss out on the show, DP convinced his wife that it was simply a dream and that everything would be okay. As they had already bought the tickets, she agreed to attend.

On arrival at the show, the couple found themselves a perfect vantage point and settled down to enjoy the aerobatic displays and the amazing aircraft.

About halfway through the show the much anticipated 'main event' started. Appearing in the distance was the distinctive shape of the de Havilland DH.110. On 20 February of that year this stunning flagship of British aeronautical design had become the first twin-engined aircraft to break the sound barrier. However, it was not just the jet itself that was of interest for flying the aircraft was the famous test pilot John Derry, a hugely popular figure at the time.

DP and his wife watched as the plane took off ready for its display. As it flew past, DP's wife grabbed his arm and said: 'That's the plane I saw in my dream – only it was silver, not black.' Using this as an opportunity to reassure his wife, DP said that this showed her dream was clearly incorrect and that there was nothing to fear. Nevertheless, she was still hugely relieved when Derry and his co-pilot, Anthony Richards, landed the aircraft safely and without incident. That evening the couple drove back to their home in Welwyn Garden City delighted that a bad dream had not stopped them having a wonderful day.

The next day, however, the evening papers carried the grim news that a DH.110 piloted by John Derry had crashed into the crowd killing 29 spectators as well as Derry and Richards. What was very odd was that the plane that crashed was, as DP's wife predicted, silver. It was not the machine that they had seen the day before. The black plane had been specially painted for the event but it had developed a fault on the Saturday morning. The first prototype was then used. This had not been painted and so was still silver. John Derry had flown back to Hatfield to collect this reserve aircraft and had flown it back to Farnborough just in time for the display.

How can confirmation bias or the law of large numbers begin to explain this event? Again, the dream was quite specific to the event. It could be argued that DP's wife was frightened to go to the air show and her fear then created a dream around this fear. However, this fails to explain the colour of the aircraft and, more importantly, that the plane they saw on the first day of the event was silver and not the colour she had dreamed, black, whereas the plane that subsequently crashed *was* black.

Interestingly enough, a few months ago I told this story to a group of my readers and one of those present, Professor Sean Street, told me that he had actually been at Farnborough on that day as a young child and had actually witnessed the crash. This was, to me, a stunning coincidence, but what was even more intriguing was that Professor Street remembered his mother saying that she had a 'bad feeling' about the event and had asked Sean's father that they stand somewhere else to watch the show and not in the place they had originally planned to go. This turned out to be where one of the engines from the crashed aircraft landed, killing many spectators. As we shall see later, this event is not so unusual. It seems that sometimes traumatic events resonate back in time with a form of signal that can be picked up by sensitive individuals.

Sometimes, precognitive dreams are absolutely specific in both detail and content. These dreams refer to people who the dreamer knows personally. Again, I find it hard to apply 'the law of large numbers' or 'confirmation bias' to these events. For example, in 1858 two brothers, Samuel and Henry Clemens, were working the steamboats that plied their trade up and down the Mississippi River. One evening their boat, the *Pennsylvania*, arrived at St Louis and the two brothers took the opportunity to visit their sister who lived in the town. After dinner, Henry decided to go back to the riverboat, leaving his brother to spend the night on land.

As soon as the young Samuel fell asleep, he saw himself standing in front of a metal casket balanced on two chairs. On top of the casket was a bouquet of white roses with a single red rose in the middle. The top of the casket was open and Samuel moved forward to look inside. He was horrified to see the body of his younger brother, Henry, inside. This was such a shock that he immediately awoke. The dream imagery was so vivid that he rushed downstairs expecting to find the casket and his brother's body. Much to his relief the room was as it always was.

The next day Samuel decided not to mention the dream to his brother but did mention it in passing to his sister. The brothers left St Louis and the *Pennsylvania* steamed down to New Orleans. Here, due to staffing problems, Samuel was assigned to another boat, the *Lacey*, while Henry made the return journey on the *Pennsylvania*.

Three days later, on 13 June, Samuel heard the terrible news that the *Pennsylvania*'s boilers had blown up just south of Memphis, and 150 people were killed or injured. Among the severely injured was Henry Clemens. Samuel immediately rushed up to Memphis, arriving the night before his brother died and sitting with him through his final hours. Exhausted, Samuel retired for a fitful night's sleep. The next morning he awoke and made his way downstairs. A large room had been set aside for the bodies of those who had died in the disaster. With one notable exception, all the coffins were of simple, unpainted pine. In the centre of the room was a metal casket balanced across two chairs. With mounting horror, Samuel realized that he was reliving his dream in absolute detail. However, one item was missing: the roses. As Samuel stood taking in the scene, one of the volunteer nurses walked into the room carrying a bouquet of roses. Set in the middle of a bunch of white roses was the single red rose that Samuel had seen in his dream.

Samuel made some inquiries and discovered that the ladies of the town, because of his brother's striking looks, had clubbed together to raise 60 dollars to purchase a metal casket for Henry.

Such was the effect that these events had on Samuel that he was to change career and become a writer. He also changed his name to Mark Twain and subsequently became one of America's best-loved writers.

The engineer's dream

Of course, it may be argued that all these examples are experiences reported by individuals who are not trained scientists. Engineers, too, must be level-headed people. In designing machines for everyday use there is no place for flights of fancy. In 1900, an 11-year-old Ukrainian boy experienced a curiously vivid dream. This dream was to stimulate the young man to follow a fascinating career. He later described the dream in his autobiography:

I saw myself walking along a narrow, luxuriously decorated passageway. On both sides were walnut doors, similar to the state-room doors of a steamer. The floor was covered with an attractive carpet. A spherical electric light from the ceiling produced a pleasant bluish illumination. [133]

As the dream progressed, the boy felt a slight vibration, one he usually associated with being on board a large ship. But he knew that this was no ordinary ship for the craft he was travelling in was flying. When he awoke he mentioned this to his parents who assured him that such a thing was impossible. Five years before this incident, the esteemed British scientist Lord Kelvin had announced that 'heavier than air flying machines are impossible'. Two years after the boy's dream, in 1902, Simon Newcombe, the director of the US Naval Observatory wrote: 'Flight by machines heavier than air is impractical and insignificant, if not utterly impossible.' However, this dream was to focus this young Ukrainian on his own future, in which he was to become one of the brave pioneers of aviation. The young man was Igor Sikorsky. A few years later he would construct and fly the world's first four-engined aircraft, the *Russky Vityaz*. On emigrating to the USA, he founded the Aero Engineering Company and designed helicopters – and flying boats.

In 1931, an AEC-built flying boat called the S42 'Clipper' was due to be delivered to Pan American Airways. Although Sikorsky had often flown the plane while it was being tested, this new version was now fitted out with all the luxury and ostentation needed to attract the wealthy sections of American society who would travel in it. As the founder of AEC, Sikorsky was invited to be on the flight deck when the aircraft was delivered. As the aircraft began its descent, he decided to go to the rear of the plane to check out the newly refitted passenger section. Until that moment, this section had been in darkness. As Sikorsky entered the hull, a light was switched on for him. He was stunned:

I realized, at that very moment, that I had already seen all this a long time ago, the passageway, the bluish light, the walnut trimmings on the walls and doors, and the feeling of smooth motion, and I tried to recall when and how I could have received such an impression, until I finally remembered the details of my dream some thirty years before.[134]

The young Sikorsky had experienced a childhood dream to become an engineer and that dream literally came true for him. Indeed, these events were to have a profound effect upon him. The later years of his life were taken up with his own personal studies into the nature of reality. In 1947 he wrote a book called *The Invisible Encounter*, which was an attempt to understand the deeper meaning of the physical universe.

It seems that aviators have a particular aptitude for precognitive dreaming and time slips. Sikorsky, Dunne and Goddard are examples of this. Indeed, Victor Goddard seemed to have led a life filled with anomalous events. In January 1946, the – by then Sir – Victor Goddard found himself in Shanghai attending a cocktail party when he heard his name mentioned. He was amazed to hear a strident English accent describing how the famous Air Marshall Goddard had been killed in a plane crash. Intrigued, Goddard excused himself from the company he was with and walked over to the small group discussing his demise. Holding court was Captain Gerald Gladstone, commander of the Royal Navy cruiser HMS *Black Prince*. Goddard introduced himself with the phrase: 'I'm not quite dead yet', adding, 'What made you think I was?' Gladstone was clearly stunned at seeing the very-much-alive Goddard standing in front of him. After a swift apology, Gladstone explained that he had been telling his associates of the night before when he had experienced a particularly vivid dream. In this dream, Gladstone saw Goddard and three British civilians – two men and a woman – in an aircraft flying over a rocky shoreline. He felt that this was the coast of either China or Japan. He knew that the scene was taking place in early evening and that they were flying through a powerful storm. He saw the plane negotiate a high ridge of mountains and then crash. 'I watched it all happen,' Gladstone emphatically confirmed. 'You were killed.' Gladstone further stated that the crashed aircraft was an ordinary transport plane, possibly a Douglas Dakota.

This story worried Goddard because he knew that the very next day he was scheduled to fly from Shanghai to Tokyo. He had no idea of the plane type but suspected that it would be a Dakota transport aircraft. However, he also knew that it was unusual for civilians to travel on such flights so he put Gladstone's dream down to simply that, a dream. Later that evening his mood was to change. He was informed that the plane would be carrying civilians, three of them: two men and one woman, just as described in Gladstone's dream. Not wishing to raise any concerns, Goddard said nothing.

Early the next morning he was sitting in a Dakota aircraft with his three predicted passengers: the Consul General, a journalist, and a young female stenographer, all British, exactly as reported in the dream. In the early evening, as the flight approached the Japanese mainland, they were engulfed by a terrible snowstorm. The ferocity was such that the captain had to crash-land the plane on to the rugged shore of an island just off the east coast of the country. Gladstone's dream had come true in all details with the exception of the most crucial one: Goddard and all his companions survived the crash.

If Gladstone's dream was a precognition, why did it fail to come true in the main element of the dream, the death of Goddard and his associates? We have discussed in some detail the Many-Worlds Interpretation of quantum physics. This suggests that all outcomes of all events take place but we only experience a single outcome every time a decision is made. Could it be that Gladstone saw one possible future but that one did not come to pass in this universe? Indeed, is it also possible that Goddard's foreknowledge brought about a series of subtle changes in circumstances that ensured that he survived. For example, he could have arrived a few minutes late for the flight. This would have delayed take-off so that the plane arrived at a crucial section of the flight later than it would otherwise have done. He could have decided to sit in a different part of the plane thus ensuring that the balance was slightly different. This might have meant that the angle of impact was altered just enough to avoid rupturing the fuel tank. The number of subtle changes that foreknowledge can bring about is almost limitless. Is this how the future was changed that evening?

This incident generated so much interest that a film was made in 1955, loosely based on Goddard's experience, called *The Night My Number Came Up* and starring Michael Redgrave. As with all film adaptations, the storyline was changed to dramatize certain events. The film proved very popular at the time. Indeed, time is such a beguiling subject that it has been the source of inspiration for many plays, books and movies.

In my opinion such fictionalized accounts allow the deeper philosophical and scientific elements to be brought to the forefront and in doing so can engender far more debate and discussion than any 'true' event might do. To illustrate this point, I would now like to move away from 'fact' and review the way in which time, this greatest of all mysteries, has been treated in the world of fiction.

CHAPTER 11

TIME, DREAMS & PRECOGNITION IN POPULAR CULTURE

Groundhog Day

Jim Morrison was one of the most iconic rock stars of the late 1960s. His lyrics contained deep reflections on the human condition; he was clearly a very well-read individual. However, sometimes it was his between-song monologues that told a great deal about the man and his philosophy. One such stream of consciousness took place at the end of the song 'Light My Fire' on the album *Live In Detroit*.

> *Well, we're all in the cosmic movie, you know that! That means the day you die, you gotta watch your whole life recurring eternally forever, in CinemaScope, 3-D. So you better have some good incidents happenin' in there... and a fitting climax.*[135]

Clearly what Morrison is referring to here is the concept we have touched upon many times in this book, the Eternal Return or the Eternal Recurrence. As we have seen, the idea that we live our lives over and over again has been a popular concept since written records began and can be found in the writings of Nietzsche, Schopenhauer, Ouspensky, O'Brien, Joyce, Eliot, Beckett and many other authors, playwrights and poets. Indeed, it has been suggested that *Groundhog Day*, one of the most popular movies of the last 30 years, was influenced by Ouspensky's novel *Ivan Osokin*.

Although the events portrayed in the film are not, technically, examples of Eternal Return, this film still touches on some of the major aspects of the philosophy. Indeed, it can be argued that the central character of the movie, Phil Conners, is the only person who is not stuck in the time-loop because he can, by his own actions, change the way in which each day runs its course.

The movie starts on 1 February when Conners, a cynical TV weatherman, is planning his annual journey from Philadelphia to Punxsutawney, Pennsylvania, to cover the annual Groundhog Day festival, which will take place the following day. This is an actual event, held in Punxsutawney every year on 2 February. The towns-folk gather well before dawn to see a groundhog called 'Punxsutawney Phil' being awoken from hibernation and removed from his hutch. According to town tradition, when the sun rises and the groundhog sees his shadow, if he is panicked into returning to his hutch he has foretold an extended winter. If he stays where he is, he has predicted an early spring.

It soon becomes clear that Conners loathes this chore and is simply doing it because he has to. It is also obvious from his actions that this man is a very shallow, but also extremely professional, individual who has nothing in his life but his job. Yet it is a job that leaves him bored out of his mind.

Travelling with him is his producer, Rita, and cameraman, Larry. From the conversations they have in the van travelling down to Punxsutawney, it is clear that Larry has worked with Conners many times and knows how to deal with the meteorologist's world-weary negativity. Rita, on the other hand, does not know Conners and quickly becomes the foil for the weatherman's snide remarks and cruel wit.

The next day, Conners is awoken by the radio-alarm clock playing Sonny and Cher's classic 1960s song 'I Got You Babe'. Conners bumps into a man outside his room and is asked some questions by the hotel owner, Mrs Lancaster and then, after breakfast, heads in the direction of the park where the main event is to take place. As he walks across town, he is recognized by an old friend of his, Ned Ryerson, who engages him in conversation. Initially, Conners assumes Ned is a fan of his TV persona and walks away with a dismissive 'Thanks for watching'. However, it soon becomes clear that Ned is an old school associate who once dated Conners' sister, 'until you told me not to'. In this way Ned jovially lets the audience know that Conners' controlling attitude to life is not just an aspect of his present personality but has been a part of him for most of his life. Conners walks away and steps off the pavement into a puddle. Ned only warns Conners of the puddle after the mishap, saying: 'Watch out for that first step, it's a doozy!'

Conners makes his way into the park with the band playing 'The Pennsylvania Polka' and spots Rita and Larry. They begin filming and Conners describes to the camera what the ceremony is all about. Again, we see evidence of his world-weary cynicism as he tries to erode Rita's wide-eyed enthusiasm for the event and what it signifies. Conners is just keen to get away from the small town and get on with his life.

On the way back they find that a snowstorm has blocked all the exit roads and they have no alternative but to return to Punxsutawney for the night. He finds this extremely frustrating, but why is unclear as it seems Conners has nothing to go home for.

Conners awakes the next morning to the radio-alarm clock and Sonny and Cher singing, 'I Got You Babe'. Conners then bumps into the same man outside his room and is asked the same questions by the hotel owner, Mrs Lancaster. He responds by asking Mrs Lancaster if she has ever had *déjà vu*. In one of the classic lines of the movie she replies: 'I don't thinks so but I could check with the kitchen.' However, this discussion is of crucial importance because he had not made this last remark to Mrs Lancaster the previous day and so her response changes the day from being a Nietzschian or Ouspenskian Eternal Return day to one that is subtly different. In other words, a new day has been created at that point. This suggests more of an Everett's Many-Worlds Interpretation than Nietzsche's Eternal Return.

Conners walks through the town and again encounters Ned. This time Conners punches Ned in the nose. In doing so he makes a huge change to this new version of Groundhog Day because this action would have changed Ned's own day in so many ways. However, in an intriguing twist, the scriptwriter has Conners again step into the puddle – even though he knew it was there.

The *byt* people

This section contains a small echo of Ouspensky's *Ivan Osokin*. In that story, Ivan is given the chance to go back and live his life again but makes the same mistakes at the same times and so ends up reliving exactly the same life. Here, the puddle becomes the symbol that even though Conners may be almost godlike in his prescience as to what is about to take place on that day, 2 February, he is clearly doomed to follow the same path unless he breaks out of what Ouspensky would call his *byt* personality.

As explained in Chapter 3, Ouspensky argued that some people exist in a circle in which they are doomed to live the same life over and over again. He called them *byt* people.

However, by breaking out of this circle of endless repetition, a more advanced human being can change their life into a spiral in which every life that is repeated can be subtly changed. In this way, the soul advances and can eventually break out and move on. As we have seen, for Ouspensky this was facilitated by 'self-remembering'. This is the awareness, however subliminal, that this life is an illusion that we are repeating over and over again.

It can be argued that all the characters, with the exception of Conners, are characters trapped in *byt*. They simply respond to Conners' subtle, or not so subtle, changes of the day. They are seemingly self-aware but unaware of what is happening to them. Conners, on the other hand, achieves 'self-remembering' automatically from the first repeat morning. He is already an advanced being existing within a spiral while all the other characters are trapped in their own circles.

In one fascinating sequence, we also get elements of Nietzsche's 'demon' in the role of Rita. In this we see Phil tossing cards into a hat, presumably to show that as he has already done this so many times that he knows the value of each card and exactly which way it is going to fall. This action signifies the frustrations of his 'life in a day' that he is experiencing. Rita points out to him that this eternally repeating day should not be seen as a curse but as an opportunity. However, even though he realizes that this may be the case, he develops a feeling of omnipotence that still draws on his negative persona. It is only when he fails to save the life of an old tramp, despite having made many attempts to do so, that he realizes that he is helpless to change the really important things. At this point Conners realizes a great truth and he verbalizes it with the words: 'It's not me, it's the universe. I am just the vessel.' This is in contrast to an earlier statement when he observes: 'I am a god, not the God.' In many ways, this is a profoundly Gnostic statement. The idea that within our own world, or 'phaneron', as the philosophers call it, we may indeed be our own god. It is just that we have not realized this yet.

I have been in the fortunate position of being able to discuss the movie with the guy who wrote it, Danny Rubin. It is clear that Danny feels he has created something that others have run away with. His motivation to write the story was not based upon Ouspensky, Nietzsche or any other philosopher. Danny informed me that he was watching a movie and he simply wondered what it would be like if the central character knew the plot. It was from such a small idea that such a great movie was developed.

The Butterfly Effect

Another movie that takes the idea of a character who knows the outcomes of his actions and then has the opportunity to put them right is *The Butterfly Effect*.

This movie, directed and written by Eric Bress and J. Mackye Gruber, was released in 2004. Initially it received a very poor critical reception. For example, the famed movie critic Roger Ebert stated in the *Chicago Sun-Times* that: 'There's so much flashing forward and backward, so many spins of fate, so many chapters in the journals, that after a while I felt that I, as well as time, was being jerked around.' Dave Kehr of the *New York Times* was even more dismissive, writing: 'Even by the lax standards of January film releases—this month is the traditional dumping time for studio films that didn't quite work out—*The Butterfly Effect* is staggeringly bad.'

However, these opinions were not shared by the public who turned out in huge numbers to view it. This brought about a curious change in the attitude of the critics. The film subsequently won the Pegasus Audience Award at the Brussels International Fantastic Film Festival and was nominated for the Best Science Fiction Film at the Saturn Awards.

The movie has an intriguing, and calculatingly enigmatic beginning when a young man bursts into an office, jams the door shut and hides under a desk. He writes a note, presumably to be found by somebody else. On this note he writes: 'It is said that the flapping of a butterfly's wings in Chicago can create a Hurricane in Peking.'

We are then flashed back 13 years to when the fearful young man is 7 years old. We are informed that his name is Evan Treborn and that he suffers from mysterious blackouts when he cannot recall what he has done. We subsequently discover that these blackouts are inherited from his father Jason, who has become so disturbed by them that he is institutionalized. Although Evan's father's 'illness' is never specifically diagnosed, it seems that it is some form of epilepsy, possibly focused on his brain's temporal lobes.

These problems do not seem to prevent Evan making a success of his life. By the time he is 20 the blackouts are part of his past. He is a well-liked psychology undergraduate with a particular interest in the mechanism of memory. However, one evening his past literally comes back to haunt him. Quite by accident, he discovers a series of journals that his younger self had written years before. He is in the process of reading a particular section of one journal to a female college friend when he loses touch with reality and finds himself experiencing events from his past in which the outcomes are different from those he remembered. This, quite naturally, intrigues him. He is keen to know if these new 'memories' represent real events in his past or are just hallucinations. Much to his surprise, Evan finds that he can travel back into his own past and change the events that took place. Even minor changes can bring about a totally different outcome. This explains why the movie is called *The Butterfly Effect* and the significance of the note that Evan leaves on the desk at the start. Small changes can bring about huge consequences as one event triggers another and another. Evan finds this out the hard way. Every time he comes out of a blackout he finds that his world has changed and that he is in a completely different set of circumstances. He finds this confusing. What is even worse is that he is also able to see the outcome of his small temporal 'tweaks' upon his friends and associates. Even when these changes are intended to be positive, somebody ends up in a worse set of circumstances. Evan ends up going back in time over and over again to try and put right the train of circumstances that he has put in motion by his actions.

The love of his life is his childhood sweetheart Kayleigh Miller. He witnesses examples of where his actions have profound effects on her and feels that he has an obligation to ensure that her life works out well for her. After a few failed attempts, he finally makes one good decision that results in Kayleigh and his other friends having lives that work out fine. However, there is a downside to this outcome. In this new universe, Evan has to ensure that Kayleigh no longer knows who he is.

The storyline is very complex and it is well worth watching to see how Evan eventually creates a series of outcomes in which all the protagonists are happy, with the exception of himself. He has to sacrifice his own happiness with Kayleigh in order to ensure that the positive outcomes come about.

In this new universe, it is made very clear that Kayleigh has not featured in his life in any way. For example, his room-mate does not recognize her name. Evan decides to burn all his journals and in so doing destroys the facilitator that allows him to go back in time. We then cut to eight years later and the Wall Street district of New York. Evan is talking on his mobile phone to somebody he is clearly in a relationship with (his wife?) when he sees a very smart, and clearly successful, Kayleigh walking towards him. They walk past each other. We see Kayleigh stop and look back. There is a hint of recognition in her eyes. Evan turns round to see her walking away into the crowds. He had not turned round soon enough to notice her looking at him.

Interestingly enough, two other possible endings were filmed.

In the first alternative version Evan looks back and catches Kayleigh looking at him. They stare at each other for a second and then Kayleigh asks: 'Do I know you?' He introduces himself. As she starts to give her name he says it at the same time. She looks puzzled and so he responds with, 'You look like a Kayleigh.' He then asks her if she would like a cup of coffee and she agrees. The movie ends at that point with the audience clearly led to believe that this meeting will develop into something of significance.

The TLE factor

In the director's cut, the ending is an altogether bleaker affair. We see again the opening sequence but this time Evan writes: 'Anyone who finds this knows that my plan didn't work and I am already dead.' He then goes back to being inside his mother's womb where he is strangled by the umbilical cord. None of his subsequent actions will have any effect because he was born dead. Indeed, in a fascinating twist, Evan's mother describes how Evan was the third of three brothers, the other two having also died at birth.

This movie applies the model presented in my book *Is There Life After Death? The Extraordinary Science of What Happens When We Die*, which suggests that we can live many lives and each decision made changes events in the future. It applies concepts from Everett's Many-Worlds Interpretation and also has elements of the stories of the great Argentine writer Jorge Borges (1899–1986), specifically his mysterious *Garden of the Forking Paths*. As I stated earlier, I suggest that the blackouts Evan inherited from his father are related to a condition similar to that of temporal lobe epilepsy (TLE). It is this enigmatic neurological condition that facilitates his falling out of time. It has been noted that Evan's full name, Evan Treborn, can be read as 'event reborn'. When he has these blackouts, his future self takes control of his past self. In 'is-there-life-after-death' (ITLAD) terminology, the Daemon takes control of the Eidolon as the blackout takes place.

The Daemon can do this because TLE involves the release of certain neurotransmitters in the brain, neurotransmitters that allow the Daemon to take temporary control. For example, towards the end of the film, Evan's 'Daemon' uses a home movie to destroy his relationship with Kayleigh before it has begun.

In another scene, Evan is in the woods with his friends before his dog is killed. The Daemon uses its foreknowledge (precognition?) to prepare his friends for what is about to happen. Both these events take place *before* Evan develops his TLE 'blackouts'. Interestingly, in his *Examiner* review of this movie, critic Mark Joseph Young suggests that a major weakness of the movie is that Evan knows about his time travelling because he keeps a journal. By preventing his own blackouts he prevents the future writing of the journal. He calls this a 'predestination paradox'. However, ITLAD can be applied to this to show that no such paradox exists because there are, in effect, two consciousnesses at work, Evan's Daemon and Evan's Eidolon.

The term 'butterfly effect' has its roots in a short story called *The Sound of Thunder*, written by Ray Bradbury in the 1950s. In this story, a time traveller accidentally steps on a butterfly when travelling back in time to the Jurassic period. In a 1969 paper outlining how chaos theory could be applied to the meteorological sciences, Massachusetts Institute of Technology mathematician Edward Lorenz used this term to describe how a small event can bring about massive atmospheric and meteorological changes over time. Four years later, he wrote a book entitled *Predictability: Does The Flap of A Butterfly's Wings In Brazil Set off A Tornado In Texas?* This is similar in wording to the note Evan leaves except in that case the butterfly is in Chicago, the tornado is a hurricane and the place hit is Peking. (At the risk of being accused of pedantry, in China, hurricanes are known as 'typhoons'.)

Unlike many of the critics, I found *The Butterfly Effect* to be a well-written and ultimately very moving film. It is successful on many levels. However, I am intrigued as to why more was not made of the 'illness' that Evan and his two brothers inherited from his father, Jason. I work with many individuals who experience temporal lobe epilepsy and they regularly report to me that time acts very strangely during their pre-seizure auras. Some have told me that it slows down to a snail's pace and others how it seems to 'fast forward'. I wonder why it was that Eric Bress and J. Mackye Gruber went part of the way down the TLE route and then decided not to follow through. I suspect it is because, in the final analysis, *The Butterfly Effect* is a science fiction love story and, as with all science fiction, it does not need to explain how things happen, just that they do happen and what the outcomes are.

Awareness of the future is a theme in both *The Butterfly Effect* and *Groundhog Day*. However, this awareness is, in a very real sense, a memory rather than a precognition. For me, one of the best movies dealing with the complexities, and more importantly the moral implications, of precognition, is Steven Spielberg's *Minority Report*.

This movie is based on a short story by the great speculative fiction writer Philip K. Dick. In my previous books I have described in great detail how this highly individual thinker presents us with some fascinatingly stimulating ideas about what it is to be a consciousness perceiving a reality that may or may not be real.

A Dickian future: *Minority Report*

In *Minority Report*, the central concept is that psychics can predict the future. As we have seen from our earlier discussions, this is not such an odd idea as it first seems. You will recall that a series of experiments by Haynes, Libet, Dean Radin and Dick Bierman and others have suggested that human consciousness can, through some as yet unknown mechanism, monitor the immediate future of its environment. If it can do this over a few seconds why is it not possible to extend this capability to a few minutes or even a few days? Indeed, once the threshold of future awareness has been crossed, even if it is only for a second or two, then it is no longer a barrier. According to the current scientific paradigm, the future does not exist – or more accurately it is yet to be brought into existence – and yet Radin and Bierman's subjects consistently showed that the future can be perceived. If this is correct, then in some very real way the future has substance that can be comprehended by our sensory apparatus. What this apparatus consists of is, of course, a whole different question.

In *Minority Report*, there are three young psychics – or 'Precogs' as they are termed – who have all been affected in the womb by drugs that their mothers took during pregnancy. This has brought about the ability to be 'pre-aware' of strongly emotional events that are about to take place in the near future. This shows certain parallels with the Bierman and Radin experiments. You will recall that the subjects of these experiments were shown a series of images projected on to a screen in front of them. Attached to the subjects were devices to measure their skin conductivity. Most of the pictures that the subjects were shown were relaxing and emotionally neutral. However, mixed in among these nice images was the occasional picture of sex or violence designed to arouse strong emotions. The subjects reacted to these pictures *before they were shown on the screen*. So, just as with Dick's 'Precogs', it seems that emotional energy can somehow override the usual temporal flow. The work of the much-maligned Austrian-American psychiatrist and inventor Wilhelm Reich (1897–1957) may contain partial answers to this mystery.

Reich suggested that all living things give off a form of energy that he called 'orgone' and believed that this energy can be detected by other beings. This might explain why many of us can sense that people have been arguing when we enter a room. There is nothing that can be deduced from the protagonists' body language or comments. It is simply a feeling that is picked up as if from the air. Reich suggested that this energy, like all energy, cannot be destroyed, it simply changes form from one type to another and so could be converted into light or sound. Is this the reason why Annie Moberly and Eleanor Jourdain were able to see a series of incidents from the past when they visited Versailles in 1901?

Orgone energy, although odd, obeys known scientific rules. It follows time's arrow in that past events, that is events that have already *happened*, are detected by somebody downstream of the temporal flow. This is perfectly understandable. It is rather like watching a movie. The movie was recorded at some specific time in the past and is available to view now. So it could be with regard to the time slips discussed above. However, Radin and Bierman's subjects, and Philip K. Dick's 'Precogs', perceive information from upstream of the temporal flow.

Information that the Precogs 'pre-conceive', such as knowledge of a future crime, appears to them in their 'mind's eye'. Sophisticated mind-interface software is used to project the images they perceive on to a screen so that they can be seen by others. The police employ specialists to work out when and where these crimes are due to take place and identify the people involved so they can prevent the crime being committed.

The intriguing moral question that is raised by this film is whether somebody can be guilty of a crime that they have not yet committed. Indeed, if the crime was to be committed in the heat of the moment, then at the time of arrest it is possible that the perpetrator will not even have experienced the emotion that would bring about the criminal act. However, if future time somehow already exists 'out there' then, in some way, the crime has already been committed, it is just that we are yet to experience it.

Indeed, a moment's reflection makes the linear model of time used in *Minority Report* seem totally impossible. If the Precogs inform the police that a crime is about to take place and the police prevent that crime from occurring, then not only does that crime not happen but it now does not exist in the future. In which case, how did the Precogs 'see' it? All they can 'see' is an actualized future. But by their preventive action the police have ensured that such an event does not take place.

To provide evidence for submission to a court of law, the police need copies of the images seen by the Precogs and for them to be 'projected' on to the screen. It is these images that are used to convict the accused person of the future perpetration of a crime that has no longer taken place. However, if the future has now been changed by the action of the police how can these images still exist, when they are images of a future that never happened?

The meaning of the film's title, *Minority Report*, is made clear as the plot unfolds. It is not my intention to ruin the plot for anybody who wishes to watch the movie but suffice to say that the central character, Captain John Anderton (played by Tom Cruise), ends up being accused of a future murder and has to clear his name. It appears that sometimes the Precogs do not agree about a future event. When this happens a 'minority report' is compiled that describes an event that was seen differently by one of the Precogs while still being agreed on by the remaining two. Now this raises some interesting questions. For example, if two Precogs see an event in one way and the third sees it in another way, which of them is correct? Or do we in fact have two alternative futures, both of which do actually come to pass – but in different universes? If we take the Everett Many-Worlds Interpretation as being the correct model of how the multiverse functions, then this is exactly what we would expect. However, the Many-Worlds Interpretation is unclear about future events because, yet again, these events have yet to take place. In other words, after the box is opened there are two 'Schrödinger's cats', one alive and one dead. The box has to be opened to bring about the splitting. But if all *potential* futures also exist in a permanent *now* then the multiverse is far, far, bigger than we can ever imagine. Every outcome of every action exists in actuality. This means that as well as all the universes that *have* come into being since the first millisecond of the Big Bang, there also exists every universe from every outcome that *will* come to pass between now and the end of time actually in existence and available to us. Not only that, but all the information contained in this timeless multiverse is also available.

If my future-orientated Many-Worlds Interpretation is correct, then the storyline of *Minority Report* becomes explicable but also brings to the table a massive moral dilemma. If all outcomes of all possible actions come to pass then it is possible that every single person on the planet will have, by accident or design (or both) murdered someone. This is because killing your spouse, for example, is a *possible* outcome in that it does not involve anything that is logically or scientifically impossible. For instance, you are more likely to kill your spouse than levitate across the room. Indeed, in a multiverse that contains every outcome of every *possible* action, not only will you have murdered your spouse countless times, but you will also have dispatched all your friends, family and relations.

In this short review of time-orientated movies, I have left out so many other examples owing to lack of space, and the argument that this book is not a film guide. Films such as *Run Lola Run*, *Twelve Monkeys*, *Triangle*, *The Time Traveler's Wife* and the classic *Dead of Night* all focus on the idea of a circular form of time where events wrap around each other. The mysteries of precognition have also been a standard plot line in many, many, movies.

I would now like to turn again to the work of the playwright J.B. Priestley. We have touched upon his writings throughout this book and I would now like to focus on a group of his plays that deal specifically with the theories of two other major subjects of this book: J.W. Dunne and Peter Ouspensky.

Priestley and his 'time plays'

Of all the great British playwrights of the 20th century, J.B. Priestley divides opinion more than any other. For some, he is a crusty, old-fashioned writer whose plays were very much of their time and have no relevance to 21st-century post-modernism. Others see him as one of the great social chroniclers whose works have contributed greatly to the modernization of Britain. For me, he is neither of these things. He is one of the most original thinkers in British theatre. His plays can be categorized into two types: the old-fashioned, and very dated, 'parlour plays' that help to pass an evening. In this category I place works such as *When We Are Married*, *Laburnum Grove*, *Mr Kettle and Mrs Moon*, and *Eden End*. However, there is a series of other plays that are revolutionary and as fresh today as they were when first performed. In this category I place all of his so-called 'time plays', each one of which focuses on a theme that we have already discussed in this book.

It is generally considered that Priestley's time plays consist of *Johnson Over Jordan* (1939), *The Long Mirror* (1940), *An Inspector Calls* (1947), *Dangerous Corner* (1932), *I Have Been Here Before* (1937) and *Time and the Conways* (1937). In my opinion the first three, although intriguing in their own ways, are not true time plays as would be understood in the use of the word 'time' applied in this book. *Johnson Over Jordan* is a meditation on the phenomenon we now know as the near-death experience (also known as the Tibetan 'Bardo' state). *The Long Mirror* focuses on another subject that fascinates me, the idea of astral travel. *An Inspector Calls* suggests an avenging spirit that appears to make a group of characters focus on their individual responsibilities for a death that is about to happen in the future. For these reasons, I will focus on the last three, *Dangerous Corner*, *Time and the Conways* and *I Have Been Here Before*.

As we have already mentioned, many commentators consider that Priestley's first ever play, *Dangerous Corner*, was also the first of his time plays. This was first performed at the Lyric Theatre in

London in 1932 – three years after the publication of Dunne's *An Experiment with Time*. However, Priestley's theme is the concept of a time-loop. The title is very clever in that it explains the plot in a subtle way. In order to prevent road accidents, a sign warning of a 'dangerous corner' is placed in advance of a sharp bend in the road. By pre-warning drivers of this danger, the potential hazard is avoided. In effect, this is what happens in the play.

As the play opens the stage is in darkness. There is the muffled sound of a gunshot and a scream. The stage is then illuminated to show four women listening to a radio play. From the subsequent conversations we discover that the location is the home of Robert and Freda Caplan. Present is Freda and her friends Betty, Olwen and Maud. Freda's husband Robert works for a publishing company. Freda offers Olwen a cigarette from a musical box, which Olwen seems to recognize. Freda asks Olwen why she is familiar with it. This seemingly innocent question sets in train a series of damaging revelations that leads to a suicide involving the muffled sound of a gunshot and a woman's scream, all of which take place on a darkened stage. The lights then go up to show an exact repetition of the opening scene. Again, the cigarettes are offered and, again, Olwen recognizes the box. However, this time Freda does not ask why Olwen reacted the way she did. As a result, there is no series of damaging revelations, unlike before, and the conversation continues without incident. The play then ends.

Clearly Priestley is keen to have his audience appreciate that a small incident can have huge consequences, and that these consequences are avoided if the incident does not happen. He is playing with alternative futures, rather like the Everett's Many-Worlds Interpretation. There is a suggestion that both outcomes have a real existence but only one outcome is experienced this time. But each incident and consequence are playing round and round in a loop of time.

However, the audience did not appreciate the message, and nor did the critics. It received extremely poor reviews and the play was threatened with closure after only three performances. Priestley held faith with both his play and his audiences and bought out the syndicate that had invested in it. As he suspected, all that was needed was for the theatregoers to gain understanding of the subtle concepts being presented. With repeated performances came increased understanding; the play subsequently ran for six months and was made into a film in 1934.

Priestley later described *Dangerous Corner* as 'pretty thin stuff when all is said and done'.[136] Yet it is clear that he felt it was well worth returning to the subject of time. It is therefore no surprise that five years later, as a much more accomplished playwright, he was to return to this theme with not one but two plays, each approaching the mystery of time from two differing, but related viewpoints: those of J.W. Dunne and P.D. Ouspensky.

The more popular of the two, *Time and the Conways*, premiered at the Duchess Theatre in August 1937. This was a study of how the optimistic post-war world of 1919 was shattered by the financial collapse of the late 1920s and the austerity of the 1930s. The unfolding events are reflected in the lives of a group of upper-middle-class characters who enjoy the benefits and endure the subsequent traumas of that period. However, woven into this morality play was a much deeper philosophical reflection upon the nature of time itself, specifically as a tool to put across to his audience the theories of J.W. Dunne. Dunne's theories had long fascinated Priestley. As already explained, in a series of books starting with his famous *An Experiment with Time*, Dunne had suggested that time is serial in its nature. That is, there are varying levels of time, all of which are used to measure temporal flow. For Dunne, time was, in its ultimate reality, a permanent 'now', similar in many ways to the models presented by Hermann Minkowski and Julian Barbour.

Time and the Conways

In the summer of 2009, I was invited to be take part in an event at the National Theatre in London. This was one of a series of pre-performance discussions known as 'Platform Events' that involve a 40-minute discussion between the audience, cast members and recognized 'experts' on the subject matter featured in the subsequent performance. I had been asked to talk about Dunne's theories of time. My fellow 'time' expert was Professor Jeff Forshaw of Manchester University. I was particularly honoured to be involved in this event because it was held before a performance of a radical reworking of *Time and the Conways* by the then *enfant terrible* of British theatre, Rupert Goold (1972–). Goold had made his reputation with his stunning direction of *Star Trek*'s Patrick Stewart in *Macbeth* and Pete Postlethwaite in *King Lear*. Much was expected of the way he would rework *Time and the Conways* and he was not to disappoint. I was keen to get across to the audience the theories of Dunne in the way I have presented them in this book: the idea that time is the fourth dimension that we perceive as creatures existing in three dimensions. From the viewpoint of this fourth dimension time does not exist. Everything happens in an eternal 'now'. Each moment is a slice of a Minkowskian time-line rather like slices of bread. This is exactly the approach Goold took in that the theatrical devices he used in the production show time as a series of snapshots similar to the famous Victorian photographer Eadweard Muybridge's time-lapse photographs of a galloping horse or a young woman skipping. In this way, Goold was able to show to his audience exactly what Dunne meant by the term 'serial time'. I suspect that Goold was motivated to show time in this way after reading the following comment that Priestley makes in his book *Man and Time*:

> *We invent time to explain change and succession. We try to account for it out there in the world we are observing, but soon run into trouble because it is not out there at all. It comes with the travelling searchlight, the moving slit.*[137]

In the play, Priestley makes indirect reference to Dunne when one of the characters, Alan, explains to his sister, Kay, that there is a book he has read that explains the true nature of time. He then goes on to say:

> *Time is only a kind of dream, Kay. If it wasn't it would have to destroy everything, the whole universe, and then remake it again every tenth of a second. But time doesn't destroy anything, it merely moves us on in this life from one peep-hole to the next.*[138]

In a series of images at the start of the play, Goold mixed the photo-imagery of Muybridge with the philosophical concept that in order for time not to destroy and recreate the universe at every moment, it must exist as an already existent series of images. It is the observer that moves from one image to the next. He showed a group of people enclosed in film-frames and as each frame moved on so the illusion of movement is created. Alan continues his explanation to Kay by talking about the concept of the 'long body' or 'shira linga':

> *The point is now, at this moment, or any moment, we are only a cross-section of our real selves. What we really are is the whole stretch of ourselves, all our time and when we come to the end of this life all those selves, all our time, will be us, the real you, the real me. And then, perhaps we will find ourselves in another time which is only another kind of dream.*[139]

From the viewpoint of 'Time Two', as Dunne termed it, a human body would be viewed as it would with a time-lapse photograph of, say, 75 years. This body would be a long, snake-like mass that starts as a tiny tail (birth) and expands through childhood, adolescence and adulthood only to start to shrink again as age takes its toll. This is the Hindu *shira linga*. From this viewpoint it is clear that time does not exist. All that exists is consciousness moving through various 'slices' of the *shira linga*, starting at the tail and exiting through the head.

This mirrors a very similar section of Ouspensky's book *A New Model of the Universe*. In a fascinating analysis he describes how he 'saw' somebody he wished to communicate with as an image of that person's whole life within the fourth dimension of time, that is, within a continuum.

In general, the play received fairly positive reviews. One can assume that this was because the plot can be followed as a simple story of the effect that time has on the characters. Indeed, a major theme is the idea of how small incidents can shape the future and make it take one direction rather than another. It also focuses on shattered dreams and unfulfilled potentials. These were themes that both critics and audiences alike could relate to. However, the Dunne themes seemed to be rather lost. In an interesting plot device Priestley uses the three acts to convey a form of time slip. The first act takes place in the drawing room of the Conway family's large home in 1919. The family have come together to celebrate their daughter Kay's birthday. This sets the scene and introduces all the characters. They are a very happy, if somewhat privileged, group who seem to have no worries in the world. The war has just finished and there is great optimism for the future. The first act ends with Kay reading a letter and going into some form of trance state. When the curtain opens for the second act the drawing room now looks a good deal more austere. We discover from a radio broadcast that the year is 1938, exactly 19 years on from the events of the first act. Through the dialogue, we discover that each one, with the possible exception of the eldest Conway, Alan, has become bitter and worn down by time. In the Goold version, it is made clear that Kay is a little confused by some of the things that are said. It is as if she feels that she is an observer of these events, even though she is part of them. As the act unfolds, resentments and tensions explode and the Conways are split apart by misery and grief. At the end of the scene, Kay and Alan are left alone on stage. Alan quotes an excerpt from William Blake's *Auguries of Innocence*:

Joy and woe are woven fine,
A clothing for the soul divine.
Under every grief and pine
Runs a joy with silken twine.
Man was made for joy and woe;
And when this we rightly know
Through the world we safely go

Priestley was very careful in his choice of poem. *Auguries of Innocence* opens with the famous lines: 'To see the world in a grain of sand and heaven in a wild flower, hold infinity in the palm of your hand, and eternity in an hour.' In many ways those last few words of the opening section of the poem even more accurately reflect the philosophy presented in *Time and the Conways*. Time is an illusion that we are fooled by. As Alan states later: 'All our time will be us, the real you, the real me.'

The second act ends with Alan saying that he will get her 'that book', clearly a reference to Dunne's *An Experiment with Time*, adding that the error is in thinking that time is snatching our lives away, but that we are immortal beings, in for a 'tremendous adventure'. Kay repeats these words and the act suddenly comes to an end. The next act opens with Kay on her own, back in the room as it was in 1919. She is clearly confused and thinks that she has been asleep and experienced a dream involving Alan and the others. It is at this point that some of the audience will spot Priestley's clever plot device in which the whole of act two may have been a dream experienced by Kay. Because audiences are used to plays in which time goes backwards and forwards, this may not seem so strange.

There is a sequence towards the end of the act in which the characters discuss where they think they will be in the future. It is during these optimistic discussions that Kay recalls her dream of the future. She becomes tearful and tells Alan that there is 'something you know that can make things better'. She then asks Alan if he 'remembers' quoting Blake to her. Alan clearly does not know what she is talking about. In an echo from the second act, she re-states the lines as Alan had done in the future. When they are again alone, Kay says to Alan that there is something he can do to change things. In this she is clearly referring to her half-remembered memories of the dream. It may be that Alan also feels a memory of the future when he responds to Kay's question with the words: 'There will be something one day, I will try, I promise.' With this, the play comes to an end.

In the Goold version, there is a wonderful device used to get across the concept of the *shira linga*. As Kay leans against a fireplace we are given a glimpse of a whole line of actresses all wearing identical clothes to Kay's disappearing into the distance. A strobe light is used to turn the line of actresses into a moving, single, figure similar to a cartoon or a series of movie stills. For the audiences who saw the 2009 National Theatre production, this was a stunning explanation of the plot – one that is denied those who have only seen less thought-through versions of this classic play.

The fact that *Time and the Conways* has been performed so many times since is evidence of its popularity. Alas this is not the case for Priestley's other 1937 production, the Ouspensky-inspired *I Have Been Here Before*. Whereas *Time and the Conways,* for all its confusing chronology, was an interesting story with effective characterization, this second play simply confused audiences. It was far too metaphysical and the characters lacked depth. Unlike *Time and the Conways,* Priestley had been working on this play for some time and had made many amendments before it was presented to a live audience in September 1937, just over a month after the first performance of *the Conways.*

It was in 1936 that Priestley first discovered the work of Ouspensky. At that time he and his family were living in a small town in Arizona called Wickenburg. On a trip to Santa Barbara in California he found he had some time to spare. While wandering through the side streets he happened upon a small bookshop. As an avid reader, he immediately entered and scanned the shelves.

One book in particular caught his eye. It was a copy of Ouspensky's *A New Model of the Universe*. I can find no information as to whether Priestley knew of Ouspensky at that time or not, but he bought the book and took it with him on his long drive back to Arizona. By that evening, Priestley had arrived at the aptly named Furnace Creek in Death Valley. He decided to stop for the night in this fascinating location and, with the silence of the desert all around him, he began reading for the first time the ideas and theories of Peter Ouspensky. He was stunned. As we have already discussed, this book presented in detail Ouspensky's model of Eternal Return. For Priestley, this was a revelation and by his return to Wickenburg he had decided to write a play based upon Ouspensky's theories. He felt that this was a way of further developing some of the issues he had touched upon in *Dangerous Corner*.

He began working on the new play while travelling across the Atlantic on a freighter. He had plenty of time to think about how the play could be developed. This was a challenge for him. Usually his writing starts with a plot, a character or an autobiography. This new play was not inspired by any of these things but by an idea. To dramatize philosophy was far more challenging and he wrote three different drafts before he settled upon a storyline.

A few months later, in January 1937, an incident was to take place that was to make Priestley question the linear nature of time. He and his wife, June, were touring Egypt. For a bit of fun they decided to visit an old fortune-teller. June was told by the clairvoyant that soon someone very close to her would be in great danger and that she would be required to travel halfway across Europe to help this person. June was also informed that the person in need would be a young female. Priestley and his wife thought nothing of this and returned to England. A few weeks later, their daughter travelled to Florence. At first things seemed to be fine. However, she suddenly became ill and June had to rush to her aid, travelling from England to Italy as quickly as she could. The illness turned out to be measles and Priestley needed to follow his wife to Italy to bring anti-measles serum for his daughter. She quickly recovered. However, Priestley was so taken with the location that he stayed for a few weeks in the small town of Fiesole that sits among the hills looking down over Florence. The fortune-teller's accurate prophecy had restimulated his interest in his new play. As he looked at the River Arno in the distance, his thoughts took him to the idea that precognition may be a form of knowledge based upon previous experiences. If Ouspensky was right in his theory that we all live our lives over and over again, then it may be possible that some people 'remember' incidents in their past lives and can use this knowledge to change things in this one. The play's structure began to fall into place. On his return to London, Priestley began the task of rewriting the dialogue of the play. He had now also decided upon a title. He was to call it *I Have Been Here Before*.

He took himself off to his home, Billingham, on the Isle of Wight. It was here that he completed both of his 1937 plays. It is clear that he found *I Have Been Here Before* a far more difficult proposition than *Time and the Conways*. Indeed, with regard to the latter, he felt that it had been written under a form of inspiration, stating that his subconscious 'shot up solutions' to some technical problems 'as fast as they were needed'. He believed that he was tapping into what he termed a 'much greater mind'. This 'greater mind' was clearly absent with regard to the Ouspensky-inspired play.

With much hard work, *I Have Been Here Before* was completed and saw its premier performance a month after its sister play. In this latter work, Priestley takes Ouspensky's interesting adaptation of the Nietzschean Eternal Return by suggesting that some individuals can become aware of their recurring life. As we have already seen, Ouspensky called this 'self-remembering' and spent the last few years of his life revisiting his old haunts to see if he could receive a glimmer of recognition of something deeper. Applying Nietzsche's Eternal Return/Recurrence to the *shira linga* concept, Ouspensky suggested that the snake-like 'long body' does not extend in a linear fashion but curls back on itself so that tail and head meet. As discussed previously, a similar symbol – a snake eating its own tail – has long been used as a depiction of eternity, particularly in alchemical circles, where it is known as the ouroborus. For Ouspensky, all time is circular and so our lives just go round and round in circles. Some of us, if we can become enlightened to our situation, can break out of the circle and ascend or descend in a spiral. However, as the spiral moves upwards (or downwards) within time we still can never break out.

The central character of *I Have Been Here Before* is a mysterious East European by the name of Dr Görtler. Priestley clearly based this character upon Ouspensky himself. Görtler is still going round in an everlasting Eternal Return but he is aware of the fact. He has attained 'self-remembering' and in doing so has become conscious of his condition. He has used this knowledge to turn the circle into a spiral and in some way has manipulated the otherwise deterministic universe that he exists within.

The play takes place in a rural Yorkshire inn called the Black Bull. The proprietor, Sam, and his daughter, Sally, are awaiting the arrival of three female guests. An elderly East European gentleman arrives unexpectedly and asks if a room is available. He is confused when he is told that the inn is fully booked. He asks questions about who has made a booking, enquiring specifically about two couples. He is informed that there was only one couple staying that night and the only other guests are three ladies. This adds to his confusion and he leaves. The phone rings and Sam is told that the three ladies have cancelled. Almost immediately, the phone rings again and another booking is taken, this time from a Mr and Mrs Ormund. Now it is Sam and Sally's turn to be puzzled. Their guest list now accurately reflects what the mystery caller had enquired about earlier. A few moments later, one of the other guests, a schoolteacher named Oliver Farrant, returns from a walk followed by the elderly East European, who is looking a good deal more relieved now that his predicted guest list has come true.

We discover that the mysterious East European (the Ouspensky-like scientist) is a German refugee named Dr Görtler. He spends the rest of the play asking leading questions of the other characters, specifically whether any of them are experiencing *déjà vu* regarding their present circumstances. All agree that they are. In the second act, Görtler explains to the assembled occupants of the inn the doctrine of the Eternal Return and how we may all live the same life over and over again. In echoes of Ouspensky's exposition on *byt* people, Dr Görtler tells them:

> *I said you might live the same life over and over again. But not all. . . some people, steadily developing, will exhaust possibilities of their circles of time and will finally swing out of them into new existences. Others – the criminals, madmen, suicides – live their lives in ever-darkening circles of their time. Fatality begins to haunt them. More and more of their lives are passed in the shadow of death. They gradually sink.*[140]

Later, Dr Görtler explains how some people manage to escape from the circle by turning it into a spiral:

> *We do not go round in a circle. That is an illusion. We move along a spiral track. It is not quite the same journey from the cradle to the grave each time. Sometimes the differences are small, sometimes they are very important. We must set out each time on the same road but along that road we have a choice of adventures.*[141]

Later still, Oliver and Mrs Ormund go out for a walk, leaving Dr Görtler and Mr Ormund alone together. Dr Görtler then asks a series of searching questions of Ormund regarding his life. On their return from the walk, Oliver and Mrs Ormund agree that they both have a huge sense of foreboding and that in some way this is related to any actions they may make in the near future. It is clear that the two are very attracted to each other and at the end of the scene they embrace.

In the third act, Oliver and Mrs Ormund announce that they are to leave together. It is here that Dr Görtler explains why he planned to be in the inn on that particular weekend. He points out that the overpowering feeling of *déjà vu* that was being experienced by all concerned was because they had all lived through these events before. He was there to ensure that these events did not spiral out of control, as they had the last time when, on hearing of the affair, Mr Ormund committed suicide. This led to the closing of the school and the ruin of all their lives. Because of Dr Görtler's intervention and following discussions with Mr Ormund in the second act, the husband was mentally prepared for the news and his reaction this time is not as extreme as it had been before. With Dr Görtler's subtle help, he has been able to come to terms with the circumstances and accept them. With the suicide averted, the school does not close and there is a better outcome for all concerned.

Curiously, Priestley has Dr Görtler claim that his future knowledge of events was received through a precognitive dream rather than simply as an example of Ouspensky's 'self-remembering'. In many ways this reflects Dunne's philosophy as much as it does Ouspensky's. Indeed, I wonder whether this is why, in her diary entry for 27 October 1937, the socialist intellectual Beatrice Webb (1858–1943) wrote the following:

Went to Priestley's play I Have Been Here Before, *based on Dunne's hypothesis that you can, if you have the gift, see forward as well as backward in time and (this seems self-contradictory) by knowledge alter the happening. The metaphysics of the play as expounded by the German philosopher were absurd but he and four other characters were cleverly conceived and admirably acted. . . Altogether the play excited, never bored, us.*[142]

This was the general opinion of the critics as well. The play was not well received by the public, however. The ideas were simply too complex for the theatregoers of the late 1930s. Sadly, this play is rarely performed and is really due for a revival. I am sure that modern audiences, used to some of the more challenging movies coming out of Hollywood in recent years, will fully appreciate the 'metaphysics' that Beatrice Webb thought to be so 'absurd'.

I am hopeful that this book may, in its own small way, help audiences appreciate exactly how much thought Priestley put into what may seem, at first sight, to be rather dated and dusty period pieces. They are far from this. I am sure that had Priestley hailed from Moscow or Berlin rather than Bradford this work would have been hailed as an expressionist masterpiece.

I could have devoted a whole book to the way 'time' has been used as a theme in films, plays, novels, music, painting and poetry – indeed I may do exactly that in the future – however, I feel that this fleeting review of the 'fictional' aspects of time has shown that this most ephemeral of concepts can be used to create great art. This is because our experience of time, or more accurately our lives within time, is one thing that every human being has in common. It is a universal perception.

When we watch movies or read books that deal with this subject there is a powerful sense of recognition within us. It is as if we know that by understanding the true nature of time we can glimpse an understanding of that other great shared experience, consciousness. This is what great art is all about.

CHAPTER 12

A NEW MODEL OF TIME?

The language trap

My object in this book has been to present a review of time and its mysteries, nothing more. However, as the book pulled itself together it became clear to me that a new hypothetical model, related to both my cheating-the-ferryman and Bohmian IMAX models, could be created. Interestingly enough, this also occurred while writing my last book, *The Out-of-Body Experience – The History and Science of Astral Travel* (2011). Indeed, it is the very model I suggest in that book that can be similarly applied to precognition and time travel.

The nature of time itself is still the greatest of all mysteries. Together we have reviewed how philosophy, theology, physics, cosmology, neurology, psychiatry and even popular media have approached this subject. Indeed it has long been argued by both scientists and philosophers that it is impossible to fully understand the nature of a system if the observer of that system is part of that system. Just as we can never see our faces with our own eyes, so it is that we can never understand the true nature of time because all our perceptions of time exist within time. We can never position ourselves outside this all-pervading dimension.

In many ways I am reminded of the philosophical concept known as the 'Incompleteness Theorem'. In 1931 the Czech-born mathematician Kurt Gödel demonstrated that within any given branch of mathematics there would always be some propositions that could not be proven simply by using the axioms and rules of that mathematical branch. He argued that we may be able to prove every conceivable statement about a group of numbers within a system, but in order to do this we have to go outside those rules and axioms and in doing so create a larger system with its own unproveable statements. The implications of this are clear: all logical systems of any complexity are, by definition, incomplete. So it may be argued in relation to our ultimate understanding of time.

Time is one system that it is impossible to escape from. It is a temporal prison in that outside it there is literally nothing. Everything we can quantify exists in time. As we have already discussed, we cannot measure time, only its duration, and even then we have to use secondary sources. A clock measures time by the movement of its hands. These are measuring distance, not time. A digital clock is simply a counter. It is calibrated against a regular sequence in nature such as the regular oscillations of a quartz crystal. As we have already discovered, the most powerful time-keeping devices available to modern science use the cycles of caesium-133 atoms. However, these are not measuring time itself. There is no known metric by which time can be measured other than itself.

I am reminded of Heisenberg's Uncertainty Principle in quantum mechanics. This states that the accurate measurement of any sub-atomic particle is restricted to knowing either its position or its momentum. We can never know both. I feel that it is the same with time. We can know with great precision how the flow of time *feels* in that it can slow down or speed up depending upon personal circumstances, but the time it takes for an accurate chronometer to measure one minute will always be one minute.

This difficulty may simply be that we are trapped within our own languages. We use one term to mean many things. We assume that the noun 'time' is referring to a single entity but it may really be many individual things that we perceive as a single something. For example, we exist within a three-dimensional space but time is a dimension in its own right. We can no more perceive a four-dimensional object than the two-dimensional characters of Edwin Abbott's famous book *Flatland* can perceive our world of three dimensions. Such concepts can be modelled mathematically. 'Bosonic String Theory' is based on 36 space-time dimensions and 'M-Theory' needs 11. If either of these theories proves to be a viable model of how the universe functions then our world is but a small part of a much greater, multi-dimensional reality. Indeed, some scientists have suggested that these multiple dimensions may explain why it is that the universe seems to have considerably less matter than it should have in order to bring about the gravitational effects observed by the movements of galaxy clusters. In other words most of our universe is missing. Cosmologists call this missing something 'dark matter'. It is called 'dark matter' because it cannot be seen. Even more puzzling for scientists was the discovery, in 1998, that the universe is expanding at a much faster rate than could be accounted for by our current knowledge of physics. This breakthrough was made by Nobel Prize-winning cosmologist Saul Perlmutter and his team on the Supernova Cosmology Project. Scientists coined the term 'dark energy' for the mysterious force responsible for this anomaly, although they have no idea what it is.

In 2006, Stephen Hawking of Cambridge University and Thomas Hertog of CERN wrote a paper that attempted an answer to this question. I hinted about this paper earlier in this book. Like many earth-shattering scientific theories, this one has seemingly failed to break out of the dry world of science journals and academic papers. This I find curious because the model presented in this paper has huge implications not only for physics and cosmology, but also neurology and consciousness itself.

The top-down approach

In order to appreciate the implications of this paper we need to remind ourselves of the work of Paul Dirac. From 1932 to 1969 this enigmatic and socially awkward genius was the 15th individual to be awarded the Lucasian Chair for Mathematics at the University of Cambridge. The second holder of this office was Isaac Newton and, interestingly enough, the 17th was Hawking himself. As you will recall, it was Dirac who first suggested the existence of anti-matter when he proposed the existence of a particle he termed an 'anti-electron'. When it was discovered a short time later and named the 'positron' it became clear that Newton's 'clockwork' universe was no longer tenable. Mankind had discovered objects that seemed to travel backwards in time, an impossibility in Newton's universe. For 30 years, from 1978 to 2009, the post of Lucasian Professor was held by Steven Hawking.

It was on 23 June 2006 that the Hawking–Hertog paper appeared in the in-house magazine of the American Physical Society. Entitled 'Populating the Landscape: A Top-Down Approach', it was a stunning attempt to explain why it is that there is so much 'dark energy' and why it cannot be detected. Hawking and Hertog's model proposed that the universe started as a superposition of all possible outcomes of all events.[143] In other words, all possible futures were encoded within the information field right from the start. At each action, the wave function of that potential universe is collapsed into an actuality that exists for a nanosecond before the next universe appears out of the energy. Now, if we apply to this the Copenhagen Interpretation, we come up with something quite interesting. As you will recall, Born and Bohr argued that all sub-atomic particles are in a state of statistical potentiality until they are 'observed'. We have already discussed in some detail exactly what is meant by 'observation' and we know many authorities have proposed that this act of observation has to be by a self-aware consciousness. As we have seen, one such authority, John Wheeler, suggested that consciousness is not only responsible for collapsing the wave function now but also for every incident in the past, including, one assumes, the Big Bang itself.

As well as suggesting an alternative model to that of Everett's Many-Worlds Interpretation, this paper also explained away the mysteries of the 'Anthropic Principle' that questions why it is that the universe seems to not only be fine-tuned for life but also seems to have got it right first time.[144] Hawking and Hertog's top-down cosmology answers both questions by saying that the universe has been fine-tuned by the automatic selection of environments in a similar way to Darwinian evolution.

Why I am so excited about this theory is that I genuinely believe that by evaluating Hawking and Hertog's model in the light of three other hypotheses I can suggest a Grand Theory of Everything that may, just may, join together the contents of this book and my three previous books into a satisfactory, and theoretically valid, model. These are John Cramer's fascinating *Transactional Interpretation of Quantum Physics*, David Bohm's *Implicate and Explicate Orders* and Ervin László's *Akashic Field*.

We will start with the Cramer hypothesis. You will recall that Professor Cramer explained that the interference patterns observed in the twin-slit experiment are brought about by forwards-in-time travelling particles encountering backwards-in-time travelling particles approaching from the opposite temporal direction. He suggested that waves travelling forwards in time, known as 'retarded waves', make up our observed universe. However, there are other waves that travel backwards in time. He calls these 'advanced waves'. Because of the way our perception of time functions, we only ever perceive what is known as 'now' the instant in which the future becomes the past. It is only at this shrinkingly tiny sliver of time that the advanced waves show themselves to us by interfering with the retarded waves travelling in the opposite direction. We can easily perceive retarded waves because they continue with us as we travel forwards in time. As an analogy, imagine travelling on a train on one railway track with another track running parallel to it. If a train running in the same direction starts to go past your train at a slightly faster speed you will, by looking out of the window, have it in view for a considerable amount of time. If the second train slows down to match the speed of your train, your view of the other train will become subjectively static. Both trains will be concurrently sharing the same general location in space (and time). However, imagine instead that the train on the other track is running in the opposite direction. In this scenario the two trains will encounter each other for only a very short time. You may be looking out of the window as the other train thunders past and it will only be in view for a second or so.

This is how it is with time. On our temporal railway track, objects that share our overall speed-through-time will remain in our perception continuously. This is why the observed world remains consistent for us. Everything that we can observe in this universe must be travelling with us. Even travelling a micro-second faster will place an object outside our perception. It will be perceived as simply being there for a tiny amount of time and then disappearing as if into thin air. Indeed, many sub-atomic particles do this constantly. From our point of view they seem to flit in and out of reality in a flash. This does not mean they cease to exist, they simply move outside our temporal frame of reference. Now, imagine the shared time frame of an observer and a particle travelling backwards in time. This will be like two trains travelling in opposite directions at virtually infinite speed. The amount of 'time' that they will share as they encounter each other must be vanishingly small – something known as 'Planck Time' – because any other quantity of time will be too large.

Where the future and past meet

According to the latest research, the smallest possible size anything can be is known as the 'Planck Length' (lP). This has been calculated as being 10^{-35} metres. At this size, space and time cease to have any real meaning. From this has been calculated Planck Time (tP), which is defined as the time it would take a photon travelling at the speed of light to cross a distance equal to one Planck Length. This is calculated at roughly 10^{-43} seconds. This is how long a particle travelling backwards in time would share our time frame and become visible or measurable. It is highly unlikely that we will ever have devices that can measure this level of precision. However, this does not mean that such particles cannot actually exist and even be produced within the laboratory.

You will recall from an earlier discussion that Richard Feynman suggested that positrons, and all other anti-particles, can be regarded as normal particles travelling backwards in time. For many years these anti-particles have been created in specialist laboratories around the world. In order to remain stable and share our temporal universe they have to have their natural temporal flow slowed down or even stopped.

The implications for the creation of anti-atoms and anti-molecules are staggering and present a real challenge for materialist-reductionist science. It means that, as anti-matter exists, anything made of matter can have an anti-matter equivalent. This means anti-matter planets, anti-matter suns and – hold on to your hat – anti-matter people. Anti-matter planets and suns form anti-matter galaxies and – ultimately – anti-matter universes. Now, if each particle of matter has its anti-matter double then everyone on this planet also has an anti-matter double living in these anti-matter universes.

But there is more. All these anti-matter universes have a time flow that is the complete opposite to our own with neither of the directions being the right direction or the wrong direction. Just like Cramer's retarded and advanced waves these alternative universes only interact for the instant that they meet each other in opposite time directions.

However, if Julian Barbour and his supporters are right then there is no 'time flow' in either direction. This is an illusion. All matter, including anti-matter, exists in a permanent 'now'. In this way time, as it is generally understood to be, is taken out of the equation.

The proposition that the universe started as a superposition of all possible outcomes of all events is intriguing in that it is an interesting new angle on the Many-Worlds Interpretation of Hugh Everett. You will recall that Everett suggested that at each quantum event the universe splits into multiple copies of itself. In doing so the universe ensures that each wave function continues without the dreaded 'act of observation' implicit in the Copenhagen

Interpretation, so disliked by Einstein. In this way consciousness was not seen as central in any way.

At each action, the wave function of that potential universe is collapsed into an actuality that exists for a nanosecond before the next universe appears out of the energy. It is this observation that brings us to the second super-theory that should be viewed in the light of Hawking and Hertog's 'top-down cosmology'.

The 'Akashic Field'

The idea that the physical universe is created out of information was first proposed by the great maverick scientist Nicola Tesla (1856–1943). Tesla suggested that there is a force field of information at the heart of the universe. Borrowing from the old Vedic scriptures, he called this field the *Akasha*. On its own, this field is passive and dormant. In order to be activated sufficiently to bring forth matter it needs a source of energy. This energy is supplied by another Vedic concept known as *Prana*. For a short period of time at the turn of the 19th century, Tesla's model proved popular. However, Einstein's four-dimensional curved space-time proved to be a far more effective explanation of observed phenomena and Tesla's model fell out of favour. However, this model shares many similarities with Hawking and Hertog's 'top-down universe'. From the first few nano-seconds of the Big Bang, the universe had encoded all potential future states of its enclosed system. Like a huge computer hard drive, the universe stores everything as a form of information that can be turned into physical reality as each wave function collapses. In effect, this means that information on everything that has happened and everything that *can* happen is encoded within this huge database. If this is the case then not only every *actual* future but also every *potential* future has an existence within this information field. Indeed, within this information field there is no time, just a permanent 'now' in which everything exists as an informational potentiality.

Hawking and Hertog present a beguiling model of reality that needs a timeless place in which the information on all potential universes must be stored. Because timelessness suggests that 'now' is an arbitrary location, all past potentialities that may or may not have come to pass in this universe but could have done so in others must also be located. This involves a huge amount of data. The questions are: Where is this information kept? How is it encoded? And, finally, how is it subsequently uploaded? As far as I am aware, Hawking and Hertog have left these questions unanswered.

The history of science is full of such unanswered questions. For me, this is where the real answers can be found, in the gaps that have been carefully ignored because to fill them would suggest that there is another reality that needs a new science to explain it. Like the medieval astronomers who invented 'epicycles' to explain the retrograde motion of the inner planets, we are creating ever more complex models in order to shoe-horn anomalous observations into our present, and somewhat creaking, scientific paradigm. However, not all scientists are trapped within this paradigm. Some are willing to take a risk and suggest real solutions to these questions, even if it means 'rewriting the rulebook'. One of the most influential of these independent thinkers was David Bohm. In his early 30s, Bohm found himself in the stifling atmosphere of Cold-War academia. As a physicist he was intrigued by quantum mechanics and in 1951 he wrote a well-received book entitled *Quantum Theory*.

However, it was at this time that he began to realize that the prevailing model simply could not explain certain phenomena. As a radical thinker, he also found himself under attack from Senator Joseph McCarthy and the anti-Communist lobby. In 1955, Bohm moved to Israel and then, in 1957, to the UK. Initially based at the University of Bristol, he moved to London's Birkbeck College in 1961 as professor of theoretical physics. It was during this time that he developed a theoretical model similar to that of Tesla. He believed that the universe was created out of something he termed the 'implicate order'. For him this was the ground state of everything. From this developed the 'explicate order', the visible, physical universe. Bohm suggested that all objects in the explicate world that surrounds us are relatively autonomous but they are derived from the implicate world, which is a field of unbroken wholeness. In his hugely influential book *Wholeness and the Implicate Order*, he likens this relationship to a flowing stream:

> *On this stream, one may see an ever-changing pattern of vortices, ripples, waves, splashes, etc., which evidently have no independent existence as such. Rather, they are abstracted from the flowing movement, arising and vanishing in the total process of the flow. Such transitory subsistence as may be possessed by these abstracted forms implies only a relative independence or autonomy of behaviour, rather than absolutely independent existence as ultimate substances.*[145]

Bohm suggested that the explicate order is extracted from the implicate order in a similar way to that in which a holographic image is extracted from a series of swirls and shadings into a three-dimensional image when illuminated by laser light. The illumination that extracts the physical universe from the implicate order is the light of consciousness. This process mirrors that of the Copenhagen Interpretation in that an act of observation is the catalyst. With Copenhagen, the observation collapses the wave function into a point particle whereas in Bohm's model the act of observation draws 'in-formation' out of the implicate order and manifests it in the explicate order. Bohm was keen to use the term 'in-formation' rather than information. By this he meant a process that actually 'forms' the recipient. This model was a huge influence upon me and I spend many pages discussing Bohm's 'implicate order' in my first book. Indeed, this is why I call the inwardly created universe that I believe we all become part of at the point of death the Bohmian IMAX. This place is created by 'in-formation' drawn up from the wholeness of the Implicate Order.

The term 'in-formation' has now been taken to another level by the creator of the third hypothesis that contributes to my new model,

Ervin László. László (1932–) was a musical prodigy, performing his first piano concert with the Budapest Symphony Orchestra at the age of 8. However, it is as a philosopher of science that he is best known, being particularly interested in the relationship between conscious experience and the true nature of physical reality. In 2004 he published his major work, *Science and the Akashic Field – An Integral Theory of Everything*. In this, László proposes that the cosmos is a field of information. Everything that exists within the universe is a manifestation of this field. Like Tesla, László was struck by the parallels between certain areas of quantum theory and the Vedic and Sanskrit myths. In recognition of this, László has termed this the 'Akashic Field' or 'A-field'.

László uses as his starting point the idea that the universe does not just consist of physical matter and energy but also contains other forces. In recognition of the huge contribution David Bohm made to this developing paradigm, he used the Bohmian term 'in-formation' to describe these forces. His definition of 'in-formation' is a:

> . . . *subtle, quasi-instant, non-evanescent and non-energetic connection between things at different locations in space and events at different points in time. Such connections are termed 'nonlocal' in the natural sciences and 'transpersonal' in consciousness research. In-formation links things (particles, atoms, molecules, organisms, ecologies, solar systems, entire galaxies, as well as the mind and consciousness associated with these things) regardless of how far they are from each other and how much time has passed since connections were created between them.*[146]

As explained in Chapter 5, the EPR paradox, put forward by Einstein, Podolsky and Rosen, suggested that – if the theories of quantum mechanics are to be believed – when two 'entangled' particles are separated they will be found to have complementary values. For example, if one has clockwise 'spin' the other will be found to have anticlockwise 'spin'. In the last thirty years or so a series of experiments have confirmed this effect. It seems that entangled particles share information in such a way that if something is done to one particle the other 'knows' about it instantaneously, irrespective of the distance between the two. They can even be on opposite sides of a room, or (theoretically) on opposite sides of the universe. However far apart they are, they can communicate instantaneously with each other. Although he had long been dead before entanglement was proved in a laboratory, Einstein was aware of the implications. He never really accepted it as a possibility, suggesting that there had to be an explanation that ensured that the barrier of lightspeed was not violated.

The Zero-Point Field

In recent years, Professor Anton Zeilinger of the University of Vienna has routinely been sending entangled particles over large distances. In 2008 he managed to bounce entangled photons off a low orbit geodetic satellite called Ajisai. This was orbiting at a height of 1,485 kilometres.[147] This feat has huge implications for communications in the future because as entangled particles communicate instantaneously this means a message can be sent from anywhere in the universe to arrive instantly anywhere else.

David Bohm used entanglement as evidence of his theory of 'wholeness and the implicate order' and in doing so also ensured that Einstein's light-speed barrier was left intact. Bohm argued that within the implicate order the two particles are entangled because, in a very real sense, they are the same particle. We, from our viewpoint in the explicate order, perceive two particles when, in fact, there is only one.

Zeilinger has now managed to entangle not only sub-atomic particles but also atoms and even molecules, including the 60-carbon-atom structure known as a Buckyball (or Buckminsterfullerene). Indeed, science in this field is developing so rapidly that it is only a matter of time before compounds may be entangled. The implications of these developments are truly astounding. If any two particles can be entangled by simply being placed in a position where they interact physically then any closely associated atoms and molecules will do the same. Now, reflect on this for a second or two. All known particles that make up the universe existed in a singular superposition at the start of the Big Bang. This suggests that every particle in the universe is already entangled with every other particle and has been since the beginning of what we perceive as 'time'. This is a staggering observation. Everything really is a single entity; it is just that our minds create separation to enable us to make sense of the universe.

For László, this all adds to the evidence that the ground state of the universe is a huge field of 'in-formation'. He believes that science has already started to find evidence for this and even has a name for it. They call it the 'Zero Point Field', a hypothetical energy source existing within what is known as the quantum vacuum.

In simple terms, it has been discovered that energy exists where there should be no energy, for example at absolute zero (minus 273.150 Celsius). At this temperature energy should vanish but it doesn't. In 1948 Dutch physicist Hendrik B.G. Casimir proposed the existence of a force arising from the quantum vacuum. In a later experiment the predicted energy force was discovered. In the 1960s, Paul Dirac, the physicist who first suggested the existence of anti-matter, showed that fluctuations in fields of matter particles (now known as fermions) were affected by the Zero Point Field. The particles changed spin, mass, charge or angular momentum. This effect was coming from a place where nothing should be. This is energy appearing out of empty space.

Borrowing his ideas from Tesla and Bohm, László suggests that the Zero Point Field is a source not only of virtually unlimited amounts of energy – unsurprisingly called 'Zero Point Energy'– but is also a source of similarly unlimited 'in-formation'. This is the equivalent of the Vedic *Akasha*. This is an all-encompassing medium that, as László states, '*underlies* all things and *becomes* all things'.

Is this where the information needed to generate Hawking and Hertog's 'top-down universe' can be found? Is this the source of all the lifetimes that are needed in order to fulfil my own cheating-the-ferryman hypothesis? Is this 'in-formation' drawn up by the holographic interaction of Cramer's retarded and advanced waves? If so, then every outcome of every decision made by every conscious being is encoded and recorded in this huge field of 'in-formation'.

If this is correct, then the past is your past and the future is your future. Is it not then surprising that occasionally we can be given glimpses of that future or that we can view a scene from the past? However, there is an important caveat to this model. Because your act of observation collapses the wave function and in so doing draws up from the field the present moment for you, this does not mean that this is an illusion populated by illusory people. I know that I have mentioned this before but it needs to be re-stated. The people, animals and objects you interface with in your own 'moment' are just as real as you are. Each version of the universe is a real, multi-dimensional place populated by real, independent entities. You are simply interfacing with the entities whose own decisions placed them in the same 'moment-universe' that you have chosen by your decisions. It is like bumping into a friend in a restaurant. You both have back-stories that placed you in the same location. This does not mean that your friend is a creation of your imagination, and so it is with this model.

Intrasomatic experience

In my last book, *The Out-of-Body Experience – The History and Science of Astral Travel*,[148] I presented a hypothetical model of reality. I call this the 'intrasomatic experience'. This suggests that normal dreaming, lucid dreaming, out-of-body experiences, astral travel and distance viewing are all aspects of the same phenomenon, the 'intrasomatic experience'. I have chosen this term quite carefully. In her review of out-of-the-body experiences, researcher Celia E.

Green first used the term 'ecsomatic experience' to describe all of the above sensory perceptions.[149] The word 'ecsomatic' suggests that the experience takes place outside ('ecso') the body ('soma'). I have turned this around in that I have replaced 'ecso' with 'intra', the Latin for 'within'. In this way I suggest that the out-of-body experience actually involves a going 'inwards' and that what is perceived as the external world is, in fact, an internal reality perceived by consciousness. I use the word 'reality' in its literal sense in that I believe that in these inner journeys the experiencer travels in other places that are just as real, if not more real, than the phenomenal world modelled from our sensory inputs and recreated within the brain.

To appreciate that the world we think is 'out there' is, in fact, an internally generated facsimile created in the mind from reassembled data sent from the senses is of crucial importance. Human consciousness never interfaces directly with the external world but is given an approximation of that world within the 'mind's eye'. So, when it is suggested that consciousness can leave the body and travel within this external world we have to ask ourselves some important questions. For example, how does consciousness free itself from the brain-reassembled facsimile and get outside? Indeed, when in an ecsomatic state, what actual senses are functioning? Self-evidently, being outside the body means being outside the brain and therefore cut off from any visual, auditory or tactile inputs. There is no longer any direct contact with the eyes, ears or skin surface. So what is receiving, processing and perceiving the information?

We have to accept that a completely new form of perception must be functioning when consciousness leaves the body, a form of perception that works using no known physical medium of transfer. It has been suggested that somehow a disembodied consciousness can sense information from some form of energy field. How this is converted into data understandable to consciousness is not explained. Of course, it could simply be that our science is not advanced enough for us to measure this subtle energy, but that really is an abdication of logic and one that leaves the apologist open to widespread, and not unreasonable, criticism from the materialist-reductionists.

My 'intrasomatic' model avoids these embarrassing questions by suggesting that consciousness never leaves the brain. This model is totally in line with modern scientific knowledge of how the brain functions. However, it is also revolutionary in that it proposes that consciousness is not an epiphenomenon of the brain: that is, that the brain somehow *creates* consciousness, suggesting that both are aspects of a deeper relationship in which they are both facets of the same thing. Indeed, how inanimate matter such as the chemicals and electrochemical processes in the brain can create self-aware consciousness is as big a problem for materialist-reductionists as consciousness existing outside of the brain is for believers in the 'soul' or 'spirit'. The Australian philosopher David Chalmers (1966–) has called the way the brain creates consciousness the 'hard problem' of science. Many believe that this 'hard problem' can never be answered by materialistic science because consciousness is not physical. It does not lend itself to a materialist-reductionist mode of analysis. A thought does not occupy physical space – it does not exist in three dimensions. As the French philosopher René Descartes (1596–1650) stated, it does not have 'extension in space'. But every self-aware human being knows with absolute certainty that they have an inner life of thoughts, emotions, memories, dreams and ambitions. They know this *empirically* – through experience. To deny this inner life is simply absurd. Daniel C. Dennett makes a strong attempt in his book *Consciousness Explained* but ends up wrapping himself up in his attempt to explain away the existence of the sentient being who is writing the book itself. This is, in my humble opinion, a person so sure in their beliefs that they deny the obvious.

The intrasomatic model suggests that we all exist within an internally generated version of reality. This model is constructed in the brain in a similar process to the much ridiculed idea of the 'Cartesian Theatre', as I have already acknowledged, a term first coined by Dennett in his hugely popular book. By this he means the naïve belief that inside our head is a little version of us viewing all the information sent to us by our senses. Quite rightly, Dennett points out that this suggests an infinite regression in that in the head of the 'little man-in-the-head' (the 'homunculus') must be another little man who, in turn, has another in his head and so on *ad infinitum*. In many ways this is similar to the infinite regression of 'observers' and 'times' in Dunne's model. This simply does not make logical sense. However, if the brain and conscious-ness are the same thing then we need go no further. The internally created facsimile is produced by trillions and trillions of small protein structures called microtubules. Each microtubule creates an 'interference pattern from single photon light with its closest neighbour'. These function like micro-holograms. Trillions and trillions of these interfaces create a three-dimensional model of the external world within the brain. This, as you may have guessed, is another aspect of my 'Bohmian IMAX', an acknowledgement of the explanatory power of Dennett's Cartesian Theatre.

It is important at this point to differentiate between information that is created from external stimuli and 'in-formation' drawn from the Zero Point Field. We all experience what I term 'The Virgin Life'. This is the first life, the one in which we experience our life for the first time. This life is differentiated from all others in that it is free of any *déjà vu* sensations and lacks an inner guiding force – the being I call 'The Daemon'. This is why on average only 30 per cent of people surveyed claim never to have had a *déjà* experience whereas 70 per cent say they have experienced at least one. This is because the 30 per cent who do not report such experiences are living their life for the first time. As their brain processes and buffers the incoming sensory data, this data is uploaded into the Zero Point Field. In this way they contribute one life to the countless other versions of themselves inhabiting other parts of the multiverse. This means a full record of every outcome of every decision of every person can be found within the Zero Point Field. It is also important to appreciate that the Zero Point Field exists in a timeless place where there is no past, present or future – just an eternal 'now'. This is how all the alternative life-routes are subsequently available when, at the end of the 'Virgin Life', the person enters the Bohmian IMAX.

From then on, our reality is a form of recording, something we all experience every second of our lives. We live within it much as Thomas Anderson does in the movie *The Matrix* before he is 'liberated'. However, this 'Black Iron Prison', as speculative fiction writer Philip K. Dick called it, is not created by aliens wishing to use humanity as a source of energy, but is simply the way in which our brain works. It buffers external information, records it and then presents it to consciousness. Indeed, does this model not effectively explain the mysteries presented by the Libet experiment, the Phi phenomenon and all the other exercises that show that consciousness, for some reason, lags behind time by as much as six seconds?

The Bohmian IMAX sources its material from the Zero Point Field. This material may include Jungian archetypes drawn up from the collective subconscious. They may include strongly held beliefs about the nature of eternal reality (is this why people who believe in UFOs see UFOs, why religious people see evidence of God everywhere, why some sensitives see ghosts or the spirits of loved ones, why mediums can talk to the dead, and why the world of the schizophrenic is full of real hallucinations?) or even intrusions of past-life memories and images.

In this way my Bohmian IMAX model can explain many psychic phenomena. Put simply, within the Bohmian IMAX, if you believe in something strongly enough it will be brought into existence in your world. Indeed, does this not explain the much touted 'law of attraction' far more effectively than those who purport to teach people how to manipulate it?

So here we have a really new model of how the universe works. There is no 'out there' at all. The external world that is presented to consciousness by the senses does not have an independent existence. It is both created for, and by, the entity that perceives it. Indeed we can further hypothesis that the idea of a singular consciousness may also be an illusion. As the great American comedian Bill Hicks once observed in a famed 'stream-of-consciousness' monologue:

> Today, a young man on acid realized that all matter is merely energy condensed to a slow vibration – that we are all one consciousness experiencing itself subjectively. There's no such thing as death, life is only a dream, and we're the imagination of ourselves. Here's Tom with the weather.[150]

If this is the case, and the Zero-Point Field model does seem to suggest this, then everything that we observe is all part of a unified whole created out of energy. In-formation is drawn up from the ZPF by consciousness and in doing so turns that consciousness into a self-aware 'observer'. The act of observation or, more accurately, the self-reflectiveness that this act imparts upon consciousness, is what creates the idea of personality and separateness. The ego-self is created by the mind in order to give context and narrative to the act of perception. This in turn then creates the illusion of individuality. In order for this independence to continue there must be a stage in which this narrative and context can unfold. This stage is time. Time is the tool in which individuation is shaped and developed. Without the backdrop of temporal flow everything just 'is'; a whole that simply exists in a timeless world akin to Julian Barbour's Platonia.

Is this simply playing with words or does it present a real answer to Augustine's famous question 'what is time?'? In answering his own question this sainted Doctor of the Church states that it can only be defined by what it isn't rather than what it is.[151] In writing and researching this book I cannot help but agree with him. Time is singularly the greatest challenge to human intellect possible because it hides in plain sight. It is everywhere and nowhere. I have found the process both challenging and enlightening. However do I really know anything more about time itself? My answer has to be no. Just as Augustine observed I have spent a great deal of time explaining the effects of this mysterious something but I have no more succeeded in isolating what it really is than any of those writers, poets, scientists and philosophers that have gone before me. We are simply left echoing Augustine's words that have echoed throughout this book:

What then is time? If no one asks me, I know: if I wish to explain it to one that asketh, I know not.[151]

And maybe that is how it should be.

CONTACT THE AUTHOR

I hope that you have found this book of interest. In writing this, and my previous books, my intention has simply been to explore in my own limited way some of the deepest and most perplexing puzzles about existence. In many ways these books are intensely personal in that I write them for myself. They are simply a series of journals or notebooks that contain my own, idiosyncratic, world view based upon half a century of reading and discussing unusual experiences with friends, family and acquaintances. Whether my conclusions have any validity are for you, my readers, to decide. Indeed I have always considered, and continue to consider, that anybody who invests 'time' (if it exists) in reading my work has invested an amount of this valuable commodity to evaluate what I have to impart. This is why I have created a series of contact points and organizations in which we can all discuss, debate, and develop the ideas presented in this book and my previous works. We have web-based groups such as my forum which can be found on my website at http://www.anthonypeake.com/forum/ and the ITLAD Walker Group which can be found on Facebook (http://www.facebook.com/groups/110161129033771/). Indeed the Walker Group as a concept now involves groups that have informal meetings in 'consensual reality'. These have been designed to be an open exchange of ideas in a convivial social atmosphere, usually in a café or bar. I am keen to set these groups up across the world so should any of you be motivated to start one yourself please contact any of the members of the Facebook Group for further details. I am also keen to hear from any readers who have experiences similar to the ones discussed in this book or any of my earlier publications. Please contact me at anthonyapeake@btinternet.com or write to me via my publisher, Arcturus.

NOTES

1 Inglis, B. *'Coincidence'* Hutchinson p. 167 (1990)

2 *Phys. Op.* fr. 2 (R. p. 16) from the Anaximander Fragments

3 Aristotle *Physics* Chapter 14

4 Aquinas, T. *Summa Theologica* 1a, 46, 1

5 'Kant's Views on Space & Time' *Stanford Encyclopedia of Philosophy* http://plato.stanford.edu/entries/kant-spacetime/

6 Nietzsche, F. *Fate and History (Fatum und Geschichte,* trans. Stack, G.J.) *Philosophy Today* (37)2, pp.154–156. (1993)

7 Nietzsche, F. *Will To Power* (note 1066)

8 Nietzsche, F. *The Gay Science* (note 341)

9 Nietzsche, F. *Thus Spoke Zarathustra*

10 Steiner, R. *Friedrich Nietzsche: One Fighter Against His Time (Ein Kämpfer Gegen Seine Zeit)* Spiritual Science Library (1985)

11 Steiner, R. *The Story of my Life* http://wn.rsarchive.org/Books/GA028/TSoML/GA028_c18.html

12 Steiner, R. *The Story of My Life* http://wn.rsarchive.org/Books/GA028/TSoML/GA028_c18.html

13 Steiner, R. *The Story of My Life* http://wn.rsarchive.org/Books/GA028/TSoML/GA028_c18.html

14 Heidegger, M. *Nietzsche volume II: The Eternal Recurrence of the Same* p. 42 Harper & Row (1984)

15 Deleuze, G. *Nietzsche and Philosophy* p. xi Athlone (1983)

16 Stambaugh, J. *Nietzsche's Thought of Eternal Return* p. 31 Johns Hopkins (1972)

17 Hishitani, K. *Religion & Nothingness* pp. 218–219, 221 (1982)

18 Hishitani, K. *Religion & Nothingness* pp. 218–219, 221 (1982)

19 *Tao Te Ching* On Hearing of The Way (41)

20 *Tao Te Ching* On Hearing of The Way (41)

21 Aristotle *Physics*

22 Whitrow, J. G. *Time in History* p. 43 OUP (1989)

23 Whitrow, J. G. *Time in History* p. 43 OUP (1989)

24 Augustine, *The City of God Against the Pagans* R.W. Dyson (ed) p. 517 Cambridge University Press (1998)

25 Aquinas, T. *Summa contra gentiles* 1, c. 66

26 O'Brien, F. *The Third Policeman* Flamingo/Harper Collins (1993).

27 Ouspensky, P.D. *A New Model of the Universe* p. 472 Routledge (1931)

28 Hunter, B. *Don't Forget: P.D. Ouspensky's Life of Self-remembering* p. 10

Bardic Press (2006)

29 Hunter, B. *Don't Forget: P.D. Ouspensky's Life of Self-remembering* p. 10 Bardic Press (2006)

30 Ouspensky, P.D. *A New Model of the Universe* p. 472 Routledge (1931)

31 Ouspensky, P.D. *A New Model of the Universe* p. 425 Routledge (1931)

32 Ouspensky, P.D. *The Strange Life of Ivan Osokin* p. 153 Routledge (1931)

33 Ouspensky, P.D. *In Search of the Miraculous* p. 250 Routledge (1949)

34 Ouspensky, P.D. *The Fourth Way* p. 116 Routledge (1956)

35 Ouspensky, P.D. *A New Model of the Universe* p. 515 Routledge (1931)

36 Pogson, B. *Maurice Nicoll: A Portrait* Eureka Editions (1961)

37 Quoted by J.B. Priestley in *Man and Time* p. 271 Aldus Books (1964)

38 Anton, U. & Fuchs, W. An Interview With Philip K. Dick *SF Eye* 14, pp. 37–41 (1996)

39 Nicoll, M. *Living Time and the Integration of the Life* Vincent Stuart Ltd (1959)

40 Pogson, B. *Maurice Nicoll: A Portrait* p. 252 Eureka Editions (1961)

41 Lupoff, R.A. A Conversation with Philip K. Dick *Science Fiction Eye* (1), 2 (1984)

42 Collin, R. *The Theory of Celestial Influence* p. 24 Arkana (1954)

43 Collin, R. *The Theory of Celestial Influence* Arkana (1954)

44 Pearson, O.P. 'The Metabolism of Humming Birds' *Scientific American* (Jan 1953)

45 Collin, R. *The Theory of Celestial Influence* p. 135 Arkana (1954)

46 Fischer, R. *The Voices of Time* Brazilla (1966)

47 Bentov, I. *Stalking the Wild Pendulum* Dutton (1977)

48 Tolstoy, L. *Memoirs of a Madman* Vol. 15 (trans. Maude, A.)

49 Luce, G.G. *Body Time* p. 24 Paladin (1972)

50 François, M. 'Contribution à l'étude du sens du Temps. La température interne comme facteur de variation de l'appréciation subjective des durées' *L'année Psychologique* 27, pp.186–204

–

52 Eliot, T.S. 'The Dry Salvages' (Quartet No. 3 of the *Four Quartets*) (1946)

53 Bennett, J.G. *The Dramatic Universe* quoted in J.B. Priestley's *Man and Time* p.273 Aldus Books (1964)

54 Gefter, A. 'Beyond Space Time' *New Scientist* 2824, p. 36. (Aug 2011)

55 http://news.sciencemag.org/sciencenow/2007/02/16-04.html

56 http://www.aip.org/history/ohilist/5908_1.html

57 Koestler, A. *The Roots of Coincidence* p. 65 Random House (1972)

58 Loye, D. *An Arrow Through Chaos* p. 114 Park Street Press (2000)

59 Greene, B. *The Fabric of the Cosmos* p. 132 Penguin (2005)

60 Peake, A. *Is There Life After Death? – The Extraordinary Science of What Happens When We Die* p. 124 Arcturus (2010)

61 Davies, P. *About Time – Einstein's Unfinished Revolution* p. 55 Viking (1995)

62 Minkowski, H. 'Space and Time' in Lorentz, H.A., Einstein, A., Minkowski,H. and Weyl, H. *The Principle of Relativity: A Collection of Original Memoirs on the Special and General Theory of Relativity* pp. 75–91 (1952)

63 Gefter, A. 'Beyond Space Time' *New Scientist* (Aug 2011)

64 Barbour, J. 'Timeless' *New Scientist* (16 Oct 1999)

65 Barbour, J. 'Timeless' *New Scientist* (16 Oct 1999)

66 Barbour, J. *The End of Time* pp.28–29 Phoenix (1999)

67 Ramachandran, V. S. *Phantoms in the Brain* p. 72 Fourth Estate (1999)

68 http://www.anthonypeake.com/forum/viewtopic.php?t=2021&sid=1c860 875750dea83b05e9c4eacec8210

69 http://www.youtube.com/watch?v=RjlpamhrId8 3 min 5 sec in.

70 http://www.youtube.com/watch?v=RjlpamhrId8 4 min 30 sec in

71 http://www.youtube.com/watch?v=RjlpamhrId8 4 min 40 sec in

72 http://neuro.bcm.edu/eagleman/time.html

73 Erickson, M.H. *My Voice Will Go With You* p. 6 W.W. Norton (1981)

74 Erickson, M.H. & Rossi, E. L. *Autohypnotic experiences of Milton H Erickson* pp. 36–54 *Am J Clin Hypn* Jul (1) (1977)

75 Cooper, L.F. & Erickson, Milton H. *Time Distortion in Hypnosis – An Experimental and Clinical Investigation* (Second Edition) Crown Publishing Ltd (2006)

76 Erickson, M.H. & Erickson, E.M. 'Further Considerations of Time Distortion' in Cooper, L.F. & Erickson, M.H. *Time Distortions in Hypnosis – An Experimental and Clinical Investigation* Second Edition Crown House Publishing (2006)

77 Op cit p. 194

78 Op cit p. 195

79 Bleuler, E. *Dementia Praecox or the Group of Schizophrenia* International University Press (original work published in German in 1911, trans. Zinkin, J.)

80 Jaynes, J. *The Origin of Consciousness in the Breakdown of the Bicameral Mind* Houghton Mifflin (1976)

81 Binet, A. *On Double Consciousness* (Chicago: Open Court) (1980)

82 Bergson, H. Memory of the Present and False Recognition in Robin Durie (ed) *Time & the Instant – Essays in the Physics and Philosophy of Time* pp.36–64 Clinamen Press (2000)

83 Blake, W. *The Marriage of Heaven and Hell* (1790)

84 Ciompi, L. 'Über abnormes Zeiterleben bei einer Schizophrenen' *Psychiat. Neurol.* 142, p. 100–121 (1961)

85 Ciompi, L. 'Über abnormes Zeiterleben bei einer Schizophrenen' *Psychiat. Neurol.* 142, pp. 100–121 (1961)

86 Bleuler, E. *Dementia Praecox or the Group of Schizophrenia* International University Press (original work published in German in 1911, trans.

Zinkin, J.)

87 Priestley, J.B. *Man and Time* p.202 Aldus Books (1964)

88 James, H. *The Principles of Psychology* p. 609 quoted from *Kelly, The Alternative*, pp.167–8

89 http://mind.ucsd.edu/papers/bhtc/Andersen&Grush.pdf

90 Kornhuber, H.H. and Deecke, L. 'Hirnpotentialänderungen bei Willkürbewegungen und passiven Bewegungen des Menschen: Bereitschaftspotential und reafferente Potentiale' (Brain potential changes in voluntary movements and passive movements of the man: readiness potential and potential reafferente) *Pflügers Arch fur Gesamte Physiologie* 284, pp. 1–17 (1965)

91 Goodman, N. *Ways of Worldmaking* p. 73 Harvester Books (1978)

92 Dennett, D.C. *Consciousness Explained* p. 115 Penguin (1993)

93 Mavromatis, A. *Hypnagogia – The Unique State of Consciousness Between Wakefulness & Sleep* p. 24 Routledge Keegan Paul (1987)

94 Soon, C.S., Brass, M., Heinxe, H.-J. and Hayes, J.-D. 'Unconscious Determinants of Free Decisions in the Human Brain' *Nature Neuroscience* (13 April 2008)

95 Cramer, John G. 'The Plane of the Present and the New Transactional Model of Time' in *Time & The Instant* Durie R. (ed) p. 183 Clinamen Press (2000)

96 http://www.bibliotecapleyades.net/ciencia/ciencia_psychoenergetics02.htm

97 Myers, F.W.H. *The Subliminal Self* (Proc S P R) 11, p. 341 (1895)

98 Lockhart, J.G. *Memoirs of the Life of Sir Walter Scott* p. 114 J.M. Dent (1957)

99 Dickens, C. *David Copperfield* Chapter 39

100 Dickens, C. *Pictures From Italy* p. 80 First World Library (2005)

101 Wigan, A. L. *The Duality of Mind* (1884)

102 O'Connor, A.R. & Moulin, C.J.A. 'Normal Patterns of Déjà Experience in a Healthy, Blind Male: Challenging Optical Pathway Delay Theory' *Brain and Cognition* 62(3), pp.246–249. (2006)

103 Neppe, V 'The Concept of Déjà vu' *Parapsych. Jnl of S.A.* 4:1, p. 2 (1983)

104 Mullan, S. & Penfield, W. 'Illusions of Comparative Interpretation and Emotion' *Arch Neurol Psychiat* 81, pp.269–284 (1959)

105 McHarg, J. 'Personation: Cryptomnesic and Paranormal – Two Contrasting Cases' *Parapsych. Jnl of S.A.* 4:1, pp.36–50 (1983)

106 106 Neppe, V. 'The Concept of Déjà vu' *Parapsych. Jnl of S.A.* 4:1, pp. 4–5 (1983)

107 Neppe, V. *The Psychology of Déjà vu: Have I been here before* Witwatersrand University Press (1983)

108 Funkhouser, A.T. 'The "Dream" Theory of Déjà vu' *Parapsych. Jnl of S.A.* 4, pp. 107–123. (1983)

109 Funkhouser, A. T. 'The "Dream" Theory of Déjà vu' *Parapsych. Jnl of S.A.* 4:2, p. 121 (1983)

110 Proust, M. *À la Recherché du Temps Perdu* (vol.3) pp. 904–908

111 Marcowitz, E. 'The meaning of déjà vu' *Psychoanalytic Quarterly* 21,481–489 (1952)

112 Neppe, V.M. 'The incidence of déjà vu' *Parapsych. Jnl of S.A.* 4:2, p. 103 (1983)

113 Neppe, V.M. *The Psychology of Déjà vu: Have I Been Here Before?* Witwatersrand University Press (1983)

114 Priestley, J.B. *Man and Time* p.207 Aldus Books (1964)

115 Swartz, T. *On The Edge of Time – The Mystery of Time Slips* http://uforeview. tripod.com/timeslips.html

116 Coleman, M.H. (ed) *An Adventure – The Ghosts of the Trianon* Aquarian (1988)

117 Coleman, M.H. (ed) *An Adventure – The Ghosts of the Trianon* Aquarian (1988)

118 Iremonger, L. *The Ghosts of Versailles* (1957)

119 Heywood, T. 'The Ghosts of Versailles, An Adventure in Time' *Fortean Times* 278: p.30 (Aug 2011)

120 Heywood, T. 'The Ghosts of Versailles, An Adventure in Time' *Fortean Times* 278: p.30 (Aug 2011)

121 Randles, J. *Time Storms* p. 85 Piatkus (2001)

122 Randles, J. *Time Storms* pp. 59–60 Piatkus (2001)

123 Randles, J. *Time Storms* pp. 59–60 Piatkus (2001)

124 http://www.parascience.org.uk/investigations/press/bold1.jpg

125 http://www.yoliverpool.com/forum/showthread.php?27794-Ghosts-and-Timeslips-...

126 http://www.anthonypeake.com/forum

127 http://www.anthonypeake.com/forum/viewtopic. php?f=19&t=2083&hilit =Nicola&sid=7df7aef95e7820442ac745bbb 2fdf347

128 Slemen, T. 'Tales of Liverpool: Timeslips' *Liverpool Echo* (18 June 2011)

129 Priestley, J.B. *Man and Time* p.254 Aldus Books (1964)

130 Flammarion, C. *Death and its Mystery* p. 121 New York. The Century Company (1921)

131 Flammarion, C. *Death and its Mystery* p. 121 New York. The Century Company (1921)

132 http://vimeo.com/2315112

133 Inglis, B. *The Power of Dreams* p.123 Grafton Books (1987)

134 Inglis, B. *The Power of Dreams* p.123 Grafton Books (1987)

135 The End of 'Light my Fire' (18:52) on Disc 2 of *The Doors: Live in Detroit*

136 *Theatre arts monthly* 22, 1

137 Priestley, J.B. *Man and Time* p.76 Aldus Books (1964)

138 Priestley, J.B. *An Inspector Calls and Other Plays* p. 60 Penguin (2000)

139 Priestley, J.B. *An Inspector Calls and Other Plays* p. 60 Penguin (2000)

140 Priestley, J.B. *An Inspector Calls and Other Plays* p. 138 Penguin (2000)

141 Priestley, J.B. *An Inspector Calls and Other Plays* p. 152 Penguin (2000)

142 Brome, V. *J.B. Priestley* Hamish Hamilton (1988)

143 Phys. Rev. D 73 123527

144 Barrow, J. and Tipler, F. *The Anthropic Cosmological Principle* Oxford Paperbacks (1988)

145 Bohm, D. *Wholeness and the Implicate Order* p. 48 Routledge & Kegan Paul (1980)

146 László, E. *Science and the Akashic Field – An Integral Theory of Everything* pp. 68–69 Inner Traditions (2007)

147 http://arxiv.org/abs/0803.1871v1

148 Peake, A. *The Out-of-Body Experience – The History and Science of Astral Travel* Watkins (2011)

149 Green, C.E. 'Out-of-the-body Experiences' *Proceedings of the Institute of Psychophysical Research* (2) (1968)

150 http://billhicks.tumblr.com

151 St Augustine, Confessions. 11.14.17 Page 214 (First World Library) 2006

INDEX

Reviews of Anthony Peake's book *Is There Life After Death?: The Extraordinary Science of What Happens When We Die*:

'This book is a remarkable intellectual adventure that has the qualities of a thriller – at times reading it is like a ride on the big dipper. *Is There Life After Death?: The Extraordinary Science of What Happens When We Die* reminds me of one of my favourite films, *Groundhog Day*. I found Anthony Peake's theory to be as thought-provoking and as exhilarating as this great film.'

Colin Wilson, author of *The Outsider*

'In *Is There Life After Death?: The Extraordinary Science of What Happens When We Die* the author, Anthony Peake, has managed to bring together in one tome an enormous amount of cutting-edge research from many different fields. This book will certainly get you thinking and make you re-examine a lot you took for granted up till now.'

Dr Art Funkhouser, author of *The Dream Theory of Déjà Vu*

'This book is beautifully written and organized and one learns something on every page, even for an old fellow like me who is familiar with much of the neuropsychology. It is rare that I get a book I can't put down, cover to cover.'

Dr Jason W Brown, Clinical Professor of Neurology, New York University and author of *The Self-Embodying Mind*

'Peake's explanation of your immortality is the most innovative and provocative argument I have ever seen.'

Bruce Greyson, Carlson Professor of Psychiatry, University of Virginia and editor of *The Journal of Near Death Studies*

'Is T̶_____ment. Peake
has th̶_____words. This
book ̶_____bout a new
understanding o̶_____

Evelyn Elsaesser-Valarino, author of *Lessons From The Light
and Talking With Angel*

'I consider this idea ['cheating-the-ferryman'] to be the most
exciting I have encountered since I first read the manuscript of
Julian Jaynes' seminal book *The Origin of Consciousness in the
Breakdown of the Bicameral Mind.'*

Professor David Loye, author of *An Arrow Through Chaos*

**Words on Tony Peake's *The Daemon: A Guide to your
Extraordinary Secret Self*:**

'[Tony Peake] undertakes a masterly, fully referenced review of
the wider fields of the neurosciences, clinical psychology,
particularly concerning strange experiences in epilepsy,
parapsychology, OBEs and NDEs, the nature of time and the
implications of quantum physics, before putting forward an
intriguing, and therefore controversial, theory.'

_____ical Network

'What̶_____sts, doctors,
psychia̶_____'s reasoning
as a pro̶_____tion of near-
death e̶_____

_____ortean Times